D DAY
THROUGH GERMAN EYES

D Day
Through German Eyes

Paperback Edition Containing Book One and Book Two

Eyewitness Accounts by German Soldiers
Of June 6th 1944

Original Material Edited by
HOLGER ECKHERTZ

Formatted and Published by DTZ History Publications
Translated by Sprech Media

ISBN: 1539586391
ISBN-13: 9781539586395

Contents

BOOK ONE

INTRODUCTION TO BOOK ONE

This book was not created by me, but by my grandfather, Dieter Eckhertz. In 1944, he held the prestigious role of a military journalist, writing articles and features for German military publications including the magazines 'Signal' and 'Die Wehrmacht,' which were widely read by German troops. Dieter Eckhertz left journalism after the war, but he continued to work on one final project, which was a series of interviews with German soldiers who had fought in Normandy on June 6th 1944, the day known to the Allies as 'D Day.'

The reason for my grandfather's interest in the German perspective of D Day was simple: shortly before the Normandy landings, he had visited several locations on the Atlantic Wall and interviewed a number of the troops there with a view to writing a feature for 'Die Wehrmacht' magazine. He was fascinated by the enormous preparations being made to defend the Atlantic coast against an invasion launched from England, and by the morale of the troops on the Wall, who were in many cases inexperienced or unfit.

Much later, on the tenth anniversary of D Day in 1954, when many Germans preferred to draw a veil over the events of the war, my grandfather made enormous efforts to track down some of the troops whose units he had visited. He encouraged these men to discuss with him their personal memories of the Atlantic Wall, their frame of mind at the time of the invasion, and their actions during the historic day of June 6th. His intention was to compile these recollections into a complete book, but the project was still in progress at the time of his death in 1955, and was never completed.

This was the state in which this material eventually came into my hands: as a collection of interviews, notes and verbatim accounts dating from 1954. Some were partial, and some included highly controversial material concerning German forces and French civilians. What comes out of this mix is a highly revealing series of factual accounts by German soldiers who experienced the full might of the Allied onslaught on D Day, especially in the bunkers and 'Resistance Points' constructed along the Wall.

I believe that these accounts show a side to the battle that is rarely seen: the motivations of individual German soldiers, their thought processes as the invasion unfolded, and the way they sought to fight back against the Allies in the violent and chaotic hours after the initial landings.

The interviewees did not, of course, think in terms of the Allied code names for the five Normandy invasion beaches (Utah, Omaha, Gold, Juno and Sword, going in order from West to East) but rather in terms of local places or the official designations of their sectors. Nevertheless, I have organised these accounts under the headings of the Allied beach names, as this is how the landings are generally discussed by historians today. I have selected one account for each of the invasion beaches, from Utah to Sword.

Throughout the book, I have included my grandfather's questions and comments in italics, as they were recorded during the discussions. The speakers, like most German people of their generation, use the words 'England/English' interchangeably with 'Britain/British.'

I should emphasise that this book does not give, and is not intended to give, any strategic overview of the landings or any tactical analysis of the engagements described. It gives a voice to several German soldiers' experiences of D Day, purely and simply, and I feel that they speak for themselves. My hope is that this book adds to the global understanding of June 6th 1944, and in a small way serves as a marker to that conflict and its many repercussions.

Holger Eckhertz, *April 2015*

Utah Beach:
The 'Tobruk' Soldier

**Stefan Heinevez was a Gefreiter (Private First Class)
with the 919th Grenadier Regiment, 709th Static Infantry
Division, based on the Cotentin Peninsula.**

*Herr Heinevez, I visited the Atlantic Wall in May 1944,
and I met some of the men in your regiment.*

I think I remember some of the men talking about your visit. You interviewed several of the troops, and asked them about their hopes and sentiments and so on. The men said that you were impressed with the situation in France.

*Indeed I was impressed. What about you, how did you
feel about your posting to the Atlantic Wall?*

In many ways, I was pleased with the posting. You see, my brothers and friends had been on the Russian front, and they had terrible stories of the conditions there. Many men returned without fingers or eyelids because of the frostbite. By contrast, a posting to France was renowned as a comfortable ride. I myself had been in Sicily in 1943, aged nineteen, fighting the Americans, and I was wounded there. This left me with a permanent limp, and for this reason I was sent to the Atlantic Wall.

Were many of the Atlantic Wall troops sent there for similar reasons?

A large number, I think, although I do not know the exact proportion. I think it was at least half of us. But of course, operating chiefly from inside bunkers and other fixed defences does not require a high level of fitness, as the activity is static; for this reason, Herr Eckhertz, people must not think that we were 'second rate' troops. I myself was a formidable operator of my 'Ringstellung' *(Ring Position or Tobruk bunker)*.

Can you give an explanation of what the 'Ringstellung' or 'Tobruk' was?

Yes, the Tobruk was a widely-used type of small bunker for local defence; this was essentially a concrete casing set into the ground, with a concrete cupola emerging at ground level, allowing a single soldier to fire a machine gun, with only his head and shoulders showing above the ground.

The designs of the Tobruks varied, but most types I saw had a concrete box about three metres square and two metres high, dug in below ground level; the cupola was a circular opening with a concrete rim for mounting the gun. My particular Tobruk had a metal shield on the gun mount, protecting the gunner. These Tobruks were sited around larger bunkers or at significant points in the zone to be defended, sometimes they were placed almost at random in the countryside as a way of making any enemy advance unpredictable in its progress.

These Tobruks were built mostly by prisoners in the construction brigades, who would dig the hole and pour the concrete under the supervision of engineers. Some Tobruks were also brought in as prefabricated boxes and placed in the ground like that. I saw some larger types of the installation which had a small panzer turret on top instead of the cupola. In these cases, the turrets came from old French or Czech tanks, and were traversed with a hand crank, having a crew of two men. But the single-man, MG armed Tobruk was the most common style that I saw.

What was the underground concrete box used for?

This was for storage of the ammunition, and for a spare man who would take over if the first operator was killed or wounded. The concept of the Tobruk was that the men would remain down in the box with the MG during a bombardment, and then one of them would come up to the cupola, fit the MG and fight any advancing infantry like that.

The advantage of the Tobruk was its easy concealment at ground level; the disadvantage of course was that the operator himself was very low down and had limited visibility.

My particular Tobruk was sited at a crossroads of unpaved tracks on sloping ground overlooking a place called Dune St Pierre, which had an important fortified house. This house was originally a civilian beachfront villa, which was now reinforced with extra concrete to the walls and a concrete roof, having narrow gun slits in place of windows, and fitted with multiple heavy machine guns and a PAK (*anti-tank*) gun. We simply called it 'the strong house,' and it had an excellent field of fire along the sea wall on the beach.

It was anticipated that the strong house might be attacked by paratroopers or partisans approaching from inland, and my Tobruk was a defence against this inland threat. We manned the Tobruk position in shifts of six hours, then a sleeping break of six hours, then another shift and so on. We slept in a requisitioned house about one kilometre away.

Our officer was in charge of about twenty of these Tobruks at various sites in the area, all of a similar design. Our officer was a very experienced man; he had been in the East as an artillery commander, and now was technically a training officer. We were connected to his command post by a telephone cable, but we had no radio set.

What was it like to man the Tobruk?

It required us to stand on a concrete plinth in the box, with our shoulders up out of the ground. The gun was an MG34 with canister magazines which did not require a second man as gun feeder, which would be the case with belt ammunition. The gun and its metal shield were fixed on a rail around the cupola, similar to the anti-aircraft gun rail on a panzer commander's turret cupola. Thus, the gun could be rotated around 360 degrees. We were ordered to constantly rotate the gun, watching for any signs of a threat.

The second man was officially meant to stay down in the underground box in case of attack; in reality, he would almost always be above ground, watching with binoculars or being otherwise useful, and we would change places regularly. As you can well imagine, Herr Eckhertz, the tedium of this task was not a burden!

The presence of the Tobruk was well-known locally, and French civilians would give us a formal greeting as they passed; there was a herd of dairy cows nearby, and the farmer was under instructions to give us a can of milk every second day. We rewarded this with cigarettes and boiled sweets from our ration. The farmer's daughter was a very charming girl of about our age, who had taken the sensible precaution of learning to speak some German words and also some English. In general it can be said that we had an excellent relationship with the local people.

Were you on duty at the Tobruk on June 6th?

Yes, I was. I had entered the Tobruk at midnight, and my comrade Sepp was on duty with me. He was a Belgian with fiercely pro-German sentiments who had volunteered to serve in the Wehrmacht, and a very clever fellow.

Did you have similar motivations to Sepp?

Yes. We both considered ourselves as the first line of defence against an attack on France and ultimately on the Reich. We must remember that, after 1943, our German propaganda changed radically in tone. Where before the message had always been '*Conquer, occupy, expand*' now the idea was '*Defend the Reich against our enemies who will try to invade it.'* Now that I think about it, this significant change, from 'conquer' to 'defend' as the main message, this happened roughly after the battle of Kursk and the invasion of Sicily. Maybe that is when the commanders and the politicians realised they must acclimatise us to being permanently on the defensive. At any rate, because of these messages, we saw ourselves as the defenders of the Reich, first and foremost.

We knew that the loss of France would be a dreadful blow if it happened, because it would give the Western Allies a platform to attack German soil in partnership with the Bolsheviks in the East. We knew that the Russians sought the destruction of Germany, and this would mean the rape and enslavement of our families under communism. This was our motivation at that time.

Did you have any indication or suspicion that the invasion was imminent on that day?

The general feeling was that the Allies would try to enter France in some form during the summer. We were told by the officers that this might happen at any time. I myself was given no specific alert or warning regarding June 6th, but, having said that, it became obvious during the hours of darkness from late evening on the 5th to first light, that something important was happening. There was a large amount of aircraft activity, even more than usual, and some continuous bombing to the south of us. The bombing was a regular occurrence, but I had never heard so many planes in the air at night before.

Our officer came to the Tobruk on his motorcycle at about one am, and he agreed that the situation was unprecedented. He told us that he had received reports of paratroopers landing to the South, and that Regimental command were 'aware of the developments.' I am sure that infantrymen throughout history have received precisely this reassurance countless times from their superiors.

The aircraft activity continued and even escalated throughout the darkness. There was a searchlight and Flak battery to the west, and this Flak fired sporadically, but the searchlights were under-powered and ineffective. I saw flames in the sky to the north at sev-eral points, which must have been burning aircraft, but no signs of aerial combat. All of this put us on edge, Sepp and me, and we awaited first light with great concern.

There began to be sounds of explosions and firing from the area South East of us, which flared up and then died away. We reported this to our officer's post on the cable phone, but the officer himself was not present.

As the light came up, it became possible to see the activity in the sky, faintly at first. There was a stream of twin-engined aircraft fly-ing north, in a disorganised formation. These aircraft had unusual black and white stripes on their wings which I had not seen before; however, from our aircraft recognition training I recognised these as C47 types, which we were told were used for personnel trans-port and for paratroopers. All of this made it clear that an airborne attack on quite a large scale was happening to the south of us, and of course this was exactly the threat that our Tobruk was positioned to defend against.

What was your personal reaction to this realisation,
and what was your comrade Sepp's reaction?

Well, I had been in action in Italy, and I felt the familiar sensation of dry throat, shaking fingers, apprehension. At the same time, though, I felt an excitement and a desire to be part of the combat, as this was my purpose and my role. I wanted the chance, to be quite frank with you, to show that despite my limp I was as good a soldier as these Allied men. I cannot speak for Sepp, of course, but he had not been in action previously; nevertheless, he remained calm and professional. He scanned 360 degrees with binoculars, and told me that there was smoke to the south, with flashes of light in the air. To the north of us, the seaward side, there was a view down to the strong house itself and it was possible in daylight to observe part of the sea between the dunes. Sepp told me that this view was obscured either by mist or smoke. As he said these words, we came under a very powerful bombardment.

The first explosion was between us and the strong house, and it was preceded by a low whining sound. The explosion was huge; I deduced from the whining noise that this was shell fire, not aerial bombing, but the power was bigger than anything I had seen in Italy. The noise made my eardrums screech, and the blast wave flattened me in the cupola of the Tobruk. When I looked round, Sepp was prone on the ground with his hands over his head, and there was a massive column of smoke and dust rising over the slope down to the bunker. Neither of us was injured, but more of these huge shells began exploding around us, and we both ducked down into the underground room of the Tobruk, me taking the MG down with me as per my orders.

This bombardment went on for about twenty minutes, and I could also hear the noise of very low aircraft nearby. Our concrete box shook and the concrete cracked in places, which was alarming; at one point I opened the cupola cover and saw a large amount of dust in the sky, also vapour trails in the air. The light was coming up fully, and the sky was becoming pale, and these vapour trails were very clear; there were dozens of them. I tried to contact our command on the cable phone, but the line did not function. When the bombardment slackened, I lifted my MG back up through the cupola, put my head out of the cupola cautiously and looked around.

The sight was very strange, and I can still see it now; it is not an exaggeration to say that the details are fixed in my memory, and I believe they always will be. To the south, the inland zone where I was to expect the partisans or paratroopers to approach, I saw, instead of an advancing enemy, that the shelling had damaged the sheds of the nearby dairy herd, and many of these animals were running out of control in the fields. It was a dreadful thing; these large cows, with their full udders, were injured, bleeding, and in some cases their hides were on fire. They were staggering or trampling in utter confusion. One began to charge towards me, obviously maddened, with its legs burning; I shot it immediately with the MG to prevent myself being trampled. That was the first shot I fired on June 6th, ironically.

Looking to the north, in the direction of the strong house on the sea wall, the shelling had created many mounds of earth and debris, and I could not see the house through the dust. However, there was a crashed aircraft there; this was an American fighter of the Mustang type, which was on its nose in the ground, on fire. Whether it was brought down by our Flak or was hit by the shell fire at low altitude, I do not know. The pilot was still in the cockpit under the bubble canopy, visibly moving, but the flames were coming from the engine very fiercely. As I watched, the wings began to burn, and then they exploded in a red and black fireball. A lot of his ammunition detonated as well, and tracer bullets shot out in random patterns all across the slope. I could no longer see the pilot.

Overhead, there were many more fighter aircraft, all with the same black and white bands on the wings and fuselage, crossing north to south at low altitude. I could not see any Luftwaffe planes anywhere, which frankly was not a great surprise to me; the lack of Luftwaffe cover was an accepted fact by that stage, on all fronts, I believe.

I did not know what to expect next, but I fastened the MG onto the shield in the cupola ring, and sighted inland towards the south where I expected an attack.

Sepp was sitting on the edge of his hatch looking down there with binoculars. I asked what he could see, and he turned to me to answer. As he did so, he was shot directly through the throat; because I was looking at him, I saw the bullet emerge from the back of his neck, causing a spray of blood and tissue. He remained upright, and another bullet hit him in the chest, causing a lot of matter to shoot out of his back, along with shreds of his uniform. He was literally shot to pieces in front of me. He slumped down, and I fired a burst from the MG to the south, although I could not see the shooters. I saw a shape appear in the air from an area of trees to one side, and from my experience in Italy I saw that this was an Allied pattern grenade. It landed short some distance from me, and although some debris hit me in the face and shoulder, it did not injure me badly.

I immediately fired on the trees, and the trunks of these trees fragmented as the bullets struck; the range was only about fifty metres. I saw no response from there, but I did see movement from my left, near the farm buildings where the injured cattle were moving around. I thought that might be one of the cows, which were still mooing and thrashing their hooves in pain; however, I clearly saw a military helmet, green, with netting, and I recognised from the enemy troops I had seen in Italy that this was an American soldier. He was in long grass, probably trying to outflank me. I shot towards him, and I saw the helmet lift up in the air and spin over. After that, I saw a man's hands moving, in the manner as if he was clutching himself, and I fired again.

Did you have any emotion during these moments?

None, to be honest. I knew that I was being surrounded, and my heart was beating very heavily, but at the same time my eyesight seemed very acute and I was watching carefully for the next threat to my position; one problem was that my ears were still ringing from the bombardment and I could hear very little.

Were you hopeful of other troops coming to your aid?

I knew that there were some armoured troops to the south and south west, but I really did not know what would happen. I believed that these Americans were paratroopers or airborne troops who were seeking to isolate the beach, which suggested that the beach would be under attack also. Although I could not hear well, I did glance over my shoulder and see the concrete roof of the strong house down at the foot of the slope; it was damaged, with big impact marks on the roof, and beyond it, between the dunes, I could see vessels on the sea itself, being mostly green or grey-coloured craft of a type I had not seen before.

I understood much later that this was the day of 'the largest seaborne invasion in history' or 'the biggest military operation ever mounted' – but that is actually all I saw of the landing itself. Just that glimpse between the dunes, with a lot of boats on the water. I think this often happens to basic foot soldiers in a war: they are in historic battles or campaigns, but their view is limited to the fields around them.

As you see, I was in a critical position. The Americans were infiltrating around me in unknown numbers, and the situation at the strong house, which was my whole purpose in being in my Tobruk, was unknown. I had no working telephone and I could not even hear properly. My comrade was dead; indeed, Sepp was still lying near me on the hatch, his body bleeding heavily but not breathing. I decided to stay where I was and continue to man the gun.

I reached down into the Tobruk and brought up several fresh ammunition canisters, and had these ready inside the cupola ring. I fired several more bursts into the trees, but could not see if I hit anything. Several shots came back, hitting the steel plate of my MG shield. The shield became deformed, but it stayed intact.

Suddenly – because I could not hear the approach – a man appeared next to me, tumbling through the air beside me. He sprawled on the ground beside the gun, and I saw he was shot repeatedly through the chest. He was a German soldier from the strong house, whom I recognised; he was carrying a rifle. I looked around, and saw several more of our troops running towards me from the direction of the beach. One by one, they were all hit by bullets, knocking them down in moments. One man was hit horribly in the head, and he lost most of his skull; another man was hit in the stomach and he writhed on the ground, thrashing his legs and vomiting. Two men threw themselves down next to me, and one was immediately hit in the neck and had his head partially severed. I fired a very long burst in an arc around the whole front of me, and this enabled the other man on the ground to get behind me, sheltered by the gun shield. He was a Leutnant, although I did not know him. Anyway, he had an MP40 (*sub machine gun*), and I was reassured to have an officer with me.

He shouted in my ear, and I could just understand what he was saying:

'They are landing tanks on the beach and burning out the strong house.'

I was confused at this, because I did not think it was possible to land tanks onto a beach; I assumed he meant they were cars.

He shouted in my ear, 'The strong house is lost. Bring the gun and leave the Tobruk.'

I said, 'You order me to leave the Tobruk?'

He said, 'We will take the men and go to the next bunkers, we will join the troops there.'

There was a further line of bunkers inland, about two kilometres south. I did not know what the situation might be there! It might be worse than this. However, more of our troops began to appear from the beach zone, and I fired off large amounts of MG bullets to cover them. Some were shot, but I also hit three Americans with Thompson guns whom I saw emerge from the trees, and they tumbled onto the ground. The Leutnant stood up, showing himself as a target, and no shots came. I was impressed at his courage. He shouted, 'Now, we move,' and this proved to be a good choice of moment.

We had a handful of men in addition to this Leutnant and myself; I unclipped the gun and I placed over the barrel a leather ring that we used for carrying it when the gun was hot. The group of us moved quickly towards the trees; one of the tracks that formed the crossroads continued past there in the rough direction of the second line of bunkers. I moved as fast as possible with my limp.

As we came level with the three dead Americans, one of them moved and seemed about to rise; he had a Thompson gun close to him. The Leutnant stooped down quickly and shot him in the head with his MP40, then shot the other two men likewise.

15

One of our men took a Thompson gun and spare ammunition magazines from the bodies. I would not have done this; I knew from Italy that if a soldier (whether German or Allied) was captured with enemy 'souvenirs' on him, then his treatment as a prisoner would be violent or even lethal; on the Eastern Front, it was an immediate death sentence, apparently. But the Thompson guns were superb items, being famous as the 'gangster guns' from the 1930s, and they were hard to resist. Armed in this way, we advanced down the earth track towards our inland bunkers. I struggled to keep up now with my limp, but I did my utmost.

After a few paces, I heard the officer curse loudly; I looked round, and saw that two of the troops had disappeared. They were literally nowhere to be seen, and there was no shooting or struggle. My hearing was recovering, and I could hear explosions from the coast and aircraft overhead, but I saw or heard no sign of those two men.

'They have deserted; they prefer to be taken prisoner,' the officer said. 'But I saw at the strong house, the Allies are not taking prisoners today, they burned the whole thing with a flamethrower, with the men in it.'

I do not know if this was true or if he said this to motivate us, but we continued, now being a few men, myself and this Leutnant.

It was very warm, and I was very thirsty. My leg was becoming painful because of my limp. We stayed in the cover of the trees, because huge numbers of aircraft were passing overhead. Some of these appeared to be twin-engined bombers, and there was a large amount of smoke rising on the southern and eastern horizons; other planes were the Jabo (*Fighter-bomber*) type, and often they would swoop down and fire on the ground ahead of us. When they fired, long streaks of white light would shoot down onto the ground, which one of our men said were rockets and very dangerous. There was a strong smell of smoke, burning rubber, and aircraft fumes.

As the breeze came from the beach area, it brought with it sounds of activity: detonations, machine-gunning and many engine noises. There was the definite sound of tank tracks; I knew these were not ours, as we had no panzers on the beach line itself.

The Leutnant gave me a drink from his water canteen, because I had left mine behind in the Tobruk. Because of the need to go up and down through the cupola, it was not possible to carry the regulation water bottle, gas mask case and haversack equipment. To my surprise, the Leutnant's water was mixed heavily with schnapps, and it was very refreshing. That Leutnant was a complete contradiction in many ways. I never knew his name.

Shortly after this, we came on a small group of civilians, who had prisoner labourers with them. As we passed, the Leutnant told them all in French to go to a cellar and hide.

Who were these prisoner labourers?

It is not remembered much, but all Reich-controlled territories had substantial numbers of prisoners of war or civilian prisoners working as manual labourers and farming or construction workers. These people were mostly Russian or Polish, mostly male, but also with women among them. I do not know the numbers, but there must have been hundreds of thousands of these people in France alone. Huge gangs of them, hundreds of them, would be at railway stations, sleeping on the wasteland beside the tracks, under the guard of a few armed engineers.

These ones that we passed on that morning of the 6th, they appeared to be farm workers, all were men. As we went by, one of them said something, made a comment – I do not know what exactly. I do not even know what language it was that he spoke. I heard a shot very close, and ducked, then looked back. The Leutnant had shot this labourer in the chest with his MP40, killing him outright. The other civilians and labourers backed away from us, and we continued onward.

Did you make any protest about this shooting?

No, I did not. It was not in our nature at the time to make protests to officers. Also, the situation was very tense and uncertain, also in all the confusion there was a real danger that some of the labourers would rise up against us and try to overpower us. I am not justifying what the officer did, you understand, but I place it in context for you.

We came on from that point into a low area where the land was flooded as a defence; our commanders had diverted the local river to disgorge partly onto this plain in order to deny its use as airborne landings or for troop advances from the coast. This floodwater was about one metre deep and covered about two square kilometres, and beyond that was higher ground where our second line of bunkers was positioned. There was a wooden walkway leading across the water, but this was bombed and burning. The only other way was to skirt around the whole flood area to reach the bunkers.

At the side of the track, there was a 'Famo' type half-track, the type without armour, parked under a stand of trees, and there was nobody present with it. Possibly the crew had deserted, or been killed away from the vehicle by the airborne troops; at any rate, this powerful machine was there for the taking, with the starting lever still working and a small amount of fuel. The officer ordered us into it, with the intention of driving it around the floodwater to the fortifications. We men bundled onto this vehicle, and one of the soldiers started it and began to drive.

Of course, this was the worst thing we could have done, because the Famo was very visible from the air. Although we drove under a long line of trees which partly shielded us, it was only a few seconds before a fighter plane came down to look at us. It came in from over the floods, and I believe it was a Mustang type, although it was moving so quickly that it was literally a blur in my vision. It fired its guns on us, and the tracer shot along the water, over the roadway and hit us in the engine and cab.

I was sitting at the back of the vehicle, and I saw the bullets smash into the sides of the cab, tearing off all the metal body plates; with no armour, there was nothing to protect the driver, and he was thrown out of the vehicle onto the road. The half-track veered around, and we ran over the driver as he rolled in the roadway, then the Famo rolled down the small embankment into the floodwater.

There was nothing to be done for the driver; his body was completely crushed open by the tracks of the Famo. The engine was on fire, and this made our presence even more conspicuous from the air. I jumped off, with the officer and the remaining soldiers plus our weapons, and we continued on foot along this track beside the water. The plane returned a few seconds later and machine-gunned the vehicle again; looking back, we saw it blow up completely as we ran on.

We found there were other troops on this track, going in the same direction, and the officer grouped them together and ordered us to work as a team. We were now about twenty in number. These men were a combination of Kriegsmarine support crews from the bunkers, Wehrmacht infantry and various Eastern recruits in the ROA insignia.

Can you explain the ROA?

This was a formation of men originally taken prisoner from the Soviet and Polish armies earlier in the war, who had now sworn an oath to us and agreed to work for the Wehrmacht; I believe they were stationed on the Atlantic Wall to keep them away from their home countries where they might defect again. We in the Wehrmacht regarded them as unreliable, although I have heard that some of them fought to the death in Normandy, fearing the consequences of being recaptured by the Allies. Whatever their motivations, these fellows ran with us along the path; were sere spread out in a long column, and we had to throw ourselves flat several times as planes came over.

Sometimes the planes fired on us, and at other times they simply flew along the road, firing at the empty pathway; they were at liberty to do as they pleased, with no Luftwaffe to challenge them at all. Several of our men were hit, and those that were struck were simply left by the path, as it was impossible to bring them with us. I remember that one man, one of the ROA, was hit in the abdomen by several bullets; his body was cut in half, I am sorry to say, and the rest of us could only step over the two pieces as we ran on.

19

Towards the end, we were fired on from ahead of us, killing one of our group, but this proved to be another German Tobruk sited near the bunker line. When this Tobruk gunner realised who we were, he waved us on towards the bunkers and called them to warn of our approach. My leg was making it almost impossible to run, and one of the Russian men helped me by letting me lean on him. I was grateful. He did not have to do that, nobody ordered him to do it, and he probably saved me from being left behind near the Tobruk.

Finally, we passed through barbed wire positions and slit trenches, and we came into the second-line bunker zone itself. This was a series of concrete blockhouse structures, three of them about one hundred metres apart, well-camouflaged, on slightly rising ground, with a good field of fire over the roadway, the floods and over an area of marshy land which separated this area from the coastline. These forts had been bombed, and there were craters all around, but they were intact. There were many vehicles jumbled up around the approaches: half-tracks, Kubelwagens, motorcycles and horse carts.

These bunker structures were what we called 'Resistance Points,' and I saw that they were armed with 75mm PAK guns, which were on wheels inside the buildings, with their barrels projecting through the embrasures, and a variety of MG positions. There were slit trenches which were crowded with troops who had retreated from the beach area, and among these was a Panzerschrek (*bazooka*) crew. There was a single 20mm Flak gun behind the bunkers to cover them.

This was a strong area to defend, as the approaches were lower-lying, difficult to cross and had little concealment. I felt more confident here, and I was seen briefly by a medic who gave me a 'soldier's cocktail,' which was a mix of morphine and amphetamine against the pain and exhaustion. I went into one of the bunkers, which had a PAK gun aimed out over the marshes. They were glad to see me with my MG34; I positioned this on its bipod mount in one of the slit embrasures, and then waited.

What was the atmosphere in this bunker?

The men who manned the bunker were questioning us new arrivals frantically. '*How many? Who are they? What weapons? Are there tanks? Flamethrowers?*' And so on. But what did we know, really? We knew there was a sizeable force approaching, with tanks of some kind, and there were also American airborne troops in the area. In this blockhouse, people were jumpy, constantly calling out that they saw something, arguing with each other; the mood was nervous. A Feldwebel (*sergeant*) came in and gave us criticism for our behaviour, and we became more orderly under his command. This Feldwebel told us that reinforcements were coming up from the south and east, and that we had only to hold this bunker line for a few hours before our panzers would arrive to push the attackers back to the beach and into the sea. This was an excellent little speech and it rallied our nerves well, because we knew that there were armoured divisions dispersed to the south.

The time now was around ten or eleven am, I think; my watch was broken in the Famo crash. I did not have much desire to know the time exactly. I felt sure that these thick concrete walls of the bunker would hold out and that we would hold the line.

I had a view of the roadway and flooded area in front, and I squinted along my MG sight, wiping all the sweat and dust from my eyes. The interior of this bunker was very humid, and quite dark, with all the troops hunched over their weapons at the embrasures, whether the PAK gun, or machine guns or rifles. I am sure that everybody's heart was beating as hard as mine, and that everyone was trying to calm themselves.

Of course, we were expecting a ground attack, but the Allies were determined to deny us the chance to fight in such a way. We heard a shouted warning: 'Jabo!' ('*Fighter-bomber!*')

I peered up through the concrete slit, and saw a horizontal line of three aircraft descending on us over the marshes at great speed. These planes had very large radial engines, which from our recognition sessions I knew was distinctive of the Thunderbolt plane.

I recall being surprised, because the planes appeared to be bare metal; the sun reflected very brightly off their surfaces. There was nothing that anyone of us could do, although I and several others fired our MGs up in an attempt at Flak defence. This was rushed and ineffective, because the Thunderbolts were simply too fast.

The Flak cannon fired, and I saw the 20mm cannon tracer fly up to seek the planes; the 20mm shells were very bright, and snaked slightly in the air. Some of these shells actually hit one of the planes in the wing, knocking pieces out. This plane lifted up and banked away, but the other two continued to descend, and they released bombs from under their wings as they approached us at probably one hundred metres height.

The bombs flew out almost horizontally from their wings, and the pilots lifted each wing in turn to release them. It is strange how the mind remembers such a detail, but in the heat of the moment, the senses are taking in all this information, and it is indelibly imprinted on the memory. The small, dark bombs, two from each plane, came tearing across the marshland and into our bunker line. The bombs slapped into the flat ground in front of us, and bounced up, tumbling over in their momentum. One bomb bounced straight past us and went between the bunkers, then another hit our roof and deflected off without exploding. It detonated somewhere behind us. From my slit aperture, I could see the blockhouse on our right; this was hit by at least one bomb, and it was covered in dust and smoke, but appeared to be standing.

The Thunderbolt aircraft came down on us repeatedly; I think there were six or eight waves of them in all. Each time, these very shiny planes flew low, flipped their wings to release their bomb load, and the projectiles would race towards us, bouncing across the ground and scattering around our position. There was no pause between the attacks: as soon as one load of bombs detonated, the next wave was on the point of unloading their bombs onto us. Our Flak hit one of the planes in the early waves; I saw this aircraft lose its propeller and engine cowling, and then the cannon tracer pierced its wings. The plane exploded in a very long streak of fire, and did not lift out of its attack run. It raced straight down onto us and hit the ground to my left, where many of the vehicles were scattered. There were huge explosions from that side, which I could not see.

The succeeding waves were not hit by Flak, and I realised that our 20mm had stopped firing. The bombs kept coming at us, and I saw one of them skip across the ground and tumble into one of the slit trenches crammed with infantry. The explosion threw up many pieces of men, weapons and clothing, all mixed together in the shockwave. I gave up looking through the embrasure; all we could do was to crouch down under the embrasures and put our hands over our ears under our helmets to protect our eardrums.

The bunker shook several times, and the explosions sent many chunks of shrapnel and debris hurtling through our concrete apertures, which ricocheted around the interior. One of the PAK crew men broke down, and began screaming. His comrades punched him to the ground and he lay sobbing there, while another man took his place.

Was there much other loss of self-control?

In fact, no; the men were well-disciplined. Some of the men produced crucifixes or rosaries and said prayers, others seemed to be simply cursing; both were inaudible, but I could see their mouths moving.

This bombing lasted perhaps a minute or two, but seemed endless. Cracks appeared in the concrete ceiling of the bunker, and large pieces fell from the upper edge of the embrasures. Some of this masonry hit our troops, crushing several limbs; these men could only lie on the concrete floor and wait for the situation to end.

When the bombs stopped, there was a pause of several seconds, and I peered out. I could see, through all the dust and smoke outside the bunker, that the blockhouse on our right had been blown open partially, there was a large hole in one side. The trench that had been hit was a horrible mess, with many dismembered bodies lying around it, many smouldering or contorted and blackened. I could hear flames and detonations from the other side of our bunker too.

Then the shout went up 'Jabo again!' It seemed that the Americans had an endless stream of planes available, which were always arriving freshly armed on top of us. These new aircraft were also Thunderbolt types; however, as they approached, I saw the white streaks of light from under their wings and the descending lines of vapour which showed they were using rockets. I had never seen rocket explosions close at hand before, and did not know what to expect.

The effect of these rockets was in some ways worse than the bombs. The warheads used some kind of incendiary material which exploded with a very intense white light and then burned and expanded with a hissing noise. I saw one of the first rockets detonate in this way against the other bunker. The white flames covered the structure and entered the hole that was blown in one side, all the time making this eerie, hissing sound. Really, it sounded like an animal hissing or breathing. The other rockets hit our line in very rapid bursts, and our zone around the bunkers was absolutely filled with the bright, pale flames.

One rocket hit our blockhouse on the wall outside the PAK gun aperture, and the explosion was completely blinding. The PAK was about ten metres away from me, and I saw many fragments of burning material pour in through the aperture and fall onto the floor around the PAK; these fragments themselves expanded and burned, until in a few moments the gun seemed to be covered in these bright, blazing pieces of material. This fire simply would not go out; it covered the PAK crew, and sank into their ammunition pile. There was complete panic and disorder at that point. The men near the PAK were consumed in these white flames, including the weeping man on the ground and several injured men nearby. The uniforms of these men peeled off in scorched pieces, and their bare skin was set alight by the fire. A round of the 75mm ammunition detonated in the flames, and the shell blasted around the interior of the bunker, glowing red with tracer. This shell smashed off the wall, off the ceiling and off the other walls – each time, it hit a man or group of men, and cut them horribly before bouncing elsewhere again.

Somebody threw open the steel door of the bunker, and I hurled myself at it. Other men were competing with me to get out of that inferno in the bunker, and we fought each other with our bare hands at the doorway. I stumbled through, over the body of a man who collapsed outside with his hair on fire, and I ran a few paces away from the structure. I made the mistake of looking back into the bunker through the door. I can tell you that the interior was a vision of hell, an obscene sight that remains with me.

The white burning material was still expanding, and burning alive the men who had not escaped through the door. Men were rolling and struggling on the floor in the flames, some were clawing blindly at the walls, trying to feel the route out, with their faces all covered in smoke because their clothing was on fire. PAK rounds and MG rounds were detonating in there, in the confined space, and the tracer was screaming from one wall to another, tearing up the bodies of men where they stood or lay. I backed away from the door, as a couple of other men staggered out after me, with their backs and legs on fire.

Finally, all I could see inside the bunker was the flickering white light of the incendiary, and many flashes of exploding rounds. All that I could hear was the screaming and groaning of men, and the strange hiss of the burning rockets as the last salvo of them exploded in front of our line.

I shook myself, and looked around for guidance. My bunker was destroyed from inside, and I could see that the bunker on the right was in a similar state; the hole in its side was issuing white flames and smoke. On my left, the third bunker had its steel door still closed, but its apertures were streaming with the incendiary flames, and there were explosions inside.

Nearby, the jumble of vehicles was completely on fire, with the trucks and precious half-tracks thrown onto their sides, and many wheels and bits of engine debris strewn about. The wreckage of the crashed Thunderbolt plane was among them, burning fiercely, with its tail rising up above the rest. Behind me, the 20mm Flak gun had been hit by bombs, and it lay in pieces in a crater with its crew. I was one of the few survivors of the attack.

What kind of incendiary was this in the rockets?

I learned afterwards that this material was a phosphorous weapon. It is a very powerful explosive chemical that the Allies were starting to experiment with. The devastating thing about this phosphorous was that the fire kept growing and expanding, and it flowed almost like a liquid, eating into anything it touched. My God, I saw some of the bodies of our troops in the trench lines that had been hit by these rockets. The bodies were reduced to skeletons, very black and charred, as all the body material was burned off and consumed. I confess that I was terrified at the sight, not knowing how soon the Thunderbolt planes would come back and strike us again. Would this happen to me within a minute, or five minutes, or six? Would I be reduced to this skeletal state soon? I was left stunned, incapable of action for a few moments.

I suppose that the psychological impact of such weapons is part of their effectiveness.

That is true; even the survivors are left fearful and incapacitated. As for me, I had no gun, my uniform was scorched and in shreds, and the morphine cocktail was wearing off, leaving me trembling and shattered. The air was full of smoke and dust, and the sun had a very harsh glare, which made it difficult to see around me. Two other men came up to me, both Wehrmacht troops, and we crouched down, considering what to do. There were no officers visible; a few other men were appearing from the smoke, but these were running away from the bunkers to the south east in complete disorder. A man appeared who was armed with a Panzerschrek (*bazooka.*) He had the firing tube but he had only two projectiles, which he carried tenderly in his arm as if they were prize rabbits. That is the way it looked to me, with my confused senses.

From the roadway, we could hear the sound of tank movement, which was rising and falling. Our view was obscured by smoke and dust, but this was thinning because the coastal breeze was strengthening across the zone. The two troops said that they were going to retreat, because the bunkers were destroyed; however, the Panzerschrek man insisted that he wanted to fire his two projectiles. He said that these could destroy any Allied tank at two hundred metres, and that we would be decorated as heroes when our own panzers arrived. It occurred to me that he was mentally confused, but I was also bewildered, and I was past the stage of being afraid for the future. For this reason, even though the two other men retreated on foot to the rear of the bunkers and left the zone, I stayed with the Panzerschrek man and agreed to operate as his loader. I took an MP40 from the body of one of our men, and two spare magazines.

We took up a position between two wrecked vehicles, a half-track and an armoured car, behind a concrete slab. This was near the crashed Thunderbolt, but the smoke from its flames was blowing away from us. We had a good view along the road track beside the flood water. The trees along the track were burning in some places, and there was debris of machinery scattered along the ground. The Panzerschrek gunner told me how to load the rocket projectile into the launcher tube, which was over his shoulder; I loaded one of the two rounds, and then rolled away as he instructed me so that the rocket blast would not hit me. I flattened myself, holding my MP40, and looked into the roadway; I could see the outline of a tank coming through the smoke from the burning trees.

This tank was very high in outline, and as it advanced on us I saw that it had a white star on the front plate. This made it very obvious, almost like a tinplate target at a fairground shooting stall. In my confused mental state, that is the image I had of this tank. The range was about 200 metres. The Panzerschrek man said 'It's a Sherman, we can finish him,' and before I could respond, he fired.

27

A huge spout of sparks and fire came out from the back of the tube, burning my face with the heat although I was away from its jet. I saw the projectile go streaking towards the Sherman, and it struck the front plate, low down between the tracks. The explosion was not large, but I saw many fragments of metal burst off the hull immediately, and the tracks stopped moving. The vehicle halted and rocked violently, and I was surprised that the machine gun in the hull did not fire; I suppose this was because the projectile had killed or injured the gunner. However, the turret machine gun fired on us, and the bullets ripped up the wrecked vehicles that we were hiding behind. We crouched behind the concrete slab, and I reloaded the rocket launcher.

The Sherman stopped shooting at us, and I heard crackling sounds which sounded as if it was burning. We peered over the concrete slab, and saw that this tank was on fire, and its crew were climbing out of the hatches. One of them had a sub machine gun, and I fired on him with my MP40, knocking him down immediately. The other crew men scattered and ran to the back of the tank. I rolled away, because I saw that the Panzerschrek man was going to fire again.

After he fired, I heard another small detonation, and I peered around the edge of the slab to see that the rocket had actually hit a second Sherman which was attempting to steer around the immobilised one. This second tank was hit on the edge of the front hull, by the drive wheel, and its track was blown off and hanging loose on the roadway. This was an incredible success for us, to have hit two tanks with two shots, and I remember feeling a sensation of great pride in this achievement. Of course, our actions were punished by the second tank, which fired on us with high-explosive. These shells blew up the vehicles near us, and showered us with debris. We were trapped behind the concrete slab, and unable to move away from its shelter.

In between the explosions, I could hear the revving and clanking of other tanks trying to manoeuvre on the narrow road. My mood changed completely. I thought that we were close to death, and close to losing our battle. The Panzerschrek man was hit by shrapnel, which hit him in the shoulder and neck, and he began bleeding heavily. He threw away his rocket launcher and took a grenade from his boot, handing it to me. I thought that he wanted me to throw it at the tanks – but what use was that? Then he told me that we should blow ourselves up rather than be captured. He was either very fanatical, or mentally unbalanced, I believe.

Did you consider blowing yourself up?

Why would I do such a thing? There was no reason to do that. We were honest foot soldiers, defending France and ultimately the Reich from aggression. But as we crouched there behind the concrete, with these high explosive rounds smashing up the wrecked transports around us, there was the noise of another tank from the south, from the direction of our lines. My spirits lifted greatly. I believed that our panzer reinforcements were arriving, at the last possible moment to assist us and defend this bunker line. I imagined a great formation of our panzers, pushing the Americans back into the sea, as the Feldwebel had promised us in the bunker. However, all that arrived was a single, solitary Stug III gun.

This was a self-propelled 75mm PAK gun on a low panzer chassis; it was renowned as an excellent vehicle in use against tanks. I had seen these Stugs used in Italy, and they had inflicted great losses on Shermans. But this was only one, and as it advanced on our position, I expected to see others behind it. There were no others, and it turned out that this Stug commander had risked his vehicle to approach the bunker line alone and assess the situation.

We gestured to the Stug, and it presumably saw us, because it drove rapidly around us and fired several shots at the roadway. I heard impacts and explosions from down there. I tried to lift the Panzerschrek man, but I was too weak and he was too heavy, and I left him lying behind the concrete. I do not know what happened to him. The Stug, having seen the situation on the road, began to reverse away slowly, still firing its gun. It did not stop for me, but the commander, who was behind an armoured shield on the roof hatch, gestured to me to climb on.

I was able to take hold of the armour skirting and clamber onto the back of the vehicle, which was extremely hot due to the engine vents. I held on there, and the Stug reversed back from the road, pushing aside many of the wrecked transports, and moved to the south, away from these bunkers. I took a look along the side of the Stug as I held on, and saw that there were three Shermans now apparently disabled in the road: the two we had hit with the rockets, and another which was also on fire and standing in the flood water. There were other tanks behind these three, and infantry moving around between them, but the immobilised Shermans were obstructing their progress. In this manner, we withdrew from the line of bunkers and used a forest track to retreat several kilometres to the south east, where a number of armoured vehicles were assembling into a small battle group in the woods.

What kind of force was this?

It was not impressive, to be frank. They were from an armoured Division to the South of the sector. There were several Stugs, several of the large armoured cars, and some infantry in Hanomags. Maybe ten vehicles in all, and thirty infantry, that is probably about all. The vehicles were heavily disguised with foliage on their superstructures, but even so, the crews were reluctant to move them out of the woods. We could see and hear the Allied Jabos overhead, swarming across the countryside at low altitude, and there was no mobile Flak gun in this group. Also, the command situation appeared to be confused; I fell into conversation with the Panzergrenadier men, and their view was that the Divisional commanders were slow in responding to the attack.

Was the word 'attack,' 'raid' or 'invasion'?
How did the men view the landings?

We all used the word 'attack' at this stage. It was only later in the day that the word 'invasion' was used more widely; at least, that is what I remember.

Was that the end of your combat on June 6ᵗʰ?

It was not. At this point, which was late in the morning, there was a lull in the fighting between the two sides. Possibly the Americans were concentrating on building up forces from their sea vessels into their land pocket; certainly, the German troops used the time to organise themselves and to bring up more vehicles and troops. This lasted an hour or so, certainly less than two hours, but all the time the Allied aircraft were moving overhead, and firing into the German zone.

As I had no trace of my unit from the original bunker, I attached myself to these Panzergrenadiers. I received medical attention from their medics, and they gave me another amphetamine tablet, which boosted my energy and my frame of mind greatly. I was armed with the MP40 I had picked up, and I obtained more magazines and grenades from these men. These troops were mostly very young men with older Feldwebel commanders; they had not yet been in contact with the Americans, and they were eager to engage them. There was also a field kitchen which gave me soup, bread and boiled sweets. I was desperately hungry and I ate all they could give me, sitting on an ammunition crate under a tree, with those Thunderbolts flying back and forth overhead.

There also came into the woods a unit of SS infantry. This was a platoon of about twenty youths who were extremely young, about seventeen, and they had been cut off from their commanders by a Jabo attack on a road to the south. They were very heavily armed, with MG34 and MP40, and these weapons looked out of place alongside their boyish faces. So all these troops and vehicles were packed together in the woods, without clear leadership and unwilling to move outside because of air attacks.

Two of the armoured cars went out to do reconnaissance of the American position and intending to take prisoners for interrogation. These armoured cars did not return, and the level of explosions and firing began to increase again after the late morning lull. Going to the west side of the woods, we could see smoke and flashes in the farmland on that side, where the land was higher and not flooded; all of this led to a great concern that we were being out-flanked and isolated.

In the end, I think after midday, the Stug commanders finally received clear orders from their Divisional command; they were to fall back to a fortified line about two kilometres south where there was German PAK artillery in emplacements. That line was to be held 'at all costs' until more reinforcements arrived. The Stug commanders told us men about this very clearly, and we began to form up into a column to retreat to the new line.

The road to the south was a route I did not know personally; it was an earth track suitable for farm tractors and so on, but it was partially sunken below ground level, and screened to the north and west by thick hedgerow of the type the French called 'bocage.' These low roads with hedge screens are typical of the Normandy and Brittany countryside. The fields to either side were believed to be mined.

This was quite a strong route for a retreat, and we began to move out along it with the armoured cars first, then Hanomags with their infantry on board in the vanguard, then the SS infantry on foot, and the three Stugs in the rear. The rearmost Stug faced backward and moved in reverse gear behind the whole column, with its gun pointing to the enemy. Because of the narrow road and the number of tight bends, the vehicles could only proceed at walking pace; the Stug crews told me this might actually be a benefit, because the vehicles were covered with so much foliage that they might look like part of the hedgerow from the air, and moving at speed would destroy this illusion! The soldier's mind finds so many hopes to cling on to in a retreat. Because of my leg injury, I took up a position on one of the Stugs, crouching among all the branches and leaves on the rear hull.

The road became increasingly sunken below the countryside, until the top of the Stug was barely level with the surrounding land. This was excellent for concealment, but of course it also meant that the vehicles could not move off the road for any reason. I heard the Stug commander say that if any vehicle broke down, the Stugs would have to run over it and continue moving. The mood was very tense;

it was hot and humid, and nobody knew how close the Americans might be, whether the Airborne troops or the beach forces.

There were parachutes visible on the ground beside the road at some points, and we saw several American paratroopers who appeared to be dead, still hanging from their parachutes in the trees beyond the fields.

One thing that we saw on that first stage of the retreat disturbed me. We slowly rounded a curve in the track, shielded by the hedgerow, and plainly visible along the top of the embankment were several dead American troops. They were in a kneeling position, with their hands behind their backs, and it seemed they had been shot methodically, then simply left where they kneeled. The crew of the Stug that I was riding on commented that this must be the work of the SS boys, who apparently had a taste for such things. It concerned me greatly that these Americans, who seemed to be Airborne troops, had been captured and deliberately executed in such a way.

Did you learn who was responsible for this?

No; and the events immediately following this lead me to think that the Allies themselves never learned of this act. This was only a few minutes into our retreat, but the next events happened with a terrible rapidity. As we all dreaded, the Jabos appeared from the south west direction, meaning that the planes could see us behind the hedgerows on our north side. There was nothing we could do about this; our destination was only a matter of kilometres away, and so the column continued to advance slowly. Hoping for the best as always, I reasoned that our vehicles were so well camouflaged that the Jabos would not notice us; at first, this seemed to be the case, as from this group of about six Thunderbolts, two flew over us without showing an interest. I am sure I was not the only soldier in that sunken road whose heart beat with relief at seeing this. But then the third and fourth planes dived down to look at us, and came racing over the roadway at low altitude, so low that I could see the pilots looking down at us from their bubble canopies. The crews shot up at them with small arms fire – but this had no effect.

The entire group of Thunderbolts swung around and attacked us from the north to the south, following along the line of the sunken road, one after the other.

The situation was absolutely hopeless for us in the column. I saw the long streaks of white vapour shoot down from under their wings, and there was barely time to take evasive action even if the sides of the road had permitted it. As it was, the vehicles were confined within the road, unable to leave the sunken channel, and the Thunderbolt rockets simply raked along the column while it was restricted in this way.

I jumped off the deck of the Stug, with the remaining energy given by the amphetamine tablet, and landed on the edge of the embankment under the hedges. I remained there, motionless, and from my prone position I was able to see the effect of the air attack on the entire column, as far as one of the Hanomags at the front, a distance of about one hundred metres until a curve in the road hid the rest of the column from me.

The American rockets poured along the column, many of the projectiles striking the fields on either side, and some striking short, exploding among the bodies of the American troops behind us. I saw that these rockets were high-explosive, which I had seen used in Italy, and I knew how destructive they could be. I saw the rockets devastate the American corpses, severing their limbs and their heads, and throwing the pieces for long distances across the fields, in trails of blood and smoking flesh. For this reason, I think the air attack destroyed the evidence of the 'executions,' if that is indeed what they were. But other rockets came smashing directly into the German troops and vehicles in the sunken road. I held my hands over my head and looked through the gap between my helmet rim above my eyes and the ground under my chin as these weapons struck us.

The sunken road was turned into an absolute slaughterhouse by these American projectiles. Their high explosives fell on the Stugs, ripping off the armoured screens on their sides and blasting away the foliage they had massed on their top decks. Two of the Stugs were hit on the engine decks, and the engine grilles burst open in big spouts of fire. The last Stug, the one reversing with its gun pointing back down the road, was hit somewhere on the upper hull, and I think that the rockets went through the hatch on the top into the crew compartment. This Stug threw itself from side to side, slamming into the embanked walls of the roadway, and I saw that the entire roof of its superstructure was being blown out. I think that all the ammunition inside was exploding, because the detonation was enormous, sending pieces of the roof whirling up into the fields. Many pieces of the crew from inside were thrown up also; the whole explosion was a real tornado of bodies and steel, every piece trailing fire and smoke as it fell to earth.

This was not the end; the rockets struck along the sunken road, exploding among the SS boys who were hurrying along there. The impacts came every second, slaughtering these boys as they ran or dived for cover. The rocket explosions ripped up the sunken track, and the high walls on either side deflected the shrapnel and debris back again, so that the path was full of bouncing, shrieking metal. I saw a group of half a dozen of these SS troops torn into pieces, with their innards ripped out and their empty bodies left burning in the road. A few of them, further ahead, ran forward to escape the carnage, but in front of them one of the Hanomags was hit by a rocket, and whether by accident or some design by the driver, it began to reverse backwards onto the SS troops behind it.

This Hanomag was blazing with fire, with all its gasoline flooding out, and it reversed out of control straight into the troops. The boys were flattened by the half-track, run down one after the other, and the Hanomag kept reversing and trampling the bodies of the troops until it finally crashed into one of the burning Stugs and came to rest.

The entire roadway was full of flames, broken bodies, shattered machinery and exploding ammunition. Some of the SS were still alive, but on fire, and the ammunition in their pouches was detonating, which was injuring them yet further. I saw one youth struggle to his feet, with his whole body on fire, and then the grenades that he carried tucked into his belt exploded, sending his limbs in different directions. Other troops crawled or dragged themselves, struggling in the pools of burning gasoline, until they were enveloped by the fires.

I waited for about a minute, then perhaps two minutes, and then for a longer time, but I don't know how long exactly. I heard the Jabos flying off to the north, and I must say that my chest was heaving very hard, making my torso rise and fall on the ground under the hedgerow. I was at a loss about what to do, in an absolute confusion. I was also hit in the back by debris, and this made it difficult for me to breathe.

I had been through a series of battles that day: the initial Tobruk fight, then the second bunker line, and now this attack on the column. Each time, the German forces were overwhelmed by vast superiority of numbers and weaponry, especially in artillery and attack from the air. I had a feeling of great despair, doubting that we could ever resist this enemy that had such machines and such resources. I was in a bad condition, physically and psychologically. The morphine and amphetamine were declining, I think, in my system, leaving me weakened and confused. The pain in my back, my chest and my leg was very severe. I struggled with myself to decide what to do.

Part of me wanted to surrender and give up the fight. But another side of my mind said that to give up now was meaningless, after so much effort, when I was close to the next line of defence. In the end, I slid down into the sunken road and made my way along its length, intending to reach our next positions. A few other survivors were doing likewise, and we had to climb over the many shattered corpses in this roadway, with many severed limbs and heads strewn around among the burning vehicles. In some cases, the fallen men were still alive, and panting or groaning miserably, and this sound was added to the crackle of the flames.

What was done to help these wounded men?

I think that nothing was done. We had no morphine or bandages, and the wounded men needed doctors, nurses and medical equipment. I had difficulty walking at all, and my breathing was very painful, so I could not carry any of them. One of these wounded was hit especially badly, with much of his stomach hanging out into the road, but he was still conscious and moving his hands. After I stepped over him, I heard a shot behind me, and I saw that one of the other survivors had put him out of his suffering with a single bullet to the head. That was a merciful thing to do, in these circumstances.

Finally, we left the destroyed column behind, and we reached the fortified line that we were aiming for. This was a strong point of bunkers with PAK guns, and it was organised much like the previous one that we had just seen destroyed by the Jabos. There, I was seen by a medic who said I had several broken ribs, and I was sent to the zone behind our lines in a horse-drawn cart which was being used to transport the wounded. I was the least wounded man in that cart. The others had lost ears, hands or eyes; many were burned, with their scalps gone or their charred uniforms stuck to their damaged skin. I felt guilty, being so lightly wounded, it must be said.

Was that the end of your war?

No. I was given several weeks recuperation at a convalescent centre in the south of our zone, although being among the able-bodied patients I was also tasked with stripping and repairing rifles and machine guns that were jammed or out of order in some way. This was not arduous work, and I found that it kept my mind occupied. I had many unwanted memories of my experiences on the 6th June, which prevented me sleeping and affected my concentration.

In the convalescent depot, of course, we followed the progress of the invasion and our defence in as much detail as possible. The mood of us recuperating men was quite pessimistic, as we had all seen

*May I ask, in your mind now, do you think of
that place as 'Omaha' or 'Vierville'?*

To me, it is Vierville. That was the name of our position, which was
a Resistance Point. I was posted there in April 1944 and we were
inspected by Rommel himself shortly after my arrival.

Did you see Rommel personally?

Yes, he was a very energetic and active man; he walked very briskly
and spoke rapidly. I did not have any dialogue with him, but he
came to our position and spoke with our officer. He asked very factual questions about the amount of ammunition we had in the post,
how old the weapons were, what we knew of the design of Allied
ships and so on. He was quite a short man, but had a very powerful
presence, although, as with all famous leaders, how much of this
was due to our expectations and preconceptions, it is difficult to say.

*What was the mood among your unit in the
days and weeks before the invasion?*

There was a feeling of great tension, because we were constantly
watching and waiting for a possible attack. We all believed that
the Allies would try to attack Europe in the summer of 1944, and
the summer was reaching its height, so a landing of some sort
seemed inevitable. The amount of bombing by aircraft and strafing by Jabo type planes was also building up enormously in May
and early June, and this had to be a prelude to some kind of event.
Our warning level went up to level 2 on the weekend before the
invasion, but, if I remember correctly, it came down again to level
3 on Monday 5th.

The waiting was very unnerving, and also the issue of constantly
worrying about what form the attack would take. Would it be by air,
or by landing boats, or in conjunction with the Communist fighters
in the French Resistance, or a combination of all these? Would it be

against us in the North, or also on the Western coast of France? All these questions plagued us, with no answers. And every day, the sea in front of our 'Widerstandsnest' (*Resistance Point*) looked exactly the same, giving us no clues at all.

Can you describe the Widerstandsnest, the Resistance Point?

This was an area of about thirty metres width and ten metres depth, set on the top of some cliffs beside one of the ravines that led down to the beach wall. The Point had a trench across its width, and several running to the rear, in jagged lines. Inside, these trenches were faced in concrete and had wooden floors with drainage points. Outside, there was a raised concrete parapet about one metre high, in which there were firing points, which were vertical slits. There were two machine gun points at either end aiming through these points. It was about three hundred metres down from the cliff to the nearest part of the sea wall, and there was a long, uninterrupted line of fire along the beach to the northwest. The guns were MG42 types, which were extremely powerful.

The Resistance Point was surrounded by barbed wire with a single exit point at the rear, and the dunes on top of the cliffs around it were mined. There were also mines hanging on cables down the cliffs, which could be dropped on any attackers from the beach. The position was open to the air, but steel covers were available to drag across the trenches in case of a bombardment; to be honest, we also used these if it rained heavily. The position had a searchlight between the two guns, and a reinforced area for ammunition and grenade storage.

Our team there was ten men: two men on each gun, the others being observers, sentries, and men intended to fire from the trenches onto the beach with rifles. A second team of ten men were either resting or working nearby; we had a small villa as a headquarters adjacent to the officer's post. We were commanded by a Feldwebel, and our officer commanded four such positions along the high ground in the area.

On the other side of the ravine that went down to the sea wall, the cliffs continued, with further Resistance Points built along there.

What were your orders in terms of defending the beach?

We were to keep a constant lookout, of course, and make regular reports by cable line to our officer's post, which was about one kilometre behind us. In case of an attack, we were told specifically to hold our fire until any enemy troops were four hundred metres from the edge of the beach; although the MG42 could fire effectively beyond 2,000 metres, this instruction was intended to ensure that we had the largest possible target area on each attacking soldier. We were told to fire at their chests when their torsos were above water, that is to say when they reached the shallows and were wading.

We were trained constantly on the importance of our task. If the Allies were allowed to gain a foothold in our sector, however slender, their huge material resources would allow them to build it up and threaten the whole of France. This in turn would give them a puppet state to use in order to harass and blockade Germany itself. The concept of the Allies actually invading Germany seemed unimaginable at the time, it must be said.

Our officers sought to educate us very thoroughly on this matter. They emphasised that if an attempted landing could be defeated by us on the shoreline, and thrown back, it would take years for the Western Allies to recover, allowing us to consolidate a defensive line against the Soviets in the East. Its effect on Western public opinion might even force the English out of the war altogether; that idea was constantly emphasised. All in all, we were fully aware of the great burden of responsibility resting on us, as the first line of defence against an attack.

What is your memory of the 6th June and the preceding days?

The preceding day, the Monday, was very blustery and wet, I remember, and we were on duty in blocks of two hours, on duty and then off. The tension was very noticeable, because of the intensity of the bombing. Throughout the weekend and the Monday, that is, the 3rd, 4th and the 5th, there were heavy raids overnight to the south east, and Jabo attacks during the daytime. The Jabos usually flew over us, and went inland, they only occasionally strafed the beach. This is something I found strange when I thought about the invasion afterwards: the level of attacks on our beach were very intense at the last minute, but very low in the previous days and weeks. I suppose this was to prevent us deducing that an attack was impending on our specific beach, but the Jabos could have caused much more disruption to us than they did before the landing.

On the 6th June, I was on duty in the Resistance Point, at the Western corner MG slot, from two am onwards. As we went up to the point in the dark, there was heavy bombing to the south again and a very high level of aircraft noise. There was Flak fire from points in a semi-circle inland of us, and further explosions in the distance. We all agreed that something was up, something was going to happen soon.

Did this cause you alarm, or fear?

I think that most of us were simply sick of the tension of waiting, waiting. An event of some kind, even an attack, would at least break the tension, the silence, the sense of foreboding that we had. For this reason, some of our men said, 'Let them come soon,' which made other men wink and laugh. But I think we all preferred to have the situation clear, to let us start fighting at last, rather than waiting.

What happened from two am up to the landing itself?

The level of noise and explosions rose and fell. As the moon was full, we could see large numbers of aircraft in the sky at times, between the rain clouds, and there were various flames and explosions in the sky on the inland side. Several times, we saw an aircraft on fire, heading out across the sea towards England, and in some cases these burning planes descended and appeared to hit the sea in the distance.

On our gun, I was the gunner, and my loader and I both had good quality binoculars. Using these, I saw that many of the aircraft were twin-engine types, and we debated whether these were bombers or something else. I know today that we were seeing the parachutist transports returning and scattering over the sea. I recall seeing one of these planes at low altitude followed very closely by another plane, which we thought appeared to be a glider under tow. These two planes descended rapidly and disappeared into the sea.

All this went on, and we became increasingly convinced that an attack from the sea would come soon, as some kind of assault was evidently already happening inland. Our officer appeared at about four am, bringing with him the 'spare team' whom he had woken, and he ordered us all to be completely prepared for a possible sea landing.

I think that first light came at about five am, and it slowly revealed the beach to us. Nothing was changed there; the sand was studded with large numbers of steel obstacles, and these were very prominent as the tide was out. The sky was overcast and the offshore wind was quite strong. As time passed, with my binoculars, as I scanned the horizon, I began to see many shapes materialise. The sea was slightly foggy out there, but I could still see first a handful of shapes, then more, and finally an absolute wall of these grey outlines stretching almost across the whole horizon.

All of us men who had binoculars stood and stared at this apparition, while the other men demanded to know what we were looking at. We handed the binoculars around for a few seconds, and many of the men took a look. Their reactions varied, ranging from curses to a kind of apprehensive laughter, or just silence. In the meantime, our Feldwebel was on the cable phone speaking to the officer's post. He came to us at the parapet and said, 'Men, they're coming now, they're coming in strength. We must be ready,' or something straightforward like that.

The whole situation was unfolding in a way that seemed almost like a dream, detached from reality. This great assembly of ships was simply looming out of the sea mist, just getting bigger and bigger, closer and closer, and nothing at all was happening on our side. I could not hear any firing from our coastal batteries further along the coast, and no Luftwaffe aircraft were visible overhead. The sea between us and the ships was completely empty, there was not a torpedo boat or a seaplane or anything.

I had a great sensation that we were on our own in front of this colossal force. It was a strange sensation: it felt like a great challenge, almost a superhuman challenge. It was unnerving but I also felt a certain relief, even excitement, that at last we would meet this enemy that threatened us. At the same time, like soldiers everywhere, I busied myself with my gun, and with getting our position as ready as possible.

At this point, a very large formation of enemy bombers came over us. These were the big, four-engined bombers, I think they were the Lancaster type. We saw them streaming towards us over the ships on the sea, and a nearby 20mm Flak gun fired on them, but they were too high in altitude. They bombed us, and we threw ourselves under the steel covers, fearing the worst. These bombs came down at an angle from the sky, diagonally out of the sky, and the explosions made the whole cliff shake and sway under us. But we realised that they were missing us, if we were the target, and the bombs hit the inland areas behind us. This was a great relief, and we laughed in a nervous, apprehensive manner as the sound of the planes moved away inland too. We climbed up and prepared ourselves, with the massive fleet of ships on the sea getting closer by the second.

The slit in the concrete parapet gave a wide arc of fire, and I practised sweeping the gun left and right, which I had done countless times in drills. Just as I was doing this, the sea bombardment began.

You must have expected the bombardment, surely?

Yes, but the intensity was astonishing. It was heavier and also far more accurate than the bomber planes that had just hit us. I had been under artillery fire on the Eastern Front, of course, where I learned to brace myself against it, both physically and mentally. That was difficult enough for me and for most others. This bombardment, however, was by warship cannons. That was obvious from the flashes that we could see on the horizon, among the many outlines of the advancing ships, and then the noise of the shells approaching us in the air. These shells made a noise similar to a gas blowtorch being run at full strength, and at first they passed right overhead. We could actually see them as bright shapes flying inland over the beach – huge shapes too, the size of a car engine or similar. They exploded a few hundred metres behind us, and then the next salvo came down much closer to us. We dragged the steel plates over our trench covers and we huddled underneath them with our guns.

The power of the explosions made the concrete of the trench ripple and fracture, and if I glanced up, I could only see enormous spouts of earth and sand hanging over the dunes and the beach. The shockwaves punched all the air out of our lungs, and made our eyes bleed. The shrapnel that flew around us was monstrous in size; I saw one piece of shell case as big as my arm, which simply fell down out of the air and jangle at the end of the trench, still smoking. But other pieces were flying left and right horizontally, screeching and smashing off the parapet and the steel roof plates. It went on and on, for salvo after salvo, with absolutely no pause in between the impacts. It was as if a gigantic hammer was falling on the beach, trying to pound it flat – that is how it felt to me.

How did the men react to this bombardment?

Most of us remained calm and disciplined. My loader was trembling as he crouched there, and as I noticed this, I realised that I was also trembling. One man, near me, could not take the stress, and he tried to run by ducking outside of the trench zone which was covered overhead by the steel screens. I saw him try to run. He was caught by an absolute storm of shrapnel, and his torso was ripped across and broken open. Absolutely ripped open, from front to back. He fell in the open part of the trench, and countless other bits of debris fell on him, mutilating him further. His body produced a lot of steam in the cool air, which filled the trench for a while. This was a terrible, shocking sight for those of us who saw it.

At one point, the end of the concrete trench was blown open by one of these shells, showering us with earth and debris. When the smoke from this cleared, it meant that we could see out of the end of the trench and down to the beach for some distance. It was possible to see the shells landing in salvos of three; each salvo made very tall plumes of smoke and debris that slowly fell to the ground.

I saw one of the shells explode inside one of the other Resistance Points about five hundred metres from us. That Point was similar in design to ours, but with a single machine gun in a concrete Tobruk bunker. The whole installation was destroyed, and pieces of concrete were thrown high into the air, with the bodies of the men who were in it. It was terrifying to watch those men flung out, knowing that the same thing could happen to us if we were hit directly. In the end, however, there was a final intense fall of shells, and then the shelling stopped altogether.

The cessation of the noise and blast waves came as a great relief, as you can appreciate. My ears were ringing, and I had blood on my face from my eyes. We knew that the halt in the shelling meant that the landing must be imminent, and so we washed our eyes in water from our canteens, and slid away the metal covers, and we slowly emerged from the bottom of the trenches. One by one, our men put their heads up over the lip of the trench they were in, or over the parapet. I lifted the MG42 back up and re-sited it in the firing slit.

I remembered that my father had told me many times that he did this as a machine gunner at the Battle of the Somme in the first war; he and his comrades hid deep in their dugouts with their guns and then emerged to fix their guns in place again before the British attacked. Now here I was, doing the same thing.

In the time that we had been under cover, the ships and boats of the attackers had come very close to the shore, and now we could see vessels which I would have called 'invasion barges' but later I learned were 'landing craft.' I did not yet know what nationality these troops were. There were very many of these landing craft approaching the beach; there were at least ten directly facing me, coming through the initial swells of the waves off the beach. They were about one kilometre from my position, I would estimate. But all down the beach, we could see more of these craft approaching. The sea was absolutely alive with these vessels, which all seemed to be the same design and colour. Behind them, there were small warships and all manner of other ships covering the sea. The sea was completely covered with this huge collection of vessels.

What went through your mind, seeing this force approaching you?

I don't recall having any conscious thought or emotion, other than anxiety that my gun might have been damaged in the shelling. I fired off a one second burst to test it. The other MG crew shouted at me to hold fire and remember our orders. I shouted at them to test their gun too, which they then did. I could hear similar short bursts up and down the cliffs, as the survivors of the shelling all quickly tested their machine guns. Then our heavier guns opened fire. These were 88mm PAK guns sited in concrete positions further along the cliffs. There should have been three in our zone, but only two fired, I assume because the other one was destroyed. These 88mm gunners were very accurate, and shot into the landing craft straight through the tall vertical bow. They fired high explosive, and the shells pierced the bow and exploded inside.

I saw one of the landing craft opposite my location being hit in this way. The 88mm shell detonated beyond the bow, and the bow door, which I then realised was a ramp, was thrown up into the air. Inside the craft, I could see a large number of troops who had been injured in the explosion, surrounded by men who were still able-bodied. They were clambering and scrabbling over each other, because the craft began to tip forward as water entered the open bow. I saw then from the shape of their helmets that these were Americans.

The 88mm gunners fired another shot into the mass of men, and this threw several of them directly out of the craft into the water. The whole craft began to sink from the bow, which made the stern of the craft lift into the air, and this movement tipped the men into the sea immediately. Wounded, or otherwise, they all slid down the inside of the craft as its tail rose and into the water. Such events were being repeated all along the beach, as these craft were hit or made to sink, or in some cases set on fire.

At that point, the warships behind them began to fire onto the beach to suppress our artillery, which had some effect. Once again we began to keep our heads down, and our 88mm guns stopped firing. But I continued to look through the slit of the parapet, and in that way I could see that, despite the losses, these landing craft were starting to lower their ramp doors and the men inside were starting to emerge and enter the water down the ramps.

What was the manner of the men's exit from the landing craft? Was it rushed or orderly?

It was orderly, very orderly. The craft were stopping at a point where the water was about chest or neck height, and the men were running down the ramps and stepping into the water, holding their guns, plunging down and then bobbing up again, with the sea up to their shoulders or chests. In most cases, the men tried to advance in the water one behind the other, with each man holding or reaching for the back pack of the man in front. It was as if they were conducting a drill or an exercise.

As the last man stepped off the ramp, the craft would reverse and hoist up its bow door, and more craft would approach the beach around it. The discipline and the skill in the way the craft were handled was impressive. And so the first of these lines of men began to trudge – that is the only word I can use, they walked slowly and deliberately – they began to advance in this way into shallower water, and the waves came to their chests, then their waists. That is when we opened fire on them, as our orders stated.

You fired your machine gun at this point.

Yes, exactly as we had planned. These troops were about four hundred metres from us. I did not sight on them individually at first, but I began firing and I swept the gun from left to right along the beach. This knocked down the first few men in each line of men; you must remember that the MG42 was so powerful that the bullets would often pass through the human body and hit whatever was behind. So it was that many of these men were hit by a bullet which had already passed through a man in front, or even two men in front. After that, I aimed more selectively, to make the ammunition last as long as possible. I fired short bursts at small groups of men and hit them that way.

What was the reaction of the Americans to your fire?

The Americans began to run, wade or stagger forwards, trying to get out of the water and onto the sand itself. They still moved quite slowly, and because of that and the close range they were easy targets to hit. In some cases, they tried to remain in the water up to their necks, perhaps hoping to be less conspicuous, and I did not fire at those men, because they showed no signs of advancing. In other cases, these troops tried to take shelter behind the anti-tank devices on the beach, which were triangles of girders sticking up from the sand. Those devices were too narrow to give any real protection, though, and those men were also hit. There were other troops who I could see removing their back packs and equipment and running onto the sand, attempting to surge up the beach towards the sea wall. I paid particular attention to these men, of course, and made sure that none of them advanced beyond a few paces.

Our other machine gun was operating in the same way as me, and between us we held back any Americans who tried to advance onto the sand in front of us. I also fired along the beach at other troops who were coming ashore further down the sand. Throughout this time, we were being shelled intermittently by the warships, and there were boats behind the landing craft which were firing multiple rockets at us in the dunes. These rockets made huge explosions, but they were falling wide of our position.

At the same time, one of our 88mm guns began firing again, and sank several more landing craft. The whole zone of the sea in front of us was now clogged with these craft, and the ones that had deposited their soldiers were colliding with the burning or drifting ones that had been hit.

If I may ask a question, how many Americans do you think you killed in this phase of the landing?

I am honestly unsure. I can say that the shallow part of the sea immediately in front of us was full of bodies, probably at least a hundred bodies, and this amount was repeated up and down the beach in front of the other gun positions. The tide was starting to come in, and these bodies were rolling and swaying with the movement of the water, and there were such things as helmets, rifles and equipment floating and rolling with them.

After the initial burst of energy and determination that I felt when the attack started, I began to feel pity for these troops, because they kept arriving in landing craft. The craft would deposit them in the shallows, and they would walk towards us through the water in the same way as the first set of troops. We fired at them in the same way, causing the same deaths and injuries. My loader was moved by this, and he shook his head, saying that the Americans should not sacrifice their men in this way.

You mentioned a short time ago your father being at the Battle of the Somme in the First War. At the Somme, it is said that some German machine gunners shouted at the advancing British to save themselves and retreat. Was there any such communication from your men to the Americans?

I am not aware of any such communication. The only time we stopped firing was when the gun barrel began to overheat, and the mechanism showed signs of misfiring. We did not want to risk the gun breaking down, so we rested it to let it cool. We took up our rifles and used them, aiming at the Americans coming out of the water. This meant exposing our heads and arms above the parapet, and it was only at this point that I noticed we received the first shots aimed at us by the American soldiers themselves.

They did not fire at you before this?

Perhaps they did, but I did not notice them firing at us before this point. The sand had various ridges in it from the shelling, and there was some natural undulation in the ground, especially a low ridge of shingle up against the sea wall, and some of the Americans had managed to take cover in these places and were firing sporadically from there. Their warships ceased their shelling at this point, I suppose because they were observing the beach and expected the combat to be at close quarters now. They began to shell behind us, blowing up the zone behind our cliffs. But the Americans who had taken advantage of the shingle ridge found it impossible to move out of them, as we fired on them as soon as they emerged. At the same time, the tide was coming in fully, so there was less and less space available on the sand for men to find cover at all. This meant that the soldiers arriving behind them had less potential space to take cover, and so the intensive killing began again. We used our machine gun again from this point on.

Was there a moment when you thought the Americans might be forced to withdraw from the beach? When you thought you might defeat the landing?

I did have such a thought, yes. I remember that one of the landing craft came close to the shallows, and whoever was in charge of it seemed to hesitate. The craft slowed and steered carefully between other craft and the obstacles, as if selecting a place to land, but it did not make a final approach. Then it turned away, making a manoeuvre as if it was trying to turn around and leave the scene. I could hardly criticise the man in charge for that. To see the situation of such carnage on the sand, with all the bodies jumbled together, and the obvious lack of cover for the men, I am not sure that I would have pressed on.

But as this craft turned away, it presented its flank to the 88mm guns, and it was shot immediately, below the waterline. The explosions tore off large pieces of its side, and the craft began to capsize rapidly as the water flooded in. I could see the troops inside as the hull rose up, the whole interior of the vessel was exposed to us. There were various vehicles in that craft, Jeeps and trucks, as well as troops. These vehicles were falling onto the troops as the floor became almost vertical, crushing many men. Other men were jumping from the sides into the sea.

The 88mm fired again into the middle of the interior, and this exploded the vehicles as they lay crushed together. I saw that whole landing craft go up in flames within seconds, and sink very quickly, surrounded by men struggling in the water. I thought, *'If many more try to turn away like that, there won't be enough Americans to replace the dead ones on the beach, and so we will win this dreadful fight.'* However, this feeling did not last for long, as we then came under heavier fire, and tanks began to appear on the beach.

Were these amphibious tanks?

I did see, in the distance, one single tank emerge from the sea. It was a Sherman type, very recognisable. I had the impression that it was coming up from the sea bed, that is how it looked to me. That was an incredible sight. I had no idea it was even possible to make tanks travel under water. I never heard of our forces being able to do such a thing. But this single tank was on its own, and it was fired on and halted by PAK guns further down the beach.

After that, I saw a very large landing craft approach several hundred metres away, and as it lowered its ramp I saw a Sherman tank come out and roll down into the shallows. This tank had some kind of screen or tubing around it, and it travelled slowly but effectively through the shallows and onto the sand, and immediately began firing up at the Resistance Points on the cliffs down there. Other tanks came out of the craft behind it, I am not sure how many, but several. At the same time, we began receiving very accurate mortar fire onto our position. So the moment when I thought that we might win was very brief.

How did the fighting develop from this point?

My memory of the closing phases of that battle are rather disjointed. My position was struck by mortar fire, which I think was coming from a mortar set up in a crater along the beach. These rounds were small calibre, but they produced a lot of splinters which flew around and ricocheted off any surface. My loader was hit in the back of the neck, and he had to withdraw from the gun slit. He had a large piece of flesh hanging loose from his neck, and it was bleeding very profusely. A replacement loader took over, bringing a new pair of ammunition boxes, and we continued firing through the slit. But these mortar rounds made it difficult to see the targets on the beach, as they produced a lot of smoke and dust, and to some extent I was firing blindly into the beach zone. I don't know if this was a deliberate smoke-screen, but it certainly made us less effective in our firing.

In addition, heavier calibre shells began to hit us again, and I think these were tank rounds coming from the Shermans. Our position was hit by one of these, and many of the men behind me in the zig-zag trenches were injured.

I then saw flashes and gunfire for the first time on top of the cliffs on the other side of the ravine that we were close to. This was a terrible moment, because it suggested that the Americans on the beach had somehow climbed up and broken through onto the cliffs, or that they had airborne troops who had joined up from inland. However this had happened, the presence of Americans up among us on the cliffs was a great threat.

At times, when the sea wind blew the smoke aside, I also saw the use of flame-throwers up on the cliffs. There were long, very bright orange spurts of flame visible through the smoke, and a strong smell of gasoline. I had a terror of flame-throwers, as my brother had told me about them from the Russian front. Therefore, when I saw through the smoke a man approaching from the sea up the beach, moving from one obstacle to another, approaching the cliffs, I was alarmed to see that he seemed to be carrying a flame-thrower gun and back pack. I shot him with the MG42 at once, and the bullets evidently ignited the fuel tank on his back. There was a very large explosion, and he disappeared completely in a fireball which went up into the air in a mushroom cloud. Both sides stopped firing for a moment, perhaps because we all saw what happened to this soldier. But then the shooting began again, more intensely than ever.

I could see hand-to-hand fighting on the cliffs directly across the ravine from me, with our troops and Americans so close that I could not fire into them because they were mixed up together. The ferocity of that fighting astonished me. Men were lunging at each other with fixed bayonets, and with their rifle stocks, and even with entrenching tools or shovels. The Americans were charging upon our German gunners in the barbed wire entanglements up there. Some men were in flames, and other men were shooting or stabbing them as they staggered on fire. I could no longer see which men were from which army, as the smoke and flames made them all a similar outline as they fought.

I was hit and wounded at this point, by shrapnel from a tank round which hit the parapet next to my firing slit. The shrapnel hit my helmet and shoulder, and the machine gun was blown out of my hands altogether. I was stunned, and I slumped down into the bottom of the trench to try to get the gun back. The gun was damaged and could not be used. The amount of shrapnel and debris flying around at this point was devastating. We could not put our heads above the top of the parapet or the trench, because splinters were constantly smashing across the top of our point. My new loader was killed outright when a splinter came in and pierced him through the ribs. This was a large piece of metal, the size of a knife, and it stuck out from his torso as he lay dead beside me.

What did you think your fate would be?

In my mind, I accepted that I was going to die. I had seen the ferocity of the fighting on the adjacent cliff, and I knew it was only a matter of time before those Americans worked their way around the ravine to where my position was. There seemed to be nothing we could do about it.

Also, I knew that we had surely enraged the attackers by killing so many of their comrades. The beach was literally piled up with corpses that we had shot. So what chance was there of the Americans showing us any mercy now?

You expected the Americans to kill you if you offered to surrender?

When I thought about the beach, the piles of bodies down there... yes, I thought the enemy would kill us all regardless of the Geneva Convention or anything like that. Would we have shown them any mercy, if the roles were reversed, if we were the attackers? I doubt that our troops would have shown much compassion in such a situation.

Our position was hit again by shells or mortar rounds, and that is the last thing that I remember of the fighting. I recall that many pieces of concrete were tumbling around, and some of these fell on top of me.

After that, I do not remember anything else until I found myself lying on my back. My ears were ringing very painfully. It took me a long time to fully realise where I was or what was happening. My head and body were very painful, and I felt very cold. When I opened my eyes, I could see the overcast sky, with smoke billowing through it, and I could hear shooting and explosions very distantly.

I turned my head, which was horribly painful to do, and I saw that I was lying among the debris of our Resistance Point. There were pieces of concrete on top of me. By moving my head, I was able to look down onto the beach over the edge of the ravine and cliff. The first thing that I saw down there was a long row of dead American soldiers. This row was so long that it stretched a very long way across the beach. They were obviously placed there carefully. I could also see wounded American soldiers, on stretchers or sitting on the sand, and there were medics moving from one to the other. They had red crosses painted on their helmets.

I now became aware of other men crouching on the cliff near to me. I saw from their boots that they were American; their boots were the only detail I could make out from my position on my back. As I became fully aware of the situation, I expected these Americans to take reprisals against me. For that reason, I tried not to move my limbs, even though the debris on top of me was very painful. I was hoping they had mistaken me for a corpse, and I wanted them to continue believing that. Of course, this could not go on for long, and after some time one of these Americans came over and stood looking down at me. He was holding a Thompson gun, I remember being able to see that, and he watched me for some time. I don't know whether he was considering killing me or what else was in his mind. Then he seemed to be discussing me with someone else, but my hearing was damaged, and anyway I could not understand English.

How late in the day was this?

I think this was some time after midday on the 6th. I had been knocked unconscious by an explosion and the Americans who initially over-ran our Resistance Point had left me in the rubble. Eventually, the men who were discussing me called a medic, and a medical orderly came and removed me from the rubble. There were two German prisoners who were carrying stretchers, and they took me down the ravine path and put me on the beach with the wounded. In this way, drifting in and out of consciousness, I spent the rest of the day lying on the beach. In the evening, some more German prisoners carried me to a ship which transported me to a prison centre in England. I was repatriated to West Germany in 1946.

What was your last sight of the beach on the 6th?

The beach was a terrible sight on that evening. There were still many bodies in the water, and medics were trying to retrieve them. The edge of the water was a red colour from the blood, I could see that distinctly. There were many landing craft vessels half sunk and on fire, and a lot of vehicles which were abandoned or stuck in the sand – Jeeps, tracked vehicles and tanks. There was a Sherman tank which had been blown up and was in pieces, with the turret lying on the beach and the tracks scattered around. There were many aircraft overhead, and smoke drifting everywhere. But it became clear to me, seeing the amount of troops and vehicles that were being unloaded from the large landing craft, that the Americans were secure in this beach head and were moving off inland now.

Were any reprisals taken against you?

No, there was no reprisal. Apart from the initial interrogation, which took place in England, the Americans took little interest in us. While I was a prisoner, I spoke with a couple of other German troops who survived in a different sector of that beach. None of them had heard of any reprisal or mistreatment against our troops from the beach.

Do you think that this battle, from what you experienced of it, could have had a different outcome?

Well, it is easy, and tempting, in hindsight, to say that *this* thing could have happened differently or *that* thing could have happened. My belief, as a foot soldier, is that we were close to throwing the attackers off the beach at that one brief moment, at least in my sector. It was the renewed heavy bombardment and the arrival of tanks which prevented that happening, I think.

I am also puzzled as to why the Americans did not damage our positions more fully before the landing. I imagine that there is a balance for an attacker to keep, between a lengthy bombardment which does a lot of damage but also signals that an attack is coming soon, and on the other hand a last-minute preparatory bombardment which forces the defenders to take cover but without letting them prepare for the attack. Nevertheless, considering their capability, I am surprised that their aircraft did not attack us more fully overnight on the evening of the 5th June or at first light on the 6th, when the bombs from their heavy bombers fell wide. I think that would have disrupted our defences and still prevented us from reacting in time by bringing up reserves and so on.

*How do you regard your involvement in this
fighting, with the passing of ten years?*

The fact is, Herr Eckhertz, that we Germans were sent there to defend the beach and the Americans were sent there to attack it and occupy it. If our roles were somehow reversed, would the Americans have chosen to fight any differently from the way that we fought? I think that they would have applied themselves to their tasks and followed their orders with the same determination that we did.

On a wider scale, now that we have time to look back and reflect on it, it seems to me that the whole situation in Normandy was really the fault of our regime in the Reich for involving the Americans in the European war at all.

What I mean is that I remember after the Japanese attack on Pearl Harbour, the American declaration of war was purely against Japan, not against their ally Germany. This made sense, of course – Germany did not bomb Pearl Harbour. We all said at the time, '*This is good, the Americans will not be involved in our war, they will keep their distance from the English in Europe.*' But then, I think it was the next day or forty-eight hours later, Adolf Hitler took everyone by surprise when he went on the radio and declared war on the USA! Why he did such an insane thing, I cannot begin to understand, even today. But that act made the Normandy invasion inevitable, because the English and Canadians could never have invaded alone, and we in the Reich could have focussed our efforts purely on the war against Russia.

If we could imagine how our lives would have been if Hitler had not done that – well, the destinies of so many people would have developed in completely different ways and forms.

—

Gold Beach: The Bunker Lookout

Marten Eineg was a Soldat (Private) with the 726th Infantry regiment, 716th Static Infantry Division, stationed in the area of La Riviere.

Herr Eineg, may I start by reading my notes of the interview which I did with you when I visited the Atlantic Wall?

That would be very interesting. Because of the disruption caused by the invasion, I never actually read your article.

In the end, because of the changed situation, it was not published. But I wrote that:

*"Marten is the sort of soldier that makes the Wehrmacht tick like a machine: twenty years of age, the battalion boxing champion, tall and widely-read. In his look-out post in the concrete dome above an artillery bunker, his wide shoulders scrape against the reinforced roof as he constantly scans the seas for signs of Allied aggression.
'They may come at any time,' he says to me, with a wink.
'With their finances, their gold and oil, they have the luxury of using England as a harbour for their ships and weapons.'
Something tells me that Marten will be ready."*

That was what I wrote about you in 1944.

I see. I do not actually remember saying that, but it sums up the mood of the time.

It was a strange time, in my view. If I may ask, what do you remember of the occasion when I visited your battery and conducted certain interviews?

I believe it was in April or May of the invasion year. I recall it very clearly, as if this was yesterday, in fact. You arrived in a civilian car and you had a battery-operated recorder, something I had never seen before. You also made notes in shorthand. I recall that you presented me with a small bottle of cognac as you left.

But I must say, Mein Herr, that in the passage which you just read to me, you changed some of the background information about me. I was not a boxing champion at all, although I certainly liked boxing. And although I was tall, I had a chronic lung condition which technically classed me as unfit for active service. Nevertheless, I was sent to France to man the Atlantic Wall.

Please forgive the journalistic licence that I showed. As you can appreciate, I was under pressure to present our forces in a certain way, with a lot of embellishment. Now that we have more liberty to speak, can you give me an account of your arrival on the Atlantic Wall and the events of 6th June?

Well, I was classed unfit when I was seventeen, in 1943. I had been a member of the Hitler Youth, like all the young boys, but I was rejected from the Labour Corps because of my problematic breathing. Nevertheless, the army doctors correctly noted that my eyesight was slightly above average, and so I was a valuable asset all the same. For these reasons, I served as a Flakhilfer (*Flak gun crew*) for several months around Munich, and was then transferred to the Wehrmacht in the west. My family were most relieved that I was sent to France, which we imagined as a true 'land of plenty.'

On arrival, I joined a beach battery sited near La Riviere. We distinguished between beach batteries, which were intended to fire at targets in the shallows or on the beach itself, and coastal batteries, which were the much larger guns intended to fire long-range at naval targets. My bunker was a concrete structure armed with two 88mm guns in embrasures, with the guns sighted on the beach itself. The bunker was positioned on a steep slope about one hundred metres back from the sea wall, giving an enfilade fire along the beach, the sea wall and the esplanade road behind the wall. My rank was Soldat and my function was to be an observer and, if an attack came, to assist with manning the MG34 machine gun which was sited in the bunker to prevent infantry assault.

We soldiers were housed in a fortified farmhouse several hundred metres from our bunker, this house being strengthened with concrete blocks, sandbags, earth ridges and corrugated iron; it was intended as a second line of defence, with a view down the slopes towards the sea front.

Our life, by the standards of what most German soldiers experienced, was frankly very soft. Our military rations were basic, but these were amply supplemented by produce from local farmers and retailers, who had no compunction about trading food with us in exchange for cigarettes, gasoline and even leather for boot-soles, none of which were available to civilians. When I read today about the French Resistance, I am impressed at their tenacity, but if the readers of such books could see the trading that went on between us and the local French, they might form a different view of life in France at that time. Well, but this is perhaps a case of history being written by victors.

When you visited us, for your interviews, I had been assigned to the bunker for about six weeks.

Now that we can speak openly, what was your
motivation in defending the Atlantic Wall?

I must say to you that the views I expressed in the interview in 1944 were definitely my views at the time.

It is overlooked, perhaps forgotten, by almost everyone today that we were there to defend Europe against the multiple threats represented by the Allies. We saw the British as an outdated Imperial force, organised by freemasons, who sought to turn the clock back one hundred years to the days when their word was the law around the world. Why should they be entitled to install their freemason puppet, De Gaulle, in France, to rule as a proxy? The Vichy government had three consistent points in its propaganda regarding the threats to the French people: these were De Gaulle, freemasonry and communism.

As for the American state, we perceived that as controlled by the forces of international finance and banking, who wished to abolish national governments and have the world run by banks and corporations. And there was the definite sentiment that both these countries, England and the USA, were being manipulated, controlled, by the Bolsheviks in Moscow. I stress that these were my views, and they were very common views, at the time. Of course, I have since changed my opinions in this regard, as I have learned more about the Third Reich, as we all have.

Did you have any personal animosity towards the Anglo-Americans?

My brother and cousin had both been killed in the East, at Kharkov, so my animosity lay more in that direction. Ironically, we had a large contingent of Russian troops with us on the Atlantic wall, who were defectors now serving in the German forces, but I had no real contact with them.

As for the English, my father had been in France in 1917 to 1918, and he confided to me that the English were surprisingly similar to us Germans in personal character, but that as a fighting force they were inconsistent, with many brave men but also a big element of shirkers and black market operators. Regarding the Americans, I think that most of us soldiers made a distinction in our minds between the American government, which we believed was a pawn of international finance, and the Americans as individuals. After all, we had all seen US films and magazines before the war, we had read about cowboys and heard jazz music, and all this was exciting and very attractive to us. But despite all this, we knew that the Americans too were intent on attacking France and destroying the unification of Europe under German protection that our leadership had achieved.

This is interesting. The phrase 'Fortress Europe' is still widely remembered today, I think, as part of Reich propaganda at the time, but you have reminded me that the phrase 'United Europe' was equally common.

Of course it was. Of course. 'United Europe' was a universal slogan. We should remember that both the Wehrmacht and the Waffen SS had huge recruitment campaigns in all the countries under Reich control, with the emphasis that people from all the countries of Europe should unite under arms and defend European unification. If we look at the Waffen SS, we see these very effective non-German units from all over Europe: the French, the famous Belgian-Walloon people under Leon Degrelle, the Dutch, Norwegians, the Croat Muslims with their 'SS' emblems on their fez hats, and so on and so on. There was a definite sense that Europe was united under the Reich, and an attack on France would be an attack on the whole structure.

One question I have received differing answers to: did you in the local German forces expect an attack or an invasion at that time, or was it a surprise, a lightning bolt and so on?

I can say with certainty that we all thought the Allies would try to enter France in the North. Some of us said there may be another small scale attack similar to the fiasco at Dieppe, perhaps attempting to capture another port such as Cherbourg or Calais, while others believed there would be a mass rebellion by the French Resistance groups, armed and equipped by the Allies. But although the phrase 'The Invasion' was widely used after June 6th, especially by the French, we did not really use it much before then. The scale of the June 6th landings when they actually happened was beyond what we had imagined possible.

For my local bunker team specifically, our officers drummed the idea into our heads that the beach was a potential target for landings and it must be defended, but at the same time they liked to tell us what a disaster the English and Canadians had made of trying to land on the beach at Dieppe in 1942. We were often shown the newsreel films of Dieppe, with all the dead Allied troops and all their wrecked tanks and so on.

There was also the danger of small-scale 'commando' type raids along the coast, which we did expect at any time. We knew the British especially were very unprincipled in these raiding parties, for example the St Nazaire atrocity in which they massacred a large number of unarmed German officers and French civilians. Incidentally, this is one point in which I have *not* changed my thinking since the war. The St Nazaire raid was a deliberate massacre by the British.

At any rate, I think our general feeling was that something would happen, but I for one certainly did not expect a major landing exclusively on the beaches, without the capture and use of existing ports or harbours. I thought that a pure beach landing was impossible, especially considering all the anti-landing obstacles which were built on the tidal range of the beach.

What were these obstacles?

These were metal girders welded in cross formations, and among them timber posts set in concrete at about 45 degrees, intended to hold up boats or other craft approaching the shore. Most of them had a Teller mine or an artillery shell attached to the obstacle at some point, being primed to detonate if a craft touched it. The artillery troops manning the two 88mm guns in my bunker regularly fired shells along the beach to ensure their ranging was accurate. Their orders were to fire on craft approaching from the sea, prioritising boats which had not yet hit an obstacle or any that had touched the beach itself. They could also fire along the esplanade behind the sea wall if any attackers managed to climb over that wall into the town.

My bunker had a substantial magazine of 88mm high-explosive ammunition, which was kept in a central pit behind the gun platforms. The MG position in which I was assigned was a concrete slit fitted with an MG 34 on a gimbal mount set into the floor.

Behind us, there was our fortified farmhouse, and then there were further inland defences, chiefly consisting of villages which were fortified and linked together with bunkers, Tobruk emplacements and Resistance Points.

What is your memory of June 6th 1944?

I would like to be able to boast that I was the first to sight the allied ships, the 'invasion armada' as the English press called it, but in fact I was not on observation duty at the time. On the Monday evening, I had accompanied two of my comrades to a small bar in the nearby town, which was friendly to Germans, and we had stayed there for several hours. They served a very light red wine which we were very fond of, and there were young ladies who would sit at our tables and speak with us.

Of course, the amount of activity in the air overhead was very noticeable. The amount of bombing had become very intense over preceding weeks, but that night the noise of aircraft engines was constant, and there was bombing to the south and west of us. All this caused the bar proprietor to close his premises early, and we went back to our barracks, under all this plane noise, with a bottle of wine which we drank in our bunks.

All these things being the case, we were asleep in the fortified farmhouse building until, at about five am, our Feldwebel stormed in and began kicking us out of bed. I am not sure of the exact time, as the situation was confused. But the Feldwebel was shouting, 'Angriff! Angriff!' ('*Raid! Raid!*') so at this early point we were thinking of the event as a 'raid,' not as 'invasion.'

We dressed and took our rifles. In all there were about two dozen men assembling in the hallway and corridors.

When we came out of the farmhouse, the light was still grey, and the air was very cool. The first thing that I experienced was the increasing noise of aircraft, which was mounting and getting louder literally with every second that passed. Overhead, there was a large volume of planes visible and coming north-south, I would say fifty or sixty aircraft, which I think were medium bombers. There were also smaller, Spitfire type aircraft behind them and several of these also at low altitude. I had not seen a fighter plane so close before; they were perhaps one hundred metres high. I experienced all of this very quickly, in a confused way, as we ran with our rifles along a sunken road which connected the farmhouse to the bunker. None of us spoke, we only followed our Feldwebel and reached the bunker quickly. We entered through a steel door which was then shut behind us, and a steel locking pin was placed across it. I began to go up to the observation point, which was my normal post, but the artillery officer ordered me to the MG position, saying that all men were needed to work the guns.

I remember that I ran into the position, which was a concrete room set into the walls, where the MG 34 was positioned at the embrasure; the embrasure was a concrete slit about one metre wide at head height, and the gunners stood on a platform to work the gun. Two men were already there, talking in an agitated way, manning the gun. I jumped onto the platform, and looking through the slit I saw the situation in the channel.

I was astonished at the number of craft; I would not like to estimate how many, but I recall that the foremost was possibly a few kilometres from the low tide obstacles, while the furthest were literally on the horizon. These craft included destroyer-type warships, tugs, and numerous low vessels which seemed to be invasion barges. There was a great variety of other boats. I was struck speechless at this sight, which I had never imagined possible. The sheer volume of craft was what amazed me. Even as I stared, more ships came into view, endlessly filling the sea. I remember, if I may be honest, that

I began to tremble, and I broke out in a sweat. I know I am not the only soldier in history to experience such a reaction when faced with the enemy, and so I feel no shame in describing this to you.

The MG gunner, who was a middle-aged man, looked at me and laughed in a bitter fashion, and he said, 'Are we sorry we started this war now?'

Then he and his loader went back to checking and readying their gun and the belts of ammunition, which were fed from metal cases from the left. I brought up more cases from the store area and I got ready to pass these to the gunners so that there would be no break in their firing. I was also trained to fire and load the gun if necessary. As I looked out of the slit again, I saw a fighter plane, I think a Mustang, coming towards us extremely low over the beach; the propeller was simply filling the visible sky in front of us. Before we reacted, this plane fired a short burst, and I heard the bullets impact on the concrete exterior of the bunker. Then the plane lifted up and disappeared over us; it was so low that I could smell its fumes.

It may sound strange, but I thought to myself, 'He wanted to kill us!' This being the first time I had seen a shot fired in earnest.

Just as I thought this, I saw many flashes of light from the ships on the sea, a huge number of white and red flames all beginning at once. Some of these appeared to be cannon from the warships, with a dense plume of light and smoke. I heard a number of these shells pass over the bunker with a loud, roaring sound and explode somewhere in the land behind us. Other weapons were a type of rocket launcher, and these rockets fired one after the other very quickly, reeling off left and right from their vessels. In moments, these rockets were landing on our bunker, and the structure vibrated as they detonated on the roof or the outside walls. Some of these weapons hit the ground in front of our post, and the explosion sent many fragments of stones and shrapnel against our embrasure, some pieces entering inside and ricocheting off the walls.

Our reaction was to duck, which I assume was the exact intention of this opening bombardment: to force us to keep our heads low, to prevent us manning our guns or observing the beach. It was effective in this respect, because the sheer number of these explosions deterred us from standing at full height on the platform. The intensity of the bombardment was agonising for me; every second there was another explosion, then another, and every one made the bunker vibrate, and sent debris in through the aperture, and the smell of explosive was very strong in the air. I put my hands over my ears and crouched on the platform, and I found the two gunners doing the same. One of them had the presence of mind to lower the MG on its mount, so that it was below the embrasure and not exposed to the shrapnel.

I thought that this bombardment would be over soon, but I found that it continued on and on. It became impossible to react, or even to think clearly, because there was no pause between the explosions, they followed in fractions of a second all the time. Frankly, I began to lose track of time, and my only thought was that I wanted this shelling to be finished. I assure you that I was not afraid to fight, but to be subjected to these colossal, ceaseless explosions was not the same as fighting. The man who was the gun loader reacted even worse than me, and he began to scream and bang his hands on the concrete wall; I could not hear his voice, but I could see his mouth and fists moving.

The steel door in our room opened, and one of the artillery officers stumbled in. As he entered, a rocket or shell exploded exactly against the aperture of our position, and a large amount of debris came in through the slit. This contained stones, shrapnel, and clods of earth. The stuff whirled around inside the room, smashing off the walls. I saw several pieces hit the officer, and pierce him in the face, going through one eye and also breaking his teeth. He flew back against the wall and slumped down. Outside in the corridor of the bunker, I could see other troops crouched against the walls, in the same position as me, enduring this bombardment.

The explosions stopped very suddenly, and the noise echoed around in our concrete space for a long time. I recall that I laughed in a crazy way, because I felt that the fighting was over. Then, of course, I realised that it had not yet begun, and I got to my feet. In the corridor, the other men were doing likewise. The injured officer lay on the floor, and we had no time to give him assistance. I raised my head over the edge of the aperture, and I saw a sight that made me almost lose hope.

The ground in front of the bunker was on fire, and full of huge craters that went all the distance down to the beach. There on the beach, a large number of troops were already coming ashore, jumping out of flat-bottomed barges that came up to the shallows. Those craft were lowering their ramps, and many men were jumping and running out. A lot of these craft had struck the obstacles, and were sinking or burning, and men were jumping from these craft into the water, some of them on fire.

To my right, I heard the *boom–crack* sound of our 88mm guns beginning to fire onto the beach. The gunners had practised so often, they were finding targets despite the numbing effect of the bombardment. I saw red tracer from our 88mms streak out repeatedly to the beach zone. The shells struck landing craft as they were lowering their ramps, in one case blowing off the steel ramp door and throwing men over the sides into the sea. That craft began to sink from the nose down, and our tracer moved onto other vessels approaching.

The two MG men raised their gun on its steel mount, both of them trembling and gasping just as I was. The gunner had great character, however, and he calmed himself and fitted the gun, and began to aim at men on the beach. The loader was not capable of doing more, though, and he went back to crouching and clutching his head in his hands. Because of this, I took over the function of loader, and I stood beside the gunner, feeding the ammunition belts, as he aimed the MG34. He said to me that these were English troops, judging from their helmets and uniforms, which were a dull brown colour. Then he began to fire.

We were firing to our right, with a clear view along the beach line. There were many men scrambling onto the sand, and a lot of smoke and explosions still happening. There was tracer coming from the other end of the beach and knocking these men down; this was a smaller MG bunker in the rocks at that end. That gunner was very precise in his selections: he put a short burst into groups of men as they exited the landing craft, sending them tumbling down the ramps, and then moved to the next one.

My gunner began to do likewise, and fired on the nearest craft, which was lowering its ramp. There was a line of men in the bow, and as they came out onto the ramp they ran straight into our tracer. One after the other, they fell over the edge of the steel plate into the sea; I think we hit six or seven men in two seconds.

What was your feeling, this being your first time in action, and participating in the killing of these men?

I was not aware of feelings. I knew that we had to stop these troops getting onto our territory, and we had the weapons to do this. Frankly, I felt a certain pride in the skill of the MG gunner, who used his gun very effectively. He was able to pin men down on the beach, forcing them to hide behind beached craft or the vehicles which were coming off the ramps, stopping them forming up and moving. In some cases, these isolated men were then hit by our 88mm fire, and the sand was thrown up a great distance into the air where the shells struck; also many pieces of men and machinery.

I remember that one landing craft was hit by 88mm as it approached the shore at speed; for some reason it then could not stop, and it crashed up onto the sand burning from the rear. Its hull struck a group of men wading ashore and crushed them down completely, utterly demolished them. I felt sick at that sight for the first time, but I continued to feed the ammunition belts to the gun.

The vessels further out at sea began to fire on us again, and more of the naval shells came down on us, the large warship rounds which we could hear approaching. I saw one of these rounds hit the ground in front of our bunker and bounce off without exploding, tumbling end over end up over our roof. But other shells hit our bunker exactly, and I believe one of them hit our 88mm positions, because those guns ceased firing for some time. I heard shouting and yelling from inside the bunker, and men calling for fire-fighting equipment. There was nothing I could do about that, so I remained at my post feeding the belts to the gun.

From your viewpoint, in your particular zone, was there ever a moment when the Allied troops might have been driven back into the sea? Was this ever a possibility?

I think that in our case this was not a possibility, because of the scale of their numbers. If we had eight or ten 88mms instead of two, or heavier guns, then perhaps the assault could have been broken up on the beach and held there. But with our 88mm guns disabled, the landing craft were able to surge up and unload, with only the MG fire to oppose them for some time.

The craft were unloading tanks at this point, and these were Churchill types. We had been trained to identify Allied planes and tank types, but these Churchills had very short, wide guns that I had not seen in our training pictures. Three of these Churchills flopped down onto the sand and began to move along up the incline to the sea wall. One of them hit a teller mine, and its track was blown off. That tank revolved in circles hopelessly, spraying sand. When it came to a halt, one of our 88mm guns opened fire at last, and hit it through the side with an armour piercing shell. My God, that caused a huge explosion in the tank; the top of the hull split open, and burning fuel poured out from the engine decks. I saw a crew man try to escape from a hatch, but he was on fire and he became wedged in the hatch opening; he burned there with his tank. The other two Churchills were also hit; one was knocked over on its side when it ran over the edge of a sand dune. The other was hit repeatedly on the turret, but it progressed to the sea wall and it fired its gun repeatedly at the concrete.

It caused huge explosions there, and the sea wall disintegrated and collapsed, forming a mound of rubble. This was presumably what the British wanted, because their men began to rush up this pile of debris and emerge onto the civilian esplanade that ran along the rear of the beach. This meant that they were now on the point of entering the town itself.

My gunner hit many of these men as they came up the debris onto the street. Several were knocked over backwards and fell onto their comrades below; others just lay there on the cobblestones. I saw some of the men who came up lose their nerve and back down again, and I am sure that I would have done the same, faced with this MG fire which was moving up and down the esplanade wherever they appeared.

I saw a large explosion among the rocks at the other end of the beach, and the German MG fire from there ceased abruptly. I think they used a bazooka or a mortar on that position. Now our bunker was firing alone, with our MG and the single 88mm operating from our embrasures.

Our MG34 was running very hot by then; the breech was glowing and it was difficult to lift the mechanism to insert the fresh belts of ammunition. The British began to fire on the bunker with rounds from their Churchills; this was very inaccurate, with the shells landing haphazardly around us, but the explosions were enormous. In effect, we were blinded by smoke and dust from this shelling, and we decided to cease firing, to conserve our ammunition and let the gun cool until the smoke cleared. We also needed more MG ammunition from the pit.

I went out into the corridor, having to step over the unconscious body of the wounded officer; his teeth were scattered across the floor. As I exited, an officer out there pointed his pistol at me and demanded where I was going. He ordered me back inside, and sent ammunition to me carried by one of the medics. I heard shots inside the bunker itself, and I guessed this was the officers firing in warning because men were leaving their posts, so I was determined not to do that. The smoke was clearing, and we could see again down onto the beach and esplanade, so immediately the MG gunner began firing.

I must say that he killed many of the British soldiers in the next few seconds. A large group of them was moving in single file down the esplanade towards us, possibly believing that our guns were knocked out. Our bullets passed right through the leading men and hit the men behind; then as they fell, the men behind were hit and so on. In moments, they all threw themselves behind a low wall beside the street, but the pathway was full of dead troops, whose bodies were issuing smoke from the impacts.

May I assume, from your earlier remark, that you had
no feeling for these dead men in front of you?

I still felt numb, but at the same time, let us remind ourselves, we the Germans were not attacking England! We were not invading America. It was the Allies attacking France, and we were there to defend the country against their assault.

Did you have other thoughts, about the progress of
the battle, and how it would turn out?

I began to doubt if our position would hold. For one thing, we were being bombarded again, with accurate artillery being fired from off-shore. These shells were causing the roof of our bunker, which was very thick, to flex and send fragments down onto us. Also, the British sent a tank up over the debris on the sea wall and this advanced along the esplanade towards us. This was a Sherman tank, a very tall target, and our 88mm hit it immediately on its front plate. However, the shell was obviously high-explosive, not armour-piercing, and it blew away various brackets and hooks on the front of the hull, but the tank continued to advance on us. I could see their infantry forming behind it, using it as cover, and although my gunner fired down the sides of the tank hull, he could not hit the men behind it.

Our ammunition belt finished, and because of the heating of the breech, the new one did not insert properly at first; also my hands were shaking, and I had grit in my eyes, so it was difficult to work on it. The gunner said, 'Come on, be quick, boy, because those troops will kill us for sure after what we've done. There's no point surrendering, do you see?'

That was a shock to me: that my actions could cause other men to take revenge on me even if I offered to surrender. The Sherman was firing on the 88mm embrasure as it advanced now, firing very rapidly with explosive, and I could see the shells detonating along the bunker wall where the 88mm was positioned. That 88mm got off one more round, which hit the tank on the right track, blowing it loose. The Sherman skidded to one side, so that its hull flank was exposed, and the 88mm fired again with armour piercing. This went into the hull above the tracks, near the engine, and that tank began to burn almost immediately.

A tall column of flame spurted up from the rear deck, and many pieces of machinery came flying out of the engine grilles. In just a few seconds, this tank was surrounded by a pool of burning fuel, literally a circle of fire. The hatches opened, and two crew men climbed out. My gunner shot them at once, and they fell off the tank into the gasoline flames. This was an unnecessary thing for our man to do, but I think he was desperate to keep the English away from our post.

Our 88mm shot the Sherman again, and this smashed a piece off the turret, sending it flying off across the beach, rolling across the sand a long way. I could actually see a crew man in the turret, apparently immobile, as the flames in there grew bigger. I began to understand what the gunner meant when he said these English would kill us for sure now.

Out of the smoke behind the Sherman, another tank advanced on us; this was a Churchill of the type with the very short, wide calibre gun. This Churchill simply stormed up the roadway, bulldozing aside the Sherman, went through the burning fuel and drove straight up to us without slowing. It was trailing burning gasoline, and although our 88mm hit it on the turret front, the round deflected off and went into a nearby house, ripping a hole in the wall.

This Churchill driver was evidently in a furious state, because he took the tank directly up to our bunker, literally a couple of metres from it, and lowered his gun to the area of the 88mm position near me. I saw the big cannon in the turret fire, and with that the whole area of the 88mm embrasure was demolished, in many fragments of concrete and debris.

I heard the explosion through the corridor of the bunker, and the amount of smoke blinded us briefly. My gunner continued firing tracer into the smoke, pouring a whole belt of ammunition into the roadway area left and right. But there was another explosion, and it was evident that the Churchill was firing his rounds repeatedly into the damaged embrasure.

I began to change the ammunition belt, and I heard the gunner curse and reach for his rifle. I looked up, over the edge of the concrete slit, and I came face to face with an English soldier who was outside. He had run at us through the smoke, and he was covered in grey concrete dust – except for his eyes, I clearly recall, which were very bright blue, and bloodshot. He was in a total rage, that was obvious. He essentially had a desire to kill us written on his face. He threw a grenade into our post, which bounced through into the corridor and exploded there. My gunner was still fumbling with the MG belt. The Englishman then fired in through the slit with a sub machine gun, the type they called the Sten gun. This produced a huge amount of fire, and the soldier must have used a whole magazine, because my gunner was hit in a devastating way in the chest and head. I was crouching down on the platform, and looking up, I saw the Sten gun punch holes in his chest, and the bullets emerge from his back. The bullets ricocheted flew wildly around the concrete walls, and several hit me, but their energy was spent and they deflected off my steel helmet and my boots, so I wasn't injured.

Were you thankful for this escape?

I had no time to think at this point. Outside the slit, there was an explosion, which was the British soldier either being hit by a shell or treading on a mine, I do not know which. Pieces of his tunic came flying in over the edge of the embrasure, burning and smoking. I left my gunner lying on the floor, as he was clearly dead; I ran out through the door and into the corridor.

Here, I saw that the whole bunker was being destroyed around us. The steps that led down to the 88mm posts were strewn with debris, and several of the 88mm gunners were crawling up them, badly injured. There were still explosions at the front of the bunker, from that Churchill or other tanks, as I thought. The officer who had threatened me with a pistol was there, and he gestured for me and another man who was running from the ammunition pit to follow him. I thought that he meant us to leave the bunker, but he directed us back into the MG room. He went in first, and as soon as he entered there was more sub machine gun fire, and also a huge explosion. I saw a very white light from inside the MG room, and a flickering glow that subsided slowly.

I looked into the MG room, and the scene was terrible. The officer and my gunner were on fire, with their limbs burned away, and the room was full of a burning powder which coated the walls and was dripping from the ceiling. I was sickened by the sight.

I believed the bunker was being overrun completely now, so together with the other soldier, I exited the building through the steel door in the rear, holding my rifle.

Outside, the situation was confused. There were still many Allied aircraft overhead, with black and white stripe marks on their wings and fuselage. I saw no Luftwaffe aircraft at all. There were several of our troops firing with rifles and MP40 from the sunken path that went to the farmhouse, aiming at the front of the bunker. These were not gunners, but cooks and so on from the accommodation staff, and they were being hit badly by returning fire. I jumped down into this sunken path. I looked around at the bunker, and saw the roof starting to sag and crack as the explosions kept striking it.

One of the soldiers said, 'The bunker is finished, we should surrender.' He threw away his rifle and raised his hands, but he was immediately shot in the head, and his skull fragmented even while his arms were stretched out. Then large numbers of the English troops began to storm up towards us from the bunker, with rifles and fixed bayonets. Our men shot down two of them, but the others kept charging, and they fell on us with their bayonets.

There was a dreadful few seconds of hand-to-hand fighting there around the sunken path. I saw one of the Englishmen stab a German through the stomach with his bayonet, and throw him aside like a sack, then move onto the next German, whom he stabbed in the neck. The soldier with me clubbed this man over the head with his rifle butt, then stepped back and shot him in the chest. The Englishman slashed at this soldier even as he slumped down, blinding him in one eye with his bayonet. An English soldier came up the slope with a Thompson gun, and shot down many Germans before he was hit by MP40.

Together with the blinded soldier, I ran low down into the sunken path, and ran along it away from the bunker. I am not sure that we had any plan, but the bunker was obviously lost as a position. Behind us, I could hear terrible screams, which I think was the hand-to-hand situation, with the English using their bayonets. Some shots came past us, but no English followed us.

We came up from the path at the farmhouse building, and immediately we were surrounded by a squad of our German troops, with one officer, demanding to know what the situation was on the beach and esplanade. I reported that the British were in the bunker and were bringing tanks up over the sea wall and esplanade. Indeed, we could hear tank engines rattling and revving on the coastal side of the farmhouse.

The officer and troops present were men I had not seen before; from their Waffenfarben (*service insignia*) I saw they were from a Panzergrenadier unit. They were armed with Panzerfaust rockets and had an MG42, rifles and MP40, so they gave me a sense of security, if such a thing was possible. The troops also assured me that a 75mm PAK was just behind us; it was only a matter of minutes, they said.

In readiness, the Panzergrenadier officer ordered us all to take up positions on the coastal side of the farmhouse, the house that we used as a barracks. We took up posts along a low ridge which had been built up as a defence with sandbags and barbed wire. It gave us a good view down the rolling slope, which was dotted with dunes and grass, to the sea defences. The slopes here were mined with anti-personnel and anti-tank mines in random patterns. The bunker was visible; this was now largely demolished, and a lot of smoke was rising from it. We saw a Sherman tank emerge from over the mounds by the ruined bunker, and this was an astonishing sight for us all.

This Sherman was fitted with a revolving drum on the front, held by two girders, on which were tied a large number of heavy chains. The drum was revolving, and the chains were crashing onto the earth with a deafening noise, raising clouds of dust and soil.

I had never seen a machine like this, but the officer shouted that this was an anti-mine vehicle, and indeed I saw several explosions under the chains as the tank came forward, these being mines that were being detonated. I was fascinated by its clever design, despite my apprehension. I could just see, behind the mine-clearing tank, two other Shermans also with these revolving drums, following it on either side; the lane they were clearing was thus about twenty metres wide.

One of the Panzergrenadiers fired a Panzerfaust, but the range was too great and the rocket fell to the ground without striking.

The officer shouted for us to hold fire, and said that the PAK gun was coming up to defend the slopes. However, the English began to fire mortar rounds on us; these small bombs fell without warning, and caused bursts of flame with a large amount of shrapnel as they exploded. Several of these mortar rounds hit the farmhouse behind us, knocking pieces off the roof, and then began to fall among us men on the ridge. A Panzergrenadier soldier a few metres from me was hit badly, and he lay quivering on the earth with blood shooting from his chest; the partially blinded soldier who came with me from the bunker was hit in the back and was unable to move any further.

What medical help was there for these wounded men?

At this point, there was none. We had to leave them as they fell, because we expected a full assault at any moment. I was sprayed with blood from the wounded Panzergrenadier, and this added to my unease. Another soldier was hit by shrapnel in the head, and his skull was completely opened above one ear, with his brain matter visible. I tell you all this because this was the experience that I had and these were the things I saw.

As the mine-clearing tanks came closer, the noise was incredible, and the pounding of the chains on the earth could be felt under us. Several times, a chain came loose from the spinning drum after a mine explosion, and the chain flew up into the air a great distance, and then came falling to the ground. One of these huge chains, which was about three metres long, fell in this way onto two of our men and knocked them both unconscious where they were crouching.

One of their comrades leaped up and aimed his Panzerfaust over the ridge, and the weapon fired, sending a jet of flame back behind it. I looked over the ridge, and saw the rocket head strike the revolving chains; the projectile was simply knocked up into the air and it went away across the slope. However, other men were stationed at the extreme ends of the ridge, and they were able to fire on the sides of this leading Sherman. The angle was acute, but they chose the target well, aiming the warheads at the wheels and tracks along the sides, and I saw the tank hit in its running gear. There was a large orange flash, and suddenly the chain drum slowed, and then stopped revolving. The tank itself stopped completely, and smoke began to pour from the rear decks. Our other men did not need a second chance, and they aimed a Panzerfaust directly onto the

Sherman's front, now that the chains were still. The rocket struck the lower turret, which was turned to the rear, and blew a hole in it which disgorged sparks.

We thought that we had stopped this tank, but the machine gun in its front plate fired on us, shooting all the way along the ridge and blowing out puffs of earth wherever the bullets hit. Also, the two similar tanks behind it came level, and continued to advance, even though that leading tank was now burning. I saw pieces of metal and tubes shooting up from the back of the burning tank as the engine burned up fiercely. The hull hatch opened, and a crew man emerged. The Panzergrenadier MG42 team immediately shot him. Again, I had the sensation that we would pay for doing such things to these people.

By this time, we had about a dozen able-bodied troops left on this ridge, including myself and the officer. We had no Panzerfausts left, but the PAK gun then arrived, towed behind a Hanomag (*armoured half-track*) which used the cover of a hedgerow. This was a large 75mm PAK gun, and the crew flew into action like devils, hauling it around and positioning it on one side of the ridge where it could fire down the slopes. The Hanomag had an MG in a shielded mount too, so we were now better armed. The PAK crew began firing within a minute, I was astonished at their speed. They immediately hit one of the two mine-clearing Shermans, striking it on the revolving drum. The drum separated from the vehicle, and crashed off onto the ground, while still revolving at high speed. This great metal cylinder raced off among the dunes, sending out bits of chain and debris that flew long distances on both our side and the English side.

The tank was undamaged, though, and it halted and began to traverse its turret around onto us, moving the main gun around very quickly. Our PAK fired again, but the round deflected off the angled front plate and went off to one side. The PAK fired another shot, and this one struck the Sherman in the tracks, causing the drive wheel to break off and spin away. However, although this tank was now immobile, its turret was fully rotated onto us, and it fired on the PAK, using high explosive. The shot went wide, but the blast lifted the gun up and rocked it, and the crew then struggled to operate it. They worked on it like devils with their hands, but nothing came of it. The Sherman fired again, and this round hit the PAK crew directly.

This was a dreadful sight, because much of the 75mm ammunition also exploded, and the debris was blasted out all around us. I am sorry to say that this was debris of the gun, its barrel and so on, but also debris of the crew: their limbs and clothing, and boots, water bottles, everything they had with them. Everything was torn apart in front of us.

The Sherman continued firing, and it landed high-explosive shells on the farmhouse, which began to burn, and on the ridge which we were sheltering behind. Some men shouted that we should surrender, but the opportunity to do this was not there, as the Sherman kept firing all along our line. Also, I had seen what happened to the man who tried to surrender at the bunker, who was shot in the head, and I was afraid of that same treatment.

In all this confusion, I heard shooting from the sunken path that led to the bunker, and I heard bullets that came from down there hitting the farmhouse walls. A moment later, a handful of English troops emerged from the path, with their bayonets fixed or with Thompson guns. They were barely twenty metres from us, and they were evidently filled with a furious energy; their eyes were staring, and they roared out incomprehensible shouts as they fired on us and charged at us.

Our MG42 team turned around on them, and shot down three soldiers in a moment. The 42 was such a powerful gun, and the range was so short, that these men were blown to pieces, almost as if by shrapnel. Pieces of their bones and flesh came streaming out behind them, and their uniforms caught fire from the heat of the bullets. I fired my rifle, and hit a man as he ran towards me. Someone shot me, and the bullet deflected off my steel helmet, making me stumble and fall on my back.

I saw one of the other English with a Thompson gun shot up the MG42 machine gun team, and he fired like a madman into all of us, knocking many of us down. Other English men came up behind him, and they charged into us, stabbing and slashing with bayonets. The Sherman held its fire, and the English troops overran the whole position. I myself stayed on the ground, with my hands visible, until an English soldier came up and pointed a Sten gun at my face.

All I could do was to spread my hands and shake my head, in an indication that I did not intend to resist any further. This man kicked my rifle away, then called for other men to come over. These men searched my pockets, then put metal handcuffs on me with my hands behind my back, and then left me lying on my side, completely disregarding me after that. I could hear the awful noise of another mine-clearing tank approaching, and of course that meant that soon their other tanks could come up from the beach and move inland past the farmhouse. The house was completely on fire, and large numbers of English troops were now grouping around it, coming up from the sunken path. I think there were almost a hundred of them, waiting to move ahead.

I assume this was the end of the fighting around your particular bunker?

Well, the German activity was at an end. What did happen, however, was that an aircraft came over the bunker zone a few moments later. I never actually saw it, because I was lying on the ground facing the house, but I heard it pass over us very low, at high speed, and I heard firing of cannons or guns. I saw many of the English troops collapse, and I realised that this plane had shot them up, strafed them, and then flown on inland. I never learned if that was a Luftwaffe plane, or an Allied plane which mistook the troops for Germans; I think it was probably the latter. But I believe that the short burst of guns killed perhaps ten men in that dense throng of soldiers around the house.

After that, I was led back down the sunken pathway to the beach zone and placed with other German prisoners in a small paved square near the esplanade.

What was your feeling at being captured?

I felt that I had held out to the last possible moment, and I did not feel ashamed of being a prisoner.

How were you treated as prisoners?

I recall that the character of the English seemed to change very quickly. When they attacked us, they were very ferocious, eager to use their bayonets. But after we were taken away to the square, we were well treated; our handcuffs were removed, we were given water, the wounded were allocated a medic who in turn asked for German volunteers to assist him. Our treatment was very humane in that respect. Having said that, many of the local French people emerged from their houses and looked through the railings of the square at us, and made insulting remarks; but of course, these were the same people we had been bartering and trading with twenty-four hours beforehand.

Some of our troops cursed the French and promised to take revenge when the English left the area – because, you must remember, we still did not know if this was a permanent occupation, despite the huge army the allies had. Some of my fellow prisoners were sure that this was a Dieppe-style raid, and they threatened the French with retaliation when German control was restored.

Was this a widespread belief, that the landings were in fact temporary?

Some of our men seemed to believe this. 'Dieppe' was said repeatedly among us. 'This is just another Dieppe, they will be gone tomorrow,' and such comments. Others pointed out the incredible resources the Allies had used, and they said that such an investment of troops and materiel would not be expended on a short-term raid. I myself agreed with this view; the number of ships and planes involved was colossal, as I had seen myself from the bunker.

One of the men there had been to Dieppe in 1942 after that raid, and he told us that the Allies had dropped thousands of leaflets by air during that attack, which said '*This action is a coup de main, not an invasion. Civilians must not risk themselves,*' or some such thing. Very sporting of the English! But on June 6th, no such leaflets had been seen, which further suggested that this was a permanent incursion into France.

Also, of course, we prisoners discussed the very obvious question of why the Allies would want to capture this particular beach, which had no harbour or port facilities. Some said that this proved it was a *diversionary* attack, and that a main attack would be made against Cherbourg, Granville or Calais. You must remember that we had no information, of course, about any other landings that morning, or the wider Allied operation. For all we knew, this was a single attack on an isolated beach.

While all this was being discussed among us, some of the exchanges that our men had with the French civilians through the railings became very angry, and the English guards fired shots into the air and dispersed the French quite roughly. One of our troops tried to take advantage of this confusion, and attempted to climb over the courtyard wall to escape; he could not swing himself over, and remained clinging to the top. One of the guards (who had impressed me as a very humane man, giving us water and supplies) well, this guard walked up to the man and shot him in the back. This was quite unnecessary, but I think he did it to keep control over us. At many times afterwards, I noticed this trait in the English: they changed rapidly from being friendly or so-called 'gentlemen' to being very ruthless, even brutal, and they could turn these different sides of their character on and off very quickly.

At this point in the day, it was still only before noon. All this had happened in one morning; it was very difficult to accept that the situation had changed so much and so quickly. Throughout the day, more prisoners were put in among us, and these men told us that they had been captured some distance inland. All the time, streams of Allied aircraft flew over us, heading inland, and others returned out to sea. One by one, the men who said that this was a temporary raid gave up the idea.

In the afternoon, the English, I recall, insisted for some reason on sending a German-speaking English army priest in among us to listen to any spiritual concerns we had; this was met with derision. I still recall the face of the army priest, who was very angry at his reception. We heard explosions and detonations from inland and from the beach throughout the day, and naval bombardments from offshore, the shells of which travelled over us with a sound like an express train going past, and always the sound of engines: planes, tanks and trucks, never stopping for a moment.

In the evening, we were taken out of the square and led to the beach. The guards made no attempt to blindfold us or to prevent us seeing the situation. The scale of the operation then became clear to us all, and most of us fell completely silent at what we witnessed.

The sea wall area was being worked on with armoured bulldozers, creating a huge ramp for vehicles to drive up. There were many destroyed vehicles and tanks, some still burning. I saw my bunker, which was collapsed in the frontal part, over the 88mm embrasures; there was smoke drifting from the rubble.

The beach was completely full of transports, including many vehicles we had not seen and we did not even know how to describe: amphibious trucks, tanks with flotation screens, enormous landing craft that were unloading whole columns of jeeps and tanks, directly onto the sand. The English had already cleared a wide lane through the beach obstacles – how they did that so quickly, I have never understood, perhaps with linked explosive charges – and this lane was an absolute highway on the wet sand and out into the sea itself. There were still many bodies, which were lined in large groups on the sand and partly covered with tarpaulins; despite our lack of religion, many of our men crossed themselves as we passed these.

One thing in particular struck many of us as amazing: all along the beach, there were no horses!

This was a surprise for you?

Yes, we found it astonishing. This huge army had brought with it not one single horse or pack-mule! All their transport was mechanised. It may sound bizarre today, but this impressed us greatly, showing that the Allies had no need of horses anymore, as they had such huge oil resources and production capacity. Because, of course, the German armies used horses for transport on quite a large scale right up until the end of the war, due to limited fuel and constraints on mechanised vehicle production. Every German unit had its stables and veterinarian officer, and here were these English without that need at all. For us, this symbolised the Allied capabilities.

We were put into a landing craft and told we were being taken to England for processing. Out to sea, there was a multitude of boats, many wrecks half-submerged, some still on fire, and in places there were bodies still floating on the water, with their clothing inflated by water. There were enormous warships simply standing stationary in the distance off shore, flying their flags as if the whole war was now concluded. In fact, the last thing I saw of the landing force was a British sailor on the prow of a battleship, scrubbing the deck with a broom. We passed underneath this great vessel, in its shadow. As we moved away, it began firing its guns inland, over and over again. The noise was deafening. Those were the last shots I heard in my war, which lasted a few hours in all.

You have given me a very frank and clear account of your
experience on that day, and I must thank you.

It is important, I feel, that these things are set down somewhere. I would not wish these things to be forgotten. These things were ten years ago, and I am not yet thirty years of age today, I am still a young fellow. And yet I feel in some ways like an old veteran, describing all these events, because they are not spoken of among either the Germans or the English. It is as if these actions never happened.

Could you describe your experiences in life to
me after D Day, up to the present?

Well, here you find one of the ironies, Herr Eckhertz. I was taken to a Prisoner of War camp consisting of huts in Yorkshire, England, where the guards treated us well. We were able to send letters, although we did not receive any in return. Various neutral inspectors from the Red Cross, who were Swiss and even Brazilian, visited occasionally. Of course, this was all too good to be true.

After a few months, I was in fear of my life there, but this was because of the other prisoners. Many of the prisoners were mentally ill, and some were SS or Hitler Youth type people obsessed with prolonging the war. Incidentally, I hope that one day the story of the POW camps in England is written; I think that there were half a million Germans and Italians in those camps, and the English, of course, never discuss them. The things that went on in those camps were completely insane. In my case, I was under pressure to join a team of ex Hitler Youth boys that had been captured in Normandy, who had a plan to break out of the camp and take control of an air base on the eastern coast. My poor physical fitness was of no interest to them; they wanted people to distract the guards with a staged rebellion to cover their escape.

This was in winter 1944/45, when it was clear that the war was essentially lost. My refusal to join this plan led to threats against my life. Some prisoners were being offered work outside the camp, and I joined this group, being assigned to work on vehicle repairs at a depot in a nearby town. After some time, I was allowed to live outside the camp in return for an oath of good behaviour; I took lodgings with an elderly lady in the town who treated me as one of the family. I still correspond with her at Christmas time. In fact, I remained in England voluntarily for two years after the war ended, working on vehicles, and then I returned to Germany where I now have a small mechanics workshop.

Have you ever returned to Normandy?

I have not done so up to now. Possibly this is something that I will do in the future.

—

JUNO BEACH: THE GOLIATH ENGINEER

Cornelius Tauber was an Oberleutnant (First Lieutenant) of engineers attached to the 736th Infantry Regiment, 716th Infantry Division, based in a unit close to Courseulles.

I believe that I met some men of your unit, Herr Tauber, when I wrote an article about the Atlantic Wall in May 1944. This was at Courselles, which is on the beach which the Allies called Juno Beach.

Yes, I was stationed near to Courselles from early 1944 up until the invasion itself, when I was taken prisoner by the Canadians who attacked the beach. I was posted to France from the Russian front, where I had been involved in building fortified positions, although I had not been in combat. My role was a military construction engineer, and this meant that I worked on many of the static beach and inland defences in the Normandy area. Static defences meant obstacles such as anti-tank devices, anti-tank ditches, walls and the concrete bunkers, in addition to fortifying buildings in the coastal and inland villages.

How did you regard your posting to the Atlantic Wall?

It was said of the troops in France that they 'lived like the Gods.' All my comrades slapped me on the back when they heard where I was going, and called me a lucky swine and so on. And you know, when I joined the 716th Infantry Division in France, I realised what a lucky swine I was. The food was excellent, and it was possible to buy virtually anything that you wanted on the black market. The weather was very mild and our barracks were remarkably comfortable, being a requisitioned house which had a heating stove, a well for fresh water and even proper beds. Every morning I thought of my brother in combat in Russia, and I felt extremely guilty. I thought it would be difficult to face him, when I knew he had been fighting in all the mud, the snow and the summer heat.

Of course, I found later in June, July and August 1944 that even such a beautiful place as Normandy could be turned into an absolute nightmare by battles between men. When you see a hundred men in a field who have been killed by artillery shells, and you cannot tell which head goes with which body, or which arms and legs; well, after that I was able to face my brother in the knowledge that I had experienced as much as him. But those spring months of 1944 felt simply too comfortable for me, despite the tension in the air from the impending invasion.

Did you feel that the invasion was imminent?

I think we all felt that it would happen over the summer. Logic dictated this. The uncertainty was over where it would fall, and what form it would take. All I could do, as a junior officer, was to lead my teams and carry out my tasks as thoroughly as possible, and to rely on all the other teams up and down the Wall to do the same in their zones. The Atlantic Wall was still unfinished in June 1944, despite Rommel's attempts in the winter and spring to accelerate the building programme.

What part did you play in this?

I was brought in as part of a programme to improve and intensify the building of the defences. The task involved strengthening the

94

existing defences and deciding on the location of the new fortifications, having them built, and fitting them with the equipment that was available. In particular, I was tasked with creating networks of strengthened houses and buildings in the inland sectors, and constructing the concrete bunkers ranging from small, Tobruk types to the larger installations for naval artillery. I was also involved in creating new types of anti-tank ditch, which had an angled floor inside the ditch and could be armed with explosives or incendiaries when a vehicle fell into it, and new anti-tank ramps made of curved concrete shapes.

Another feature we introduced was the Goliath type of tracked explosive unit, being a small vehicle on caterpillar tracks which was operated remotely and filled with a powerful bomb. We were building landscapes which would channel an enemy attack into places where the attackers could be damaged by these Goliath vehicles. A lot of this work was still in progress when the invasion actually happened on June 6th.

Were you involved in the combat of the 6th?

Yes, indeed. My barracks was located close to a defensive sector designated B19 at Courselles, where we had started to construct defences which could be exploited by using the Goliath.

Forgive me, but can you explain this Goliath more fully? I am not familiar with the machine.

Goliath was a small vehicle about the size of a wheelbarrow or similar. It had a petrol engine and ran on tracks like a small tank. Its body was packed with explosives equivalent to a Stuka-type bomb, and it was operated by wires which trailed from behind it, connected to a control unit held by a soldier. The operator would start its engine and control its speed and direction through the wires, sending it close to a target and then detonating it remotely. Although it was designed for offensive purposes, it was felt that it could be used in defence also, for example by sending it out from bunkers against formations of tanks or assemblies of troops, where a bomb of that size would cause a very destructive blast wave.

We actually had large numbers of these useful machines in readiness; in that particular sector of B19, we had a store of about twenty-five of them.

We had built a quite complex defensive belt around that zone, with several Resistance Points between civilian villas, armed with PAK which fired down onto the beach. Any tank trying to exit the beach would need to skirt a series of anti-tank ditches in the dune area, and this would bring them into the arc of fire of the PAK guns. It was intended that, as tanks bunched up on the beach waiting to move out, being delayed by the PAK guns, we could then send out Goliath machines from a concealed bunker point built for that purpose, destroying the enemy tanks on the sand.

At Courselles, the Goliath bunker, as we called it, was thus positioned on the beach. It was incomplete, but it had a roof on it and was perfectly concealed from the sea by concrete shapes which were painted to resemble the local rocks. It was in this Goliath bunker that I saw combat, in my capacity as an engineer officer.

What happened on June 6th?

I had returned from a site inspection of a new bunker which we were planning in the north, and I got back to the officers' barracks around midnight. Even then, there was substantial aircraft noise overhead, and I stood outside the barracks for some time with some of the other officers who were based at the barracks, discussing all this. It didn't sound like a heavy bomber raid, because the aircraft were lower and their engine noise was lighter. There was a constant drizzle, and the clouds were lit in part by the moon, I remember. Shapes of aircraft were noticeable moving under the clouds, going north to south. Flak fire was shooting up at the aircraft, in a sporadic way.

To some extent, we were accustomed to aerial bombing, but this was the largest movement of aircraft that we had experienced. In the end, we went into the barracks; one of the officers opened a bottle of cognac, which we shared. The mood was philosophical, in the sense that if this was an attempted invasion, or some form of initial attack, this might be our last night of comparative peace. This proved to be correct, of course. We began to receive communications by messenger that attacks were happening to the south west, involving gliders. The officers with me were a mixture of infantry, engineers and artillery men, and everybody went off to their unit at that point. None of us knew what was happening exactly, but the situation was evidently escalating. I think we were all glad of that cognac.

I myself collected ten men of my team from the nearby men's barracks, who dressed hurriedly. We went to the zone of fortifications at B19, which was about thirty minutes on foot. There, I spoke briefly to the commander of the PAK guns which were sited in the Resistance Points between the houses, and we agreed to have the Goliath bunker on the beach ready for possible use. I left five of my men up in the main fortifications, and took five down into the Goliath bunker on the beach. The bunker was accessed by a tunnel shielded by a concrete casing; this casing was camouflaged with foliage and stones to make it seem part of the seafront. The concealment of the whole Goliath bunker was extremely effective. The bunker itself was a concrete circle with a domed roof, at the lower end of the tunnel, and because we had surrounded it with our painted 'rocks' it was impossible to see from the beach side.

In the bunker, we had three Goliath machines ready to operate. There were a further five lined up in the covered tunnel. Each Goliath was armed with its bomb and filled with enough gasoline to enable it to travel about a kilometre. The bunker had a narrow opening onto the beach, shielded at the front by the rocks, and we could send the Goliaths out onto the beach through this. We could observe the beach through a vision slit and also through a periscope we had built into the roof, giving good visibility of the beach forward and partially to the sides.

Did you have any other armament other than the Goliath devices?

The men had their rifles. We had intended to equip the bunker with a machine gun, but this had not been fitted as yet. The real purpose of the post was to be a hidden launching point for the Goliaths, rather than a machine gun point.

It was now about three am, and with my five soldiers I checked and double-checked each Goliath, and we started the engines to warm them. This filled the bunker with fumes for a while. We were all quite calm, although I myself was filled with uncertainty about what would happen if a landing came onto the beach. My feeling was that any landing would have to be repulsed almost immediately. If the Allies built up men and vehicles on a beachhead, especially tanks, it would be difficult to ever dislodge them, because of the very weak level of Luftwaffe cover and the strength of their air forces. I knew that my Goliath machines were a key part in this rapid repulse of any attack.

Were you confident of victory?

I simply had no idea of what would happen. Would a force even come from the sea? I didn't know. Perhaps it was an airborne attack, or perhaps the sea landings were happening elsewhere on this coast, or even elsewhere in the country. There had been rumours for several weeks that the Allies would try to take over Paris as a propaganda coup – perhaps this was in progress? In the Goliath bunker, we had no radio set or telephone, and had no understanding of what was in progress elsewhere.

But I did feel confident that my bunker and my team would give a good account of themselves if the enemy arrived. We were not politically sophisticated, any of us, but at that time we trusted the state message that an attack on France was an attack on a united Europe and on the Reich itself.

What was the feeling towards the English, Americans
or other forces that you might meet?

I myself had little understanding of them as a culture. I think there was a grudging respect for the English after the North Africa campaigns were lost, but on the other hand their performance in Italy was quite slow and cautious. The Americans we were more afraid of, possibly, because of their industrial power. It was said they waged war the way a rich man wages war, with lots of machines and no worry about the gasoline or the amount of ammunition. But almost all of us had lost someone in the Allied bombing attacks on German cities, and this made us bitter.

To be frank, though, when you are in a bunker in the dark, waiting for a possible attack, your thoughts are focussed on immediate concerns.

How did the time pass?

The bunker was cold, and the exhaust fumes of the Goliaths hung in the air, stinging my eyes. It was a relief to put my face to the vision slit and get some fresh air into my eyes. The mood was tense, and I made what encouraging comments I could to the men. They were all either older men in their forties or inexperienced youths below twenty. Our engineering teams were made up of these men from 1943 onwards. These men tried to joke and reassure each other, but this was half-hearted. We could hear aircraft passing continually over us, both low-level fighters and bigger planes which sounded as if they were higher up.

First light was starting to break, and through the vision slit I could see the beach, which was looking very wet and pale in this light. The sand extended about three hundred metres down to the sea, and our anti-tank girders were set every two or three metres in this zone. There was a light mist hanging on these girders, and also on the sea itself. This was a time of extreme tension and waiting, as the light grew stronger, helping to illuminate the inside of the bunker and my men's grim faces. I took the opportunity to remind them of their tasks, which were to prepare the Goliaths, bring further Goliaths down from the tunnel, and to defend the bunker with their rifles if needed. As I spoke these words, which were intended to build confidence, a massive barrage of explosions began on the beach and on the dunes above us.

I heard the sounds of falling shells, which was a roaring noise very different to a falling bomb from an aircraft. This roaring was unusually loud, sounding like a heavy engine being accelerated. When the explosions began, I realised that they were of an enormous calibre, much bigger than any artillery I had heard before. I had been bombarded before in Italy, but this was a different order of magnitude. The explosions made the ground shake and they pummelled our ears with shock waves, which appeared to pass through the slits in the bunker and travel through the inside spaces. The best we could do was to crouch down and put our hands over our ears. The flashes from the explosions were very bright, and they lit up the bunker walls as if they were lightning bolts.

One of my men, who was the youngest and least experienced, broke down under this attack and began to weep sorrowfully. We all heard his sobs in the occasional pauses between the shell detonations. Another man also suffered, and he tried to run out of the bunker, into the covered tunnel. A Gefreiter (*corporal*), who had his wits about him, tackled this man and threw him back onto the floor of the bunker. However great the pressure, we could not tolerate men acting like that. All this went on for an extended time, and several times I looked through the periscope on the roof to see the beach. There was a vast amount of smoke, dust and debris flying around, and some of the steel defence posts were blown over or in pieces. It was difficult to make out the sea itself, but the water appeared at times as a green band at the edge of the beach. It was close to sunrise at this point and there was more colour visible in what I could see.

Looking along the beach, I could see the PAK Resistance Point between the houses near us at a higher level, and this appeared to be damaged but intact. At this point, one of my troops from that upper bunker came running down the tunnel into our bunker in a breathless state. Over all the sound of the shelling, he yelled,

'They're coming, Herr Leutnant.'

He brought the information that a large formation of ships was sighted off the coast and was advancing on our beach. He had no specific details about numbers or strength, but this appeared to be a very large attacking force. I ordered him to go up and return with any more information that was available. In the meantime, the shelling paused, which felt suddenly strange after all the noise. The men who had lost control pulled themselves together and apologised for their behaviour. This was the least of my worries, but it was a sign that they might pull through psychologically. I ordered one of the Goliaths to be brought to the exit door, the door onto the beach which was shielded with rocks.

We started the Goliath's engine to warm it again, and the rattle of the little device was almost comical after the great bombardment. The unintended amusement was a way of breaking the tension, the stress. Our grins were wiped away, though, when we heard aircraft coming over the beach very low, and the sound of cannon fire.

Through the vision slit, I could see aircraft overhead; they appeared to be Hurricane types. They were strafing the beach, dunes and buildings. We heard many of the cannon shells hit our bunker, but they did not penetrate the concrete. I heard a single Flak gun respond to them, but this fell silent very quickly. These Jabos came back repeatedly, and it would have been suicide to step out of cover at that point. I saw that their cannon shells were tearing the beach up and breaking pieces off the surrounding rocks. When these planes left, there was a second or two of calm, literally no more than that. I used the bunker periscope to try to observe the sea.

I could make out various flashes offshore, and lines of light which were evidently rockets. These rockets were flying over our bunker and exploding behind us, or in some cases smacking onto the beach and blowing up there. They burst with a bright orange light and spread many shrapnel pieces at very high speed. I saw one rocket bounce off the sand without exploding and sail off up into the rocks, turning end over end like a stick.

Finally, when the beach was absolutely covered in debris, and the smoke began to clear, I saw tanks approaching from the sea. I was very surprised at this, because I knew that the Wehrmacht could adapt tanks to cross rivers and lakes underwater, but these tanks seemed to be entirely amphibious. They were Sherman class tanks, this was clear from the rounded turret. They were fitted with what seemed to me to be canvas boxes or screens around their hulls, and they were literally swimming towards the shore. I was astonished to see this – they were not on rafts, or being towed, but somehow swimming under their own propulsion. As an engineer, I simply could not understand how the Allies got these tanks to do that. But of course, this was also the exact situation that my Goliath machines were intended to counter.

I could see three of these tanks, although my view was limited. Our PAK guns were firing on them from the Resistance Points. I ordered my men to move the first Goliath to the beach outside the exit door. The Goliath was controlled by a man with a unit built onto a plywood holder, and I gave him directions as I looked through the periscope. I ordered him to drive the Goliath out onto the beach, and I looked down from the periscope to see the machine rattling off through the door. It unwound its control cables behind it from a drum, which allowed us to steer and detonate it remotely. It disappeared from the doorway, and through the periscope I could see it advancing across the beach towards the edge of the sea. This was exactly the plan: that we would detonate the machines as tanks came onto the beach and engaged the PAK guns or were held up by the PAKs.

I could see splashes in the water as our PAK gunners in the Resistance Point shot at the Shermans. I saw one PAK round deflect off the nearest tank's turret and actually fly up into the air for a great distance. Then another round hit that same tank, and pierced the armour of the turret by the gun mantle. The tank continued to advance, but it was trailing smoke, and it fell behind the other two tanks, which were now coming up out of the shallows onto the beach itself.

Several more large shells began falling on us at the seafront line, not from the tanks but from offshore. I could see the outlines of many ships behind these Shermans – a huge number of ships, and some of them were firing large calibre guns. One of these shells struck the rocks in front of us, and shook our whole bunker to the core. The blast wave knocked me over, and I lost sight of the Goliath through the periscope. When I looked again, I saw that the Goliath was stationary on the beach, and appeared to be damaged, with one of its tracks missing. Then the operator told me that the machine was not responding. He tried repeatedly to make the device move with the controls, but the shell blast must have severed the control cables. This meant we could not steer or detonate the device, and all this time the Sherman tanks were advancing on the beach.

The one that had been hit by PAK was now capsizing and burning, and crew men were climbing off it, several of those men were also on flames as they jumped into the water. Our machine-gunners were firing now, but I could see their bullets bouncing off the front plates of the Shermans, making bright sparks.

I ordered another Goliath to be sent out, and this one disappeared out of the doorway in the same manner as the previous one. The men watched it go with very tense faces. They could not see the beach outside, but through the periscope I could follow the progress of the new Goliath towards the Shermans. I gave directions to the operator, '*Straight ahead, turn right, now straight again*,' and in this rudimentary way we steered the device towards the tanks among the flying debris. I was hopeful that we would knock out at least one of these attacking tanks, but as the Goliath approached them, it tipped into a shell crater and did not emerge. The operator tried to move it forwards and back, but I think it had fallen on its side and was immobilised. It was about twenty metres from the nearest Sherman, which was firing on the Resistance Point and the dunes, and machine-gunning along the beach. I gave the order to detonate the Goliath, as there was nothing else to be gained from it. It made a substantial explosion, and all its machinery went whirling out across the beach for hundreds of metres. The blast made the Sherman rock from side to side, but the tank kept firing and moving.

Did you have doubts about your Goliath system at this point?

Yes, I began to see that we would need to be quite fortunate to make it effective against tanks, because it would need to be completely adjacent to them to blow them up. It might be more suitable against landing barges, and in fact I could see several barges approaching on the water. I told the men to start up another Goliath, and to bring more down from the covered tunnel in readiness. The men were actioning this when the situation changed and we found ourselves under infantry attack.

Because the periscope only gave a forward view of the beach, I did not see where these infantrymen came from. I think they must have landed from the sea some distance to my left, and were now moving along the beach towards the Resistance Point and the houses. There were about twenty of these troops, in British type uniforms, armed with rifles and Thompson guns. I found out later that all these men were in fact Canadian in origin. They passed about ten metres in front of our bunker without seeing us, because we were so well concealed among the rocks. One of my men, without my order, fired through the vision slit, and he shot down one of these Canadian troops. This was a grave mistake, because it revealed our location. The shot soldier was writhing on the sand, and he was producing a lot of blood. The others took cover and pointed at our position. I took in these details in a strangely detached way, although my mind was racing, thinking what we should do next. One of the Canadians who came into view had a flamethrower unit, which was a tube attached to a tank on his back – it was very obvious to see.

We had no time to react to this. I began to give the command to fire again through the vision slit and the doorway, to hit the man with the flamethrower, but this flamethrower operator turned straight onto us and fired his unit.

What was the experience of being under flamethrower attack?

The experience was terrifying, I must say. The unit produced a long sheet of flame which shot directly towards us in the bunker. The light of the flame was blinding, and the speed of its action was astonishing. In a second, the flame hit the doorway onto the beach and the fire entered the bunker. The flame was based on some kind of gasoline mixture, and this liquid splashed wildly as it poured in, and it burned fiercely. It caught two of our men immediately, and set them on fire. Their uniforms went up in thick flames and smoke, and they threw themselves about, crashing into the other men and flailing their arms. They screamed as they thrashed about. I can still hear these screams in my mind, Herr Eckhertz. The flamethrower fired again, and the flames raced in directly through the door, soaking the nearest wall in the burning liquid.

Many of the flames splashed onto the waiting Goliath, and set that on fire. All the men who could still move leaped for the exit door to the exit tunnel, and I was in no state of mind to resist their retreat, frankly. The flames were pouring down the wall, and the whole bunker was full of smoke and the stench of this gasoline. The two men who had been hit were enveloped in flames, still moving but no longer screaming. I jumped for the doorway to the tunnel, and behind me there was the noise again of the dreadful flamethrower shooting its flames in from the beach. I ran into the tunnel, where our stored Goliath machines were lined up, and I followed the men as they ran like rabbits up the tunnel to the bunker area at the top. The light, noise and the smell of the flames was behind us all the way.

I think the Canadians burned that bunker out completely. The Goliath down there did not explode, though, or at least I did not hear it explode. Everything was now confused and dislocated. My memory is of arriving at the top of the covered tunnel and stumbling out into the light, not really knowing what was happening. I had my pistol in my hand, and I ran straight into a Canadian soldier who had a rifle with a bayonet fixed. We literally collided with each other. The shock of this stunned me, because I thought I would be in a strong position up at the Resistance Point. This Canadian gave a shout and swung at me with the stock of his rifle, and smashed me in the face across my eyes. I fell back onto the ground, blinded.

Was this the first time you had been in hand-to-hand combat?

Yes. I was not prepared for it, mentally or physically. This man was determined to kill me, that was clear. It may sound strange, but the realisation that he wanted to kill me suddenly filled my mind, with the knowledge that I therefore had to kill him first. This all lasted barely moments, just fractions of a second. I could barely see him, but I knew he was raising his rifle over me, either to shoot or to stab me with the bayonet. I fired up at this figure with my pistol, not aiming properly but just pointing it at his outline. I fired twice, and sprays of blood from him blew back at me. Then his shape disappeared, and I could see the open sky, which was completely crisscrossed with aircraft trails. I became aware that fighting was taking place all around me, with men fighting at close quarters around the entrance to the main PAK point. The Canadian that I had just shot was lying beside me, apparently dead.

I could not understand where these Canadians had sprung from – they must have traversed the sea wall at a point along the beach, and charged up to the PAK here. They were attacking us like men possessed by devils, I can tell you that. They had blown open the door of the main PAK bunker, and they were firing inside and throwing grenades in there. Others were shooting down our troops who were appearing from trenches on the other side, and there was frantic shooting between the two groups. Everything was very confused. In this chaos, I rolled over and threw myself into one of the slit trenches that ran back from the bunker. I landed on top of two bodies: a German soldier and a Canadian soldier, who had shot and stabbed each other with their rifles. They were both very young, and their dead faces looked quite similar. I saw this as I crawled over them along the trench.

Didn't the Canadians pursue you here?

The situation was very uncertain on all sides. There was a lot of shooting and tracer going over the top of the trench, and shrapnel flying across as well. I didn't know where I was going, but I still only had my pistol and my vision was blurred with blood from where that soldier hit me in the face. I rounded one of the corners of this trench, and came into contact with three German soldiers who were also retreating away from the Resistance Point. They were well-armed, with MP40 machine pistols and grenades. Together, we hunched down and scrambled along this trench to its furthest point, where it met a path that led away from the beach sector and went inland towards our next line of defences.

These men told me that there was a force already assembling at the next Resistance Point. I told them that we should get up out of the trench and join this force, and fight from there. Being an officer, I went up over the top of the trench first and scrambled down the path to a point where it was not visible from the seafront area. The man who followed me was hit by a mortar burst, and his arm and face were torn off. He died in a few seconds. I confess that I took his MP40 immediately and shouted to the others to follow. That was the nature of this combat, we had to keep moving quickly, regardless of losses.

The other two men jumped over the trench and came with me, and together we crouched and ran off along the path towards the next Resistance Point. I knew this Point well; it was a Tobruk-type installation with an old French tank turret mounted on a concrete ring, and several machine gun points. The approach was mined, and in our haste one of the two troops with me went off the path and onto the minefield. There was a small explosion and he fell forward, making horrible sounds. I saw that his legs were blown off below the knee, and his trousers were burning, showing his shin bones in the smoke. His whole body was convulsing in response to the injury, and as he thrashed about he set off another mine under his body. This blew a large piece out of his chest, and he went still. I did not even have time to react to this dreadful sight.

With the remaining soldier, I reached the Resistance Point in a few minutes. We were almost killed by a Tobruk machine gunner who fired on us, injuring the man with me very badly. I managed to carry this man the last few metres to the Point, and left him in a trench at the rear face.

What was the time at this stage?

I think it was about eight am. So this was about ninety minutes after the initial landings. The Resistance Point had a phone cable, and a Feldwebel there was relaying information to a command point deeper in the defensive belt. I added my information: that the Goliath and PAK bunkers were destroyed, and the Allies were bringing tanks directly onto the beach.

Throughout this time, mortar and rocket rounds were landing in our vicinity. We could also hear the sound of tanks on the breeze from the dunes, and many explosions along the beach side. All this suggested that the attackers were to some extent in charge of the beach, and they had tanks preparing to move out towards us.

There were about thirty men at this Resistance Point, including a local infantry officer, a man whom I knew well. We agreed that this Point could be held if we made great efforts and rallied the men. We tried to motivate the men by reminding them of the need to push the Allies back into the sea, and the danger to us all if they gained a foothold on the coast.

How did the men respond?

Most were very positive. A minority, who were mostly older German troops or Eastern troops, were quiet, and I suspected their hearts were not in the fight. On the other hand, some of the men aged forty-plus, and some of the Eastern men, were also positive, so it was not a simple distinction of '*all* the older/eastern men had no appetite for the combat.'

Who were these Eastern troops?

These were not the official ROA troops, who had their own leaders and insignia. These were Polish, Ukrainian or Baltic men who had been enlisted or had volunteered for the Wehrmacht, and wore the same uniforms as the German troops, serving under the same officers. We must remember that at this stage in the war, the German armed forces were a kaleidoscope of European nationalities and languages. This to some extent bolstered the idea of the 'United Europe.'

How soon did you expect the next wave of attack to come?
And how strong was this Resistance Point?

I expected to see the Shermans within minutes. The clear path to the beach zone between the minefields was just wide enough for a tank to pass; this was deliberate, in order to force tanks onto this passage so that they could be destroyed and the access would then be blocked, holding up any advance. The distance from the beach sector to this Point was about four hundred metres.

As for the Resistance Point, the old French tank turret at the centre was a very solid 'Char B' type, with thick armour, mounting a medium-calibre anti-tank gun. It was crewed by men in an underground chamber who had extensive supplies of ammunition. There were two MG42 machine guns in emplacements at each corner, connected by a series of trenches, and all these guns had an arc down the path and the slight incline towards the beach zone. The approaches were mined, other than the track, and there were entanglements of barbed wire around the perimeter. So this was not a bad position to hold, at least in the short term. I took up a position in one of the trenches beside the tank turret, armed with my MP40. I took over an informal command of the fifteen men, approximately, in this trench, and I urged them to be watchful.

Did you think this would prove to be a short-term engagement?

My hope was that the forces in the deeper zone would come forward to reinforce us, or that we would delay the Allies long enough to enable us to fall back to the next defensive line, having done a good job here. I myself was in an aggressive and positive frame of mind. I felt that I had done my utmost in the Goliath bunker and in the hand-to-hand combat, and I had the feeling that I might make a name for myself in this battle. I exhorted the troops to be ready, and the men lined the slit trenches with their weapons aiming down the slope. We had a few seconds, no more than that, of expectation, and then the Canadians came up from the beach.

The first thing they sent was a Sherman type tank, which came onto the edge of the path through the minefields and fired on our Point immediately. Its first shell exploded beyond us, but then a second shell hit the French tank turret and blew up there. The French turret still functioned, and fired back. This turret crew had been training constantly to land their shells exactly where the Sherman was positioned, and they hit that tank immediately. The shell deflected away across the minefield, but the impact made the Sherman rock on its wheels, and it began to reverse.

Our French gun fired again, and this hit the Sherman on the front plate, somewhere near the tracks. I saw the track fly off to one side, and the whole tank jolted and moved very slowly. Our gun fired again, and hit the Sherman on the front plate, which caused a shower of debris and sparks.

By now our men were cheering. The Sherman turned its flank as it jerked around in reverse. Our gunner shot it through the side of the hull, and flames leaped up from its rear deck. I saw the engine covers blowing up into the air, and the rear wheels went spinning off into the minefield. Several crew members emerged from the hatches, and at once our machine gun teams opened fire on them. The machine gunners shot wildly at first, and three of the crew were able to jump clear. But then our gunners focussed their fire and hit the tank, and the last two crew who climbed out were shot down on the front of the hull, with their bodies draped over the gun barrel.

Our gunners in their enthusiasm kept firing, and those two tank men over their gun were ripped to shreds, with their limbs falling off and their bodies exploding with spurts of flame. I shouted to the machine gunners to stop firing, but in their eagerness they shot off unnecessary amounts of ammunition, spraying the whole area with fire before they stopped.

Behind this wrecked Sherman, I could see columns of fire rising into the sky, which I guessed were from the work of the flamethrowers on the bunkers. I was glad that we did not have to face those flame-throwers anymore. I shouted encouragement to the men beside me. I felt very confident at this point. I almost considered taking a group of troops back towards the beach, so that we could make contact with the sea again and become a focal point for reinforcements coming up from the inland sector. I must admit that I had a mental image of myself leading this heroic counter-attack, and becoming famous due to our resilience. I was very excited, full of energy, full of hope.

How long did this last?

Perhaps a minute. Perhaps less. Then another tank came out to attack us. This new tank that emerged from the bunker area was a different model. I recognised it from films of the Dieppe raid as a

Churchill series, with heavily armoured covers over the tracks, and a squared-off turret. This tank edged past the burning Sherman tank, pushing it aside. It set off some mines beside the track, but these were anti-personnel mines and they did not break its tracks. Our French gun turret fired, but the shell bounced off the Churchill's front plate and tumbled away into the dunes. Our French gun fired again, but again the round ricocheted off, and this worried me, because this Churchill was advancing on us quite quickly, and firing with its main gun. It fired high-explosive shells which blew up one of our machine gun emplacements at the corner of the Resistance Point. The crew of the machine gun were thrown out of their trench, and they lay badly injured on the barbed wire in front of us. They were moving and crying out for help, but of course there was nothing we could do for them in the situation.

Our French gun kept firing, but I think the gunner was panicking by this point, because he missed that Churchill twice. The Churchill fired once again, and this round exploded directly on the French turret. It knocked the whole turret off its concrete base, and the thing went rolling away to one side. The gunner remained in the open concrete ring, with his whole body emitting smoke and flames. I think he was alive, but stunned and unable to move.

At this point, looking from this poor man to the British tank, I became aware that this Churchill was different in some way from the photographs we had seen in our training sessions, in which we were taught about the strengths and weaknesses of the different Allied tanks. The training lectures had made no mention at all of what I saw next, as the tank halted: there was a burst of flame from a point in the tank's hull plate at the front.

So you were facing the type of tank known as the Churchill Crocodile?

After the war, I learned that 'Crocodile' was the official name for the thing. We came to know it as a Flammenpanzer (*flame tank*), and it had a hugely demoralising effect on our troops.

What form did its attack take in this situation?

This initial burst of flame from its front hull was only a few metres long, and it set fire to the ground in front of it. The range by now was about two hundred metres from us. One of the troops in the slit trenches fired a Panzerfaust, but this fell short and failed to explode. The Panzerfaust in June 1944 was still the earlier model with a very limited range, you see. You had to be one hundred metres or less. Now, after that initial burst of flame, the Flammenpanzer began to fire at full power – and the effect was completely horrific.

It produced a jet of fire, which was a burning liquid of orange-yellow colour. This roared out towards us at a very high speed, climbing perhaps ten metres up into the air. The front of this flame jet spread out to left and right, so that it produced an absolute curtain, or a solid wall, of flames. We all watched, stricken dumb by this apparition. The flamethrowers I had seen before were hand-held devices, such as the one at the Goliath bunker, and they were bad enough! This machine was a hundred times more powerful. This huge wall of flames collapsed down onto the ground in front of our position, so that it fell onto the two wounded machine gun men who were stranded on the barbed wire. They were swallowed up in this inferno of flames.

The heat burned our skin and hair, and the smell of the gasoline fuel was sickening. The flames poured all over the front of our position, and they went gushing into the slit trench there. There was quite a row of men in that trench, with their rifles at the ready, and this all happened so rapidly and in such an unexpected way that they had no time to escape. I think there were a dozen men there, and they were set alight at once. I saw that the whole trench was filled with this burning liquid, and the men in there were incinerated where they stood. The heat was so intense that I couldn't breathe properly, as these flames were about twenty metres away from me.

How did the other men at the resistance Point react to this?

There was a panic, which seized us all, including myself and the other officer. We saw the spout of flame die down, as the Churchill ceased firing, but I was gripped by a terror of what would happen if it fired its flames again. We would all be swallowed up in that orange-yellow fireball. I leaped from my trench, as did all the other men around me, with no thought for rank or discipline. Some of these men were cut down by machine gun fire from the Churchill, and they tumbled around us as we, the surviving men, either threw our hands in the air in surrender or ran to the back of the Point away from the tank.

I was among this latter group, which was about half a dozen men, and we ran to the Eastern side, getting away from the Flammenpanzer. I still had my MP40, but some of the men had dropped their guns and were simply running like civilians – no weapon, no helmet, just fleeing that wall of fire. Two of us were hit by machine gun fire from the Churchill, and in the end it was only myself and three men who managed to jump down into a sunken track and run along that, intending to reach the nearest German line to the rear. At one point, I looked back, and I saw a huge column of smoke rising from the area of the Resistance Point, which I assumed was now burned up completely.

The three men with me, who appeared to be inexperienced, were very shocked by this encounter, and they asked what chance they had of fighting against such machines. I told them that the Flammenpanzer was a panzer like any other, and we could have destroyed it with a PAK gun or if we had got closer with a Panzerfaust. But these men remained very low in morale because of what they had seen.

How did the day develop and end for you?

After several minutes running along this track, we came around a curve and ran into several German troops on a Hanomag (*armoured half-track*) under an overhanging hedgerow. They shot at us before they realised who we were, and killed one of the men with me. Such killings were regrettable, but inevitable when troops are rushing blindly in such a situation.

These Hanomag troops were dressed differently from us: they had camouflage uniforms and their helmets were coated with foliage. They were armed with the most modern weapons, including the MP44 sub machine gun and a Panzerschrek weapon, in addition to Panzerfausts. They were a reconnaissance group from an SS Panzergrenadier regiment to the south, and they quizzed us at length about the situation on the coast and what we had seen. They exuded confidence, and this gave heart to me and the two surviving men with me, even though the body of our third man was still lying in the road in front of their Hanomag. They offered us drinking water, which we took eagerly, while their NCO spoke on a radio set with their command.

There was now a strange calm. The skin on my face was burning painfully from the heat of that Flammenpanzer. I leaned on the embankment of this sunken road, and composed myself mentally after the action I had been in. The time was mid-morning, and the day was becoming brighter and more humid. There was a constant noise of aircraft overhead, and through the branches of the hedgerow, which concealed the Hanomag, I could see large formations of Allied bombers moving south. There were also numbers of planes towing what appeared to be gliders. All these aircraft had conspicuous black and white stripes on their wings, and it was obvious that there were no Luftwaffe planes in the sky, not a single one to be seen.

At frequent intervals, Jabo type planes raced along the fields beside us at low level, strafing the sunken tracks. To move out of the cover of this hedgerow, even on foot, would be virtually impossible because of these planes. From the coastal sector, there was substantial shooting and the noise of explosions, but this did not seem to be getting closer.

What went through your mind in this lull?

The reality of the situation now sank into my mind. I accepted that this was the major invasion that we had thought might come, with the full resources of the Allies in all spheres, air, land and sea. My duty in the midst of this historic battle was to find the remnant of my unit and fight onward with them, whether as an engineer or in some other capacity. But the confusion of the whole situation made this unrealistic for the time being. And so I waited with this SS reconnaissance group, while they observed the coast and made reports on their radio. The two men I had brought with me seemed to be very glad of the pause. But this lull only lasted about ten minutes.

The Panzergrenadiers began to prepare to move out from under the hedgerow, by piling more and more foliage onto their vehicle to try to camouflage it. They planned to move East along this sunken track, to observe the Allied advance in that area. However, one of their men returned on foot from that direction and said that three Allied tanks were advancing on a sunken road that intersected with our track. In fact, we could see a blur in the air about three hundred metres distant over the fields at the top of the embankment, which looked like exhaust fumes or dust from tanks.

I cautioned these troops that there were Flammenpanzer tanks in the area. The soldier who had seen them insisted that these were normal Sherman type tanks, which were advancing inland in a line of three, with about fifty metres space between each one.

These Waffen SS men became very enthusiastic about the prospect of engaging these three tanks with their Panzerschrek. The difference in mentality between these SS troops and the troops I had led at the bunker was remarkable. These soldiers were very eager to attack the tanks, and when one of them was ordered to remain with the Hanomag, he was highly indignant. I left the two men from the bunker with him, and I accompanied these Panzergrenadiers, because by this stage I was determined to fight back in some way against the invasion, after the series of defeats I had been involved in already. These troops did not want me to accompany them, but I insisted, and they agreed to hand me a Panzerfaust.

There were six of these troops plus me. There was the two-man crew of the Panzerschrek, plus four SS troops with automatic weapons. We had three Panzerfausts with us. We advanced along the sunken track, until a point where it bisected a larger road, which was also partially sunken. The Panzerschrek team positioned themselves to fire along the track towards the crossroads, and the other troops concealed themselves among the ferns and foliage that were growing along the sides of the raised walls of the track.

The idea was for the Panzerschek to fire on the leading Sherman, blocking the crossroads, and then for the rest of us to enter the crossroads and fire on the following tanks with the Panzerfausts. All this was decided in a very cool manner, in just a matter of seconds. We could already hear the noise of approaching tanks from the bisecting road, and we took up positions among the ferns and foliage along the side of the sunken track. We primed our Panzerfausts with the firing lever, being careful not to touch the trigger blade underneath as we waited. A few moments later, the noise of tank tracks became very loud, and a Sherman tank appeared in the crossroads, advancing quite slowly, with its gun pointing straight ahead.

Our Panzerschrek team fired as soon as it appeared, and the rocket gave out a huge trail of gas and sparks as it shot forward. This rocket hit the Sherman just above the rear set of running wheels, and there was a sizeable explosion as it detonated. It appeared to penetrate into the engine compartment, because the rear deck of the Sherman immediately lit up with an orange fire, and various pieces of metal flew into the air behind it. The whole tank ground to a halt, rocking on its wheels, making a shrieking noise of metal and a hiss of flames. The SS men rushed forward at once, and without hesitating they ran into the edges of the crossroads and looked left to where the other tanks might be. I joined them, and kneeling at the edge of the crossroads I saw another Sherman, looking very clean and dripping with water, starting to reverse back down its road. I remember wondering why it was dripping water, and then I realised that it had come straight from the landing craft on the beach, presumably without even stopping.

The machine gunner in the Sherman's hull evidently saw us, because he began firing, but this was quite wild, and the bullets smacked into the earth walls of the track, and even into the rear of the burning Sherman behind us. I sighted on the retreating Sherman and squeezed the trigger blade. The heat of the Panzerfaust rocket scorched my already burned face, but it flew directly onto the Sherman and exploded on his front plate.

An SS man beside me fired likewise, and he hit the tank slightly higher up. The two explosions caused the Sherman to go out of control, and it slammed into the side of the earth wall, covered in smoke from the impacts. It tore down a whole landslide from the embankment, and this blocked the road very effectively. The Sherman came to rest across the sunken road, with its track broken and its front drive wheel racing around at high speed, throwing out bits of the track. The third man with a Panzerfaust fired into its side, and this projectile blew a hole in the edge of the hull.

We three men who had fired the Panzerfausts threw the spent tubes away. We all looked at each other, and then there was a massive explosion which made us all retreat out of the crossroads. From around the corner of the sunken track, we took a look at the Sherman we had hit, and the machine was exploding to pieces in front of us. It was rocking back and forth, and the turret was partially blown off the hull. From inside, I could see huge explosions in the crew compartment, as the ammunition in there blew up. I imagine that it was fully loaded with shells, and coming straight from the beach it had possibly not even fired a shot before it was hit. Everything was blowing up in there, and sparks from it were setting light to the hedgerows on either side. Beyond this tank, I could just make out another tank reversing away, through the smoke.

I felt extremely elated at this success. I felt that I had contributed to throwing back the invasion, and that we might have a chance of resisting the entire attack if we could use our precious weapons in the way they were intended. The Panzergrenadiers began to run back to their Hanomag, saying that they would drive quickly into the cover of a wood to the south, and from there make their way east to do their reconnaissance as planned. As I turned to leave, though, I saw a sight which shocked me and made me doubt what we were really trying to achieve in this fighting.

What was this sight?

It was beside the first Sherman that we had hit, the one that was knocked out with the shot from the Panzerschrek. That Sherman was on fire very heavily, with a stream of flames blasting up from its engine deck. I wanted to get away from it, in case its ammunition exploded, but I also saw two crew members lying by the tracks on the road. The tank men appeared to be unarmed. They were lying face down, with the backs of their heads severely damaged. I thought at first they might have fallen from the tank, but the Panzerschrek crew were putting their pistols back into their holsters. They winked at me and said it was time for us to leave. It was clear to me that the Panzerschrek men had shot the tank crew as they came down from the tank, in the back of the head.

This disturbed me greatly, as it was against the way that I thought we should conduct the war. I knew the reputation of the Waffen SS as very ruthless fighters, but this was an unnecessary and brutal action. Of course, there was nothing that I could do after the event.

Did you criticise the SS men for this, or did you protest?

No, I did not. Everything was happening too quickly. That Sherman began to explode, and shells began to fly out of the open hatches and spin around in the hedgerow overhead. I retreated from it, and I joined the Panzergrenadiers in their Hanomag.

We raced along the sunken track to a point near a forested area. I remember being amazed at how fast this big half-track could travel with a full crew. We shot up out of the sunken track using a farmer's gateway, into a field at ground level, and went straight into a wood so that we were barely out in the open for any length of time. The SS men knew the area extremely well, and one of them told me that they had been training here for several weeks.

In the woods, we crossed on a forestry path and moved over to the Eastern side of the battle sector. There were several Jabo aircraft, which were British Typhoon class planes notable by their large radiator intakes, circulating over the woods, as if they knew we were in there. One of these planes fired rockets down at random into the wood, and this caused huge explosions which set off fires among the trees, and made the tree trunks crash down near us. With their knowledge of the area, the SS team steered into a thick part of the wood, and although the going was slower, we must have been completely hidden there from any pilot in a plane overhead.

We finally arrived at a small base on the edge of the trees, which had a sunken road leading inland and a large number of troops dislocated from their units seeking to rejoin their brigades. I recognised several men and officers from my regiment , and I disembarked to join them. By this time, it was around midday, and there was talk of a coordinated counterattack using the armoured units dispersed to the south. I actually saw a line of Panther tanks on the edges of a neighbouring copse, all being armed and refuelled by their crews. There was a definite feeling that our resistance to the attack was being organised fully.

With the various troops from my unit, I joined a truckload of men which was being sent South to reform in the afternoon of the 6th. On the way South, we passed small groups of panzers and Stugs concealed among the trees or in the sunken roads, and we shouted encouragement to them. Our progress was constantly interrupted by Jabo aircraft overhead. We always had to jump from the truck and run into ditches or under trees to take cover. I think it took three hours to cover ten kilometres. There were many shells bursting in the fields, which seemed to be coming from offshore guns, and large numbers of dead and injured cattle around. There were also homeless French civilians who were moving about with their possessions, and obstructing the progress of the military.

I remember that all of this was taking place in the perfectly beautiful landscape of the Normandy valleys, with their sparkling streams, ripe corn, apple orchards and pear orchards. Here and there was a perfect little French chateau or villa, and then around the corner was a group of German trucks that had been bombed, with body pieces spread all over the road and evening hanging from the trees. All this was on the still, warm evening of the 6th June as we went South. Truly, this was an instance of paradise being turned to hell by the hands of mankind.

If I may return to the case you mentioned, of the executed British tank crew. How common were such events in Normandy, do you think?

I really cannot say how common certain things were. I did not have an overview of the campaign. The situation was changing so rapidly, and was so intense, that I did not have the luxury of reflecting on what happened that day. I fought on with some elements of my Division up until the nightmare at Falaise, and then I was able to retreat eventually across the Seine and join an engineering unit working on the West Wall, where we were much needed.

But, since you have asked the question, let me give you an example from the other side. Around the time of the retreat towards Falaise, when we were being hounded by the Allied Jabos in every daytime hour, I was sheltering at the side of a road under some trees. Along the road came a German ambulance truck, which was an Opel wagon, clearly marked out with huge Red Cross signs painted on its roof and doors. These signs were perfectly clean and clear, as if the crew had recently cleaned them to avoid any misunderstanding. I watched this ambulance come slowly down the valley, and I watched two Mustang aircraft swoop over it. They went over twice, so they could not have failed to see the Red Crosses. The third time that they came over, they machine-gunned that ambulance truck. The bullets blew the truck apart, and the truck tipped over. The wounded men inside were thrown out across the road. There were female nurses in that truck also, who were blown apart with their wounded. I can tell you that, after dark, for the sake of decency, we put all the different body parts into a ditch at the roadside. Perhaps they are still there today.

I ask you, Herr Eckhertz, how different that was from the event I saw at the crossroads in the bocage country on June 6th? Was it better or was it worse, as an example of human behaviour? I do not know the answer to that question.

You have told me very explicitly about your experience on June 6th. I am grateful for the candour you have shown in describing these events.

These events should not be forgotten; that is my main concern. The experience of the soldiers on all sides is recorded quite rarely, other than in commercial cinema films and so on, which are a mockery of what we experienced. I hope that my experiences can be kept on record, and I fervently hope that none of our children's generation will have to experience what we on all sides experienced in Normandy. That is my most fervent wish.

—

Sword Beach: The Battery Officer

L.T.J. Wergens was a Leutnant (Second Lieutenant) of artillery with the 716th Infantry Division based at Merville near Franceville.

Herr Wergens, you were stationed at one of the larger gun batteries in the Normandy sector. Can you give some background to the German batteries in the sector?

Indeed. The static Atlantic Wall defences were generally speaking in two classes: coastal fortifications and beach fortifications. The coastal fortifications were large fortress type batteries equipped with heavy calibre guns usually of naval origin, being guns of up to 21cm calibre as one would find on a light battleship. These coastal batteries were either in cliff top locations or slightly inland, and they were in some cases quite large fortresses, containing ten or more sub-bunkers of varying designs.

These sites were supplemented by the beach or land sites, which were intended to fire on craft approaching at much closer range or at targets actually on the beaches. These sites were mostly equipped with 88mm or 75mm PAK type guns, and supplemented by machine gun positions to prevent infantry assault. These bunkers sometimes extended some distance inland in layers or belts, with the additional use of flooded land, obstacles and minefields to break up any attacking force and manipulate its progress to the defenders' advantage, by pushing attackers into the fire of the PAK guns.

The Merville Battery was somewhat unusual in that it was some distance inland from the shore, and was equipped with comparatively light guns because the heavier guns it was intended to house were not yet ready for installation.

So it was that I was assigned to the Merville battery as a gunnery command officer in early 1944, while it was still being completed. My role was to command the use of one of the guns in a heavy concrete casemate.

Can you describe the battery, its organisation and construction?

The battery consisted of a group of reinforced concrete bunker buildings on a plateau facing towards the sea in the distance. There were four main gunnery bunkers, each one originally designed to be equipped with a 21cm naval gun, with an arc of fire of ninety degrees. In reality, from my arrival to the invasion itself, the bunkers were equipped with much smaller guns of only 10cm calibre. This was an interim measure. We were still waiting for the 'real guns,' as we called them, to be fitted when the invasion happened. As things stood, we would be able to fire on the beach zone forward of us, and against any movement inland from the beaches over the plateau. That was our role.

These guns were sited in concrete casemates and fired through a horizontal embrasure. They had a steel shield on the gun itself. In addition, there were ten other bunker buildings, which had various uses including range-finding domes, Flak guns of 88mm and 20mm calibre, ammunition storage, water supply, mess hall, power generator, command centre and so on.

The bunkers were connected by trenches covered with concrete or steel slabs, and the artillery bunkers had underground chambers intended for use in prolonged siege-type situations as medical centres. The concrete used for the walls and roof of the bunkers was about one metre in thickness, reinforced with metal rods. The bunkers had a rounded design intended to offer optimal resistance to blast forces. In the rear, facing away from the sea, the bunkers had access doors of armour plate and electric fan ventilators ducted to the outside.

The battery had a complement of some one hundred men in all. These were chiefly gunnery crews, of course, such as my team, but also included staff officers and their assistants, medics, cooks, observation teams, maintenance teams and guards with side arms. It was intended that the battery could remain under siege for up to three months, with sufficient rations and generator fuel kept on site for this event; the water supply came from an aquifer and could not be interrupted. It was a remarkable structure, and it featured prominently in propaganda of the time, which is where I think you became involved in 1944.

Yes, I was able to visit the battery and see some of the bunkers; we took some photographs which did not reveal any important information, and these were intended to be used as generic public images of the 'Atlantic Wall' and 'Fortress Europe.' I remember being astonished at the scale of the battery structure and the resources that went into its construction.

It was built in early 1944 by enforced labour, of course. The bunkers were very well planned and constructed, and gave us all great confidence. It is no exaggeration to say that we felt impregnable there on the plateau. The danger in such a feeling, obviously, is that a fortress itself may be impregnable, but if it can be surrounded and isolated; there is the risk.

What was the morale, the spirit in the bunkers in the summer of 1944, just before the invasion?

We were eager to take delivery of the larger guns and install them in the bunkers. We were rather embarrassed about the smaller guns we had, but this was in hand. The spirit was very positive. Our troops at the bunker were not front line soldiers, but morale was excellent. We took care to keep the battery troops fully educated on their mission, both tactically and in terms of the direction of the war.

What message did you convey to them about their
purpose in manning the fortress?

Before I answer that simply, let me give you, Mein Herr, some background to the morale issue. Let me say firstly that, contrary to what some people may believe today, the mood in early to mid-1944 among the German forces was not disheartened. Far from it. It is true that we had lost the North African oil supplies, but, equally, the American arrival in Tunisia had been unimpressive. Italy was holding firm, and the Allies were expending huge resources on the war there for no great purpose at all. The Allies showed no signs whatever of doing the logical, rational thing and invading the South of France. There was certainly concern about the Eastern Front, and we all knew dreadful stories about the intensity of the fighting there, but the disastrous collapse of the central Army Group in Russia had not yet happened.

Above all, we in the officer class were well-informed enough to know that the underlying trends in the war situation were far from discouraging. Industrial production was not only holding firm under the air bombing, but actually rising in early 1944. The air bombing itself had hardened the men's anger at the Allies and their resolve. Everyone had lost civilian relatives, friends and neighbours to the bombing, almost without exception.

Most importantly, however, was the matter of the German weapons and machines. The regime had shown us photographs and films of the platoons of the enormous Tiger B panzers, and the Messerschmit 262 jet aircraft, and we knew about the new, super-sized U Boats entering service. The regime had also deliberately spread rumours about the presence of futuristic rocket weapons which could cross entire continents or oceans; we found out later in June that these existed and were actually stationed close to us in France, and were called V1. These weapons were more advanced than anything the Allies possessed, we were sure of that, and there were constant themes of 'Wunderwaffen' (super weapons) in the state propaganda, hinting that these machines which we already knew about were simply the forerunners of what Germany would soon produce.

Today, of course, we know that this was mistaken, and that the practical ingenuity of our engineers had already peaked in mid-1944 with the V1 and the V2; from then on, everything was purely designs on paper. But we must remember the great boost that these weapons and hoped for weapons gave to our morale at the time.

All of this we condensed into our messages to our artillery troops who manned the battery bunkers. We did not have 'political education' in the way that the Red Army had this, but we included these ideas in our address to the teams at inspection and training times during the day. The troops were very receptive, very motivated, and discipline was good. I am not exaggerating when I say that the general spirit of the bunker was first class.

With such a large garrison, was there a relation-
ship with the local French civilians?

Well, that is a difficult question. The battery was intended to be a sealed unit, and obviously no civilians were allowed near its perimeter; I think the exclusion distance was five hundred metres. But a hundred men must be allowed a certain relaxation, and there was a tendency for some men to visit the local towns. Not at night, that was not permitted, but in their leave periods in the day, they would visit. Our guards would double as police and patrol these towns, and any drunkenness was punished.

Nevertheless, there were cases of venereal disease associated with the towns, and we learned that certain men were forming 'relationships' with French women that they met in their leave hours. This was an obvious security risk. For this reason, from March 1944, leave visits to the towns were blocked. To compensate for this, we installed a cinema facility in the mess hall and a football pitch behind the battery.

And was this an effective compensation?

There were grumbles and wisecracks, of course.

And so, from what you have explained, I have the idea of well-motivated, well-informed men, in a well-engineered battery, quite heavily armed and well-prepared. That is the impression I had at the time when I visited. Can we now come on to the events of June 6th, and what happened on that day?

June the 6th, yes. You must give me a moment to collect my thoughts, because the day was so revolutionary, if that is the right word.

Did you have any indication, any warning, of the impending invasion?

Well, there was no specific bulletin from the commanders saying, *'Prepare for invasion on the 6th,'* if that is what you are thinking. Our alert level was raised to level 2 (level 1 being the highest) on the weekend before the invasion, but this had happened before without consequent attacks, and so it was somewhat ambiguous.

What we were informed of, and this was very useful, was the high level of allied bombing along the northern French coast and inland at transport junctions. This bombing had been visible to us locally throughout the April/May period, with large fleets of aircraft overhead and the noise of bombs to the south and east. We were informed daily of the increasing intensity of this bombardment, and we drew our own conclusions that this suggested an attack would be made imminently.

At the same time, in the first days of June, the sea in front of us became surprisingly low in activity; we noticed a definite reduction in reports of enemy shipping passing between England and France. This seemed suspicious rather than reassuring, as if the Allies were concealing something. With all these things put together, the evening of June 5th was tense and expectant, just like June 4th and 3rd and the days before that.

Were you on duty in the night of the 5th/6th?

Yes. My bunker was the most westerly of the four heavy gun bunkers. The bunker was actually quite cramped inside, because the walls were so thick and the ceiling was low. Its interior space was about ten metres by twenty metres, and the breech of the gun took up a lot of this space. This gun was installed on a turntable which rotated left and right in the concrete floor. The shells were kept behind metal shields on the wall beside the gun; there was a mechanical lift to hoist ammunition from the underground chamber up to the firing platform. There was also a metal trap door giving access by steps to the underground rooms, which were equipped for a siege.

I had a control section in the rear of the bunker, equipped with a phone to the battery's central command, but my preference when on duty was to be at the embrasure, observing the plateau and the sea with binoculars, and then moving around the interior checking on the men's readiness.

We had machine gun teams in concrete and sandbagged circles at the perimeter of the battery, and these reported to us at intervals. The slopes in front of us were mined with anti-personnel mines and protected with barbed wire to prevent infantry assault.

The 5th of June was a cool evening, and there was some mist on the sea. It became a rainy night and the moon was full. At about midnight on the 5th/6th, that is the Monday night, we were bombed for about twenty minutes by aircraft at high altitude. Our Flak gun's searchlight could not locate the bombers. Fortunately, these bombs did not damage our bunkers other than throwing debris in through the apertures, which was soon cleared away. After that, the noise of aircraft, which had been noticeable, became very conspicuous indeed. The noise suggested even more air activity than on the previous nights.

I have heard people say that 'there was no Luftwaffe' or 'the Allies controlled the air' but in my case I clearly saw, through the embrasure, a twin-engined night fighter pursuing an Allied bomber out over the sea, and shooting it up with tracer. Both aircraft went off into the clouds, firing at each other. After that, there were long pathways of aircraft going in both directions overhead, far more intense even than the regular raiding formations.

We also had a phone contact from a battery to the East saying that gliders and paratroopers were being seen behind the coastal zone. When I heard that report, I put my men on maximum alert and brought up the second shift of men from the barracks behind the battery, to act as external guards and replacement crews. I also ordered ammunition to be brought up from the underground chamber, gas masks to be ready and the periscope rangefinders to be raised, which were projecting up looking over the embrasure. All this was in place by about one am, so we were well prepared. The men ate a meal at about that time, being soup in canisters from the canteen, cheese and the excellent French bread which was brought in each day.

I remember that meal well. The sea wind was coming in through the embrasure, and our interior lights were all off, so we were lit only by the moonlight through the concrete slit. The men ate in an eager way, as if they wanted all possible energy for the fight that we all suspected lay ahead of us. That is the way it seemed to me at the time.

You yourself did not eat this last meal?

I had some soup in a flask, I remember. I also took a minute in the command post at the back of the bunker to write a few words to my wife, and I placed this letter in a metal cigarette case in my tunic left chest pocket. Like many troops, I partly hoped that, in the event of my death, my wife would somehow receive the letter. I also partly believed the old soldier's story that the power of such a letter, being placed over my heart, would deflect shrapnel or bullets. Just as I buttoned that inside my pocket, we heard firing from outside the bunker.

The sound was only distant, but it was definitely there. It appeared to be coming from the land side, not the sea or the plateau. At the same time, I received a phone call telling me that paratroopers were landing and moving outside the battery, to the South East.

I told the men that action was imminent, and to remember their training and responsibilities. They saluted as one man, and went to their posts.

Did you see anything of these paratroopers at that point?

I was able to extend our periscope up over the top of the bunker roof and turn it around to the inland side. It was difficult to make out anything there, but I kept watching. I also had my men watching the seaward plateau with binoculars, of course, and reporting to me on what they could see. The tension was very great, as we all knew it was now a matter of time before an attack came. There was Flak fire from the South, and there were flares going into the sky on the horizon.

Then, after some time, as I looked through the periscope towards the rear of our site, in the moonlight I could see a descending shape which did not appear to be a parachute. This was a large shape, and it appeared to be emitting fire and sparks from the tail end. I believed at first that this was a large rocket of some kind, or even some form of jet-propelled aircraft. Then I realised that it was in fact a simple glider, which was on fire, presumably from being hit by the Flak. It slowly reared up and flopped down directly onto our position, still on fire. It landed so close that it went below the line of sight of my periscope, but immediately there was gunfire from that side of the position. Our guard troops there were fighting against these glider attackers, whoever they were.

Out to sea, there was nothing unusual to observe in the dark, and there was no report of activity on the plateau. I had the men send up a white flare to illuminate the plateau, so that we could be sure. I therefore considered that this assault might be a localised, commando-type raid, rather than part of a full scale invasion – but of course, there was no way of knowing what eventual form this would take.

What did you know of the situation outside the bunker?

I telephoned up to the observation room, and received a report of close quarters fighting between airborne troops and our men in the battery positions to the rear. It was reported that these troops appeared to be English, and they were causing and receiving substantial casualties. I said, '*It was only one glider, and how many troops can they carry in a glider?*' But what was happening, I later learned, was that the glider troops were creating a gap in the defences for the paratroopers outside the position, and these paratroopers were storming in onto the battery itself and surrounding the bunkers. So we were to some extent under siege from that point on.

What was your feeling, to be besieged in this way?

It was an agonising feeling, because our whole purpose was to fire onto the plateau and the coast, which was still empty. The twenty men locked inside my bunker were simply unable to fight back against this assault from the land side. I could hear explosions and shooting near the back of our bunker itself, coming through the metal door at the rear. At the same time, when I tried to use our telephone again, I found the line was dead. We were not equipped with a radio, and so we were cut off from information. I listened at the steel door, and I could hear debris from explosions hitting it repeatedly. This was a great shock to me, because, if the enemy troops got onto the roof of our bunker, or close to the embrasure, they would be able to fire in onto us or throw grenades in at us.

I ordered several men to come to the door with rifles and be ready to force back any attempted entry here; at the same time, I shouted from the seaward embrasure for troops to come to our assistance. However, there was no answer or signal from troops on that side of us.

In this way, we had to endure several minutes of waiting, as fighting took place outside our bunker, without knowing the real situation. The men became frustrated, and offered to break out through the rear door to clear the approaches. I did not permit this, as opening the door during action was forbidden by orders, and we did not know the enemy's strength outside.

The situation was brought to an end very violently, when the enemy began to fire their guns into the ventilator system at the rear of the bunker. This caused pieces of the ventilator fans to smash off, and a large number of bullets came out of the ventilator ducts and ricocheted around the inside of the bunker. These bullets hit two of our men, one of whom was killed instantly, and the other was blinded.

I ordered sandbags to be brought to block off the ducts. As the men were bringing these across from under the embrasure, two small bombs came out of the duct tubing, evidently having been thrown in by the enemy outside. My men shouted warnings and threw themselves flat on the floor away from these bombs. I took in the situation with a heart that, frankly, was pounding with sheer dread. In appearance, these bombs were like large grenades, grey in colour. One of my men had the intelligence to throw the sandbag that he was holding onto one bomb and cover it. However, the other bomb remained on the floor. I went to grab a sandbag from another man, who was backing away from the bombs, when both bombs exploded.

The one under the sandbag did not detonate properly, and caused only a lot of dust and smoke; however, the loose one on the floor exploded fully, and caused a very white flash which spread an incendiary material out, in a ball several metres wide. This incendiary ball was horribly blinding, and it hung in the air for what seemed like a long time. I was transfixed at the sight, as I had not seen an explosion like this before, and I did not know what it meant. Then the fireball collapsed onto the floor, and spread out in a manner I would describe as volcanic. This white burning matter enveloped several men nearby, who were flat on the floor, and it took hold of their bodies completely. Their uniforms were burned off in moments, and their bare skin was blackened and charred. Whole pieces of their flesh became black in moments, and began to disintegrate.

These men screamed and convulsed in a dreadful way, and the other men backed away from them in a rush. I shouted for order to be restored, and for a fire extinguisher. I also had the men throw more sandbags onto the ventilator ducts to prevent more bombs coming through them.

Your ammunition was not set off?

Our immediate ammunition was kept in a steel-clad unit on the opposite wall, so fortunately it was not detonated. The trapdoor to the lower chambers, where there was the main ammunition store, was also not touched by the flames. There were two hundred rounds of high-explosive down there, and an explosion would probably have demolished the entire battery.

Were the men who were burned saved?

This was not possible. The extinguisher was used on them, but they were severely burned. I think that two were dead, and a third was alive but moving in a terrible torment. His neck and chest were completely burned open, and his skin was smouldering even after the extinguisher was applied. It was inconceivable that anything could be done for him. A Feldwebel asked my permission to put him out of his suffering with a merciful shot, and I gave the permission for this, so he was shot cleanly in the head. I would have wished the same thing for myself in such a condition.

What was the effect on the men?

There was much cursing and denouncing of the English. We could hear the attackers outside, kicking or beating at the steel door to gain entry, and there were other explosions in the air ducts from explosives that they threw in there, but these explosions were muffled by the sandbags. The air inside the bunker was now full of smoke and charred particles, and the men who were away from the embrasure donned their gas masks. All this happened in the space of a few seconds, perhaps twenty seconds.

What was your state of mind?

I was in an absolute fury at this situation, as we were being steadily choked and suffocated instead of fighting properly as we were intended to. I tried to look through the periscope to see the situation, but the optic was cracked and not operable.

I ordered two men to climb out of the main seaward embrasure with MP40 guns, in order to shoot down any enemy who were on the roof or trying to reach down to the embrasure. As soon as they climbed out, there was shooting and they were both hit by shots from the roof area. They fell out of the concrete slit, onto the mine-field area underneath, and they were blown up badly by the personnel mines there, which were positioned to stop the enemy getting close to the front of the bunker. I took an MP40 and went over to the embrasure to see the situation.

Just as I approached, I saw two hands appear from the upper edge of the slit. These were the hands of the enemy, surely, because these hands were holding a Thompson sub machine gun, which was clearly silhouetted against the sky outside. The gun muzzle was smoking slightly. This soldier was presumably lying on top of the roof and reaching down with his gun. I can tell you that an absolute storm of fire was directed at this man, from my gun and the men's rifles, and before he could fire, the gun was shot out of his hands and it went flying off into the minefield.

I could now hear the enemy troops outside, talking and shouting in English. I could hear them saying the words 'bomb, man, fire' which sounded like the words we have in German. The fact was that, if we did not have infantry remaining outside to guard against a close attack like this, there was nothing that we could do to drive off these assailants. We had a small supply of stick grenades, and I took one of these and primed it, then attempted to throw it out of the slit up onto the roof.

As I reached out, I was shot through the forearm, and I dropped the grenade, which exploded below. I was stunned from this wound and the explosion, and as I gathered my senses I saw one of these English soldiers reach down and throw in another of the grey-coloured incendiary bombs which they had used on the air ducts.

This bomb exploded against the gun shield, and it covered the shield in that bright incendiary material. The shield was thick enough to withstand this, but some of the incendiary fluid shot around the edges and hit the men in the gun crew, causing terrible burns. I knew that, with one or two more of those bombs, our whole bunker crew would be wiped out. I decided that the gun position was simply indefensible in the current state of the combat.

Did you decide to surrender?

No. I hated the idea of surrendering to a lightly armed force. I knew that the German infantry around our sector must surely be arriving imminently to fight off the attacking troops. It was inconceivable that they would not come to assist us against a small airborne force. I therefore ordered the men to open the trapdoor which led down to the lower chambers, and to take cover in there. I ordered the firing mechanism from the gun to be removed and brought with us. The men obeyed rapidly, and in a few seconds they were moving down into the underground space. The wounded were brought down as carefully as possible, and medical supplies were available in the underground rooms.

As I followed the men down the steps, I saw the English attackers jump down from the roof onto the ledge of the embrasure and begin shooting wildly into the interior, absolutely spraying the inside with bullets. There were two of these men, and they had sub machine guns which they simply jerked left and right, filling the whole bunker with shots.

I caught sight of their faces, and I can tell you that the glimpse alarmed me as much as anything I had seen that day.

Why did their faces alarm you?

Their faces were set rigid, in an expression of absolute hatred. Sheer hatred. This worried me. Why would men, who were the same race as us, who were physically similar to us, why would they hate us in this way? Why would they want to burn us alive, when we were protecting Europe? What was the origin of this hatred? I had no answer to such questions.

I dropped onto the top step of the underground chamber, and I secured the steel door over us. I could only use one hand because of the wound in my forearm, which was extremely painful. The steel plate was echoing with bullets which were deflecting off it. Below the door, we had a concrete block which rolled on two girders to sit across the trapdoor entrance. I operated this block across the steps. We were now sealed into the underground chamber, with the enemy running loose in our bunker overhead.

How long could you last out down there?

Oh, a very long time. There was dry food stockpiled there which would last many weeks. Water was limited, but there were medical supplies. There was a single electric lamp which gave a feeble light, worked by a hand crank dynamo. There were two air vents which ran to concealed covers outside the bunker, and as long as these were not blocked we could breathe. But my hope was that we would only have to wait an hour or so until the surrounding German troops counter-attacked and took back the battery.

Of course, above us, we could hear the sound of the enemy moving about in the bunker now. It was a dreadful sensation, knowing that they were in our superb bunker, no doubt intent on destroying our guns. The immediate danger was that they would use explosives to open the steel trap door and drop their incendiary bombs down into the chamber. The walls down there were lined with ammunition for the gun. I think there was probably twenty tonnes of explosives in there. These shells were unprotected, and might be set off by an incendiary or even a bullet. We had extinguishers ready, and the men pressed themselves back against the walls.

We crouched there and looked up at the roof over us, as the English up there began to set off explosions and smash our equipment. We heard their voices in a muffled way through the steel door. It was extremely hot and smoky in the chamber, and sweat ran down my face as I crouched there, wrapping a bandage around my wounded arm and looking at the trap door.

Several times, we heard the enemy soldiers treading on the trap door, or stamping or kicking at it. They must have known that we were underneath, because where else would we all have gone? At one point, we heard an explosion directly above us on the steel plate itself, suggesting that the enemy were trying to blast it open to get at us. The thought of those incendiary grenades coming down into our confined space was horrifying. Some of my men began praying, while others kept up a stream of muttered obscenities directed at the enemy, vowing a dreadful revenge for this humiliation.

All this went on for about fifteen minutes in all, and then the explosions above us stopped. I listened at the steel plate, and could not hear footsteps or impacts up there. Some of the men asked me not to open the door, while others told these men to shut up and begged to be allowed up there to fight on. I told all the men to shut up, and I rolled aside the concrete slab on its girders, then listened again before opening the trap door slightly.

What did you see out there?

The bunker was so full of smoke that it was impossible to see anything except a faint blur which suggested that first light had come, if not dawn. It was close to five am. I could hear shooting from the distance, and also German voices shouting closer at hand. This told me that we had been relieved by a counterattack and that the English were being driven off. I opened the trap door fully and climbed up into the bunker. Slowly, the smoke and dust cleared and daylight came in through the embrasure. It became apparent what had happened.

The enemy had set off several explosive charges around the gun breech, and had tried to detonate the bunker ammunition also. There was an explosive pouch stuck between the 10cm rounds, with electric wires, but this had not gone off. This was fortunate, because it would probably have blown the floor down on top of us in the chamber. It was clear that the gun was damaged and needed extensive repair work. As we examined this, we opened the rear doors to ventilate the bunker, and found a large group of German troops outside, firing into the distance.

The attackers had essentially completed their mission, if that was to disable the guns for the time being. Now they were retreating down the slopes towards the nearby village, exchanging fire with our men as they went.

I saw one of our quadruple 20mm Flak guns on a half-track carriage that had been brought into the battery site, and this was firing below horizontal at the retreating enemy.

Around the bunker, there was a lot of destruction. The glider which had come down was crashed very close behind our bunker, with its tail part burned off. There were two dead English troops visible hanging out of the glider, and many more scattered around the battery, between the bunkers and even on the roofs of the bunkers.

They had black paint on their faces and wore red berets. They were armed with the 'Sten' type gun which we knew to be very effective at short range, but liable to jamming. In fact, some of these English troops seemed to have picked up German MP40 guns during the combat. There were also many dead German troops, both our artillery men and the infantry which had relieved us.

I took all this in within a few seconds, and then my attention was drawn to the air overhead. There were huge numbers of aircraft in progress across the sky, which was still a grey-white colour. These were both bombers and what appeared to be transport planes.

We were immediately strafed by a fighter plane which dived on us from over the headland, and our Flak cannon with great versatility raised its barrels in an attempt to fire back at this aircraft. This plane, which was a Spitfire type, shot up the Flak cannon and smashed open its half-track bed, so we were without air defence. We went quickly back into the bunker.

What kind of order was restored at the battery?

Our men were already working on the guns in each of our four bunkers. Of the four guns, the enemy had driven off the gunners from three of them. We were the only ones who had remained with our gun in the underground chamber, which I was proud of. The damage done was serious. Our gun and one other were badly damaged and would have to be extensively re-machined. Two others were less seriously hit, and work was underway on them already to try to bring them back into action. At this stage, I was seen by a medical orderly who examined the wound in my arm. By this stage, it was impossible for me to move my arm at all. This was bleeding heavily, and the diagnosis was that the bones were broken, hence my inability to use it. I was urged to retreat from this sector to a field dressing station inland, where the wound could be treated.

As my gun was out of action, my commander ordered me to go to the dressing station and then return later in the day, taking with me the various walking wounded from the battery. A truck was found to take us, and as I waited for the wounded men to board it, I used binoculars to scan the sea in the distance beyond the plateau.

At that point, the full dimensions of the attack became clear to me. The horizon of the sea was filling up with vast numbers of ships. Anyone who was present will confirm that the horizon was literally filled from East to West with vessels. I could not make them out, but there appeared to be a huge variety of types, including substantial warships. Above them, this constant stream of aircraft flew inland, making the air itself vibrate with their noise. There was the sound of heavy bombing from further inland.

We were all struck speechless at this sight for several seconds, as we had not envisaged the full scale of the onslaught that was about to hit us. Above all, there was no sign of our forces fighting back on sea or in the air. The sea between us and this oncoming horde was completely empty and featureless, and there were no dogfights or aerial battles taking place overhead.

I tried to remove myself from the ambulance truck, because my natural inclination was to be present in combat when this massive force arrived. But my commander ordered me again to leave, and to return later when my gun was in a state to be operated. Reluctantly, I went to the field hospital and had the bones in my arm set. This journey, of a few kilometres, was full of risks in itself, as the Allied Jabo aircraft began to strafe continually along all the inland roads to disrupt the defending transports. We were constantly taking refuge under trees or in ditches as these aircraft, apparently without any opposition, roved across the inland landscape.

Did you rejoin the battery that day?

To my great regret, the events at the battery overtook us all. Although we held the battery on the 6th itself, later in the day it was cut off by the Allied troops, and those of us in the hospital zone were unable to rejoin it. In effect, the front line was between us and the battery. The battery held out for some time until later in the month, remaining as a fortress-type installation behind the Allied lines until it eventually surrendered.

I myself was ultimately reassigned to a series of batteries further west, on the Brittany coast, and these were in turn isolated and cut off by the Allied advances in July. I was eventually taken prisoner at a point near Cap Gris Nez, and went into captivity under the Americans.

How important do you think it was for the Allies to capture your battery?

I think they overestimated the capacity of the guns at the battery. These were 10cm guns, not the long-range warship guns which some of our installations were equipped with. Our guns would have been a danger to them in their landings in our area, but not to the extent that we could have obstructed the landings completely.

Nevertheless, I can appreciate that they saw a need to eliminate the guns at that early stage for the sake of security, considering they would have to be eliminated sooner or later in the campaign anyway. It was certainly a brave and audacious assault, to use a glider and paratroopers in that way in the darkness; but remember, we did in fact retake the position and defend it from then on. Like so many things in war, the real significance of this battle is rather hard to judge in retrospect.

—

Postscript To Book One

By Holger Eckhertz
April 2015

I very much hope that the reader has appreciated these translated accounts, and found in them some new insight or perspective of June 6th 1944. For me, detached in time from both the interviews and the events themselves, I find that there are several main themes to these statements, which I would like to briefly highlight.

Firstly, there is the *motivation* of the German troops, which repeatedly returns to the question of 'defending France' or 'defending a united Europe' against various international forces. I found this surprising when I first read the interviews, but, when I investigated German propaganda of the late war period, I found that this was in fact a very common message. The presence of the idea in the interviewees' statements shows, probably, how effectively this idea was communicated by the regime's propagandists.

Secondly, and connected to this, is the *surprise* described by some interviewees when they were confronted by the Allied troops' aggression and determination. This is partly a tribute to the professionalism of the Allied soldiers, many of whom, of course, were in combat for the first time. But it also reveals a certain lack of understanding among some of the German soldiers being interviewed, who seem to regard their mission in France as non-threatening to the Western Allies. How widespread such an attitude was at the time can only be a matter for conjecture today.

The third element which I notice very strongly is the *lack of resources* available to the first-line German defenders of the Atlantic Wall when confronted, especially, with the newest weaponry and air superiority of the Allies. It is possible, of course, that the speakers are in some ways dramatizing the reasons for their own defeat, but we are left with an impression of overwhelming force. We know that as the Normandy campaign progressed, the land battles became more even-handed, especially as German armour arrived in strength.

One last thread which strikes me is the role that *luck* plays in a soldier's survival or death. Those of us who have never been in action surely cannot imagine the stress which comes from knowing that the path of a bullet or shell, falling almost at random, might immediately kill you, or might pass you by. Such stress must surely be common to all combatants, whatever their motivation or uniform.

—

BOOK TWO

Introduction to Book Two

Day (the name which the Allied media gave to the Normandy landings of June 6th 1944) is an event which has been viewed very largely from an Allied perspective. Considering the colossal challenges which the Allies faced, and the bravery with which their troops carried out the landings, this is in some ways understandable.

Having said that, however, I have been astonished at the interest which greeted Book One of these accounts by German soldiers who experienced D Day. So many people around the world have been fascinated and intrigued to read the words of the German defenders of the Normandy stronghold – words which have been almost lost to the historical record.

This new book presents a different series of accounts, some of which I deliberately excluded from Book One. To be frank, when editing Book One, I felt that some of these testimonies would be distressing to French people whose parents or grandparents had been in Normandy in 1944, because of the way in which some of the German interviewees describe their attitudes to the French population. After much thought, however, I have commissioned a translation of these interviews, as I believe that these glimpses into the Germans' presence in Normandy deserve to be known and understood.

For readers who have not read Book One, the background to these interviews is that my grandfather, Dieter Eckhertz, was employed during the second world war as a writer for German military propaganda magazines such as 'Signal' and 'Die Wehrmacht.' He visited the Atlantic Wall and the Normandy area in the spring of 1944 to collect interviews with the troops for such propaganda, and was fascinated by the enormous fortifications being built under General Erwin Rommel's command. Ten years after D Day, in 1954, he made it his personal mission to track down German survivors of the Normandy landings, in order to record their experiences. Meeting one veteran put him in touch with others – until he had assembled a portfolio of such interviews which eventually came into my hands in 2014, in the form of unedited notes and transcripts which were untouched since they were first made 1954.

I would like to emphasise that the interviewees whose testimonies are recorded in this book demonstrate a wide range of attitudes to their wartime experience. Some were remorseful for their service in the German forces; some appeared to have changed only slightly, while others, as the reader will see, were conflicted, traumatised or otherwise affected by the cataclysmic events of June 6th.

Taken as a whole, I believe that these testimonies offer us a rare and crucial insight into the psychology of German foot soldiers in 1944, and above all a unique glimpse of the onslaught of June 6th from the defenders' viewpoint. I don't doubt for a moment that these interviews will be controversial. Nevertheless, these are among the human voices of D Day - and surely they deserve to be heard in all their human form.

Holger Eckhertz, *July 2015*

THE CONCRETE PANZER

Gustav Winter was a Gefreiter (Private First Class) with the 726th Infantry Regiment, 716th Static Infantry Division, stationed near Colleville, inland of the American Omaha beach.

Herr Winter, you said in your letter to me that you started the war in the panzer forces, the elite panzer troops as you said, and then you finished the war on the Atlantic Wall in Normandy. How did that come about?

You see, Herr Eckhertz, the Normandy invasion was a bitter experience for me, because I had been transformed from a panzer crew man into a *static* panzer crew man, and so I was fighting in a panzer but unable to move.

Can you explain what you mean by that? In what way were you in a static panzer?

Oh, the static panzers were an important part of the Atlantic Wall, and later the West Wall between Germany and France, and the defences inside Germany also.

You see, if a panzer is damaged in action, especially in the running gear, engine or hull, and if that panzer was an older type, say a Panzer III or one of the Eastern European machines that we used, it was often not worth the time and the steel to repair it fully. But of course, it could not be wasted. If it was not melted down, it could be used as part of the fortifications.

The static panzer which I was assigned to in Normandy was an old Panzer III which had no engine or drive wheels. It was encased in concrete, literally set in a concrete box, and this box was positioned down in the ground so that the turret could operate at ground level. It had to be in a concrete box, because the ground was mostly sand, which was unsuitable for digging a normal emplacement. Because there was no power, the turret was traversed by a hand wheel, and the panzer only held two men: the gunner and loader. We called it 'der Betonpanzer' (*'the concrete panzer.'*)

Where was this concrete panzer located?

On the dunes, just back from the sea itself. Our panzer had a field of fire onto the seafront and the beach, and the intention was that we would fire on any enemy that tried to come up off the beach, as they came up over the dunes at that point. The purpose was to keep the enemy pinned down on the beach at that point, preventing him moving inland. In that sense, we were part of the main line of defence, after the machine guns and artillery that were positioned to fire along the beach itself.

For me, it was very strange to be in this concrete panzer, because I had taken part in the France and Russian campaigns in a real Panzer III, which at that time was the workhorse of the Wehrmacht panzer forces. To come from those dramatic campaigns, which were full of glory and movement, to a concrete panzer set in the sand dunes…this was a difficult transition for me to make.

This is what I want to understand - why were you assigned to this unit in Normandy?

This was because I suffered very badly from frostbite during that first winter in Russia, in 1941. We had no winter clothes at that time, and in the unheated panzers the temperature could go down to minus twenty or thirty celsius. We in the armour suffered less than the infantry, but still, remaining for twenty four or thirty six hours in a steel box at minus twenty degrees, without enough fuel to use the engine, this will damage a man.

As you can see, I lost the little fingers on each of my hands, because my gloves were torn, also the tip of my nose, and my toes were damaged as well. I was no longer the handsome panzer boy after that, although I suffered far less than many of the others...

...I remember one crew in Russia who were stranded in the ice when their fuel ran out; they froze to death inside their panzer. When we eventually got to them, they had to be lifted out with a winch, like statues, one after the other. We lined them up on the ice, like marble statues of men. So I considered myself lucky to lose two fingers and my nose, and to have a limp.

I was transferred to be a panzer training instructor, but it was felt that my frostbite wounds would unsettle the cadets, and so I was made a truck driver in the auxiliaries. Finally, because I was a skilled panzer gunner, I was moved to the Atlantic Wall and I ended up with the Static Infantry on the concrete panzer. I learned to use the gun controls with my eight fingers well enough. The mechanics adapted the gun system for me, with extra grips on the control wheels. My assistant, my loader, was a Czech-German boy who was not very bright, but very enthusiastic. We were a happy crew, just the two of us.

Was this concrete panzer part of a system of fortifications?

Yes. In that area of the dunes, there were several strong points covering the exits from the beach. Apart from my concrete panzer, there was a PAK *(anti-tank)* gun on a turntable inside a steel shield, and a number of the small concrete bunkers for one or two men. We were spread out on that plateau in the dunes, just within sight of each other. There were also trenches for infantry, and behind us there were some houses we used as barracks, which were linked together and mined to make fortresses.

Did you consider these to be strong defences?

Well, in the East, they would have been considered quite weak, especially against an enemy expected to use panzers. But there on the French coast, it seemed to me that it was pretty unlikely that the Allies could land with large numbers of panzers. We knew they had landing craft which could bring a panzer onto dry land, because they had used this in Italy. But France was not Italy. They would need thousands upon thousands of panzers to invade France, and how could these possibly be carried across the water from England to all arrive at once? We had no idea of the organisation that the Allies were capable of, you see.

Also, on many of the beaches, the sand between high and low tide was completely covered with girders that had Teller mines, which were there to blow the tracks off panzers if any tried to come ashore, and also the Belgian gates. All this made the beach defences seem stronger.

What were the Belgian gates?

They were large, steel frames with rods that stuck out, and were meant to damage panzer treads or flat-bottomed boats. I don't know why they were named that. There were thousands of these things stuck in the sand, and other girders or posts with mines or artillery shells primed to explode...those beaches were a murderous place. Personally, I couldn't see how an invader could come ashore and move off the beach in any kind of strength, and so I was not greatly worried by the thoughts of an Allied landing.

On the other hand, some of the other men manning the other bunkers around me were very anxious with 'Invasionangst' *('Invasion Anxiety.')* This mean that they thought about the invasion too much and they became weighed down with the thought. You must remember that we were isolated there on that damned plateau of dunes, and all day we had to stare through our binoculars at the sea, which was only about one kilometre away, not knowing what devilish things might appear out there.

What was life like for you in the bunkers on the plateau?

Apart from the uncertainty, we in the infantry had a comfortable life before the invasion came. The local French people were not supposed to come close to the bunkers, but in reality they would come and trade with us, offering food. They had bread, milk, cider, eggs and even fresh meat, which was unavailable to Wehrmacht lower ranks. In return we exchanged things like cigarettes, bootlaces and lamp oil, which the French couldn't get hold of at all.

We would also catch seagulls and cook them, and further inland there were a lot of rabbits to be hunted. It's strange that my memory of those months before the invasion is so full of food, but that is how it was. We would say, 'Fill your belly on French ham and cider, because tomorrow you may be transferred to the East, where there is only hard biscuit and snow to eat.' Some of our bunkers were little storehouses of contraband food and liquor, and the officers would take their share when they inspected us. This would never have happened in the panzer troops, of course, but standards of conduct in the Static Infantry in France were different.

Did the Germans form relationships with the French?

The relationship was generally friendly. The French would complain bitterly about the Allied bombing, which was ruining their little towns and villages, especially around the transport routes. Many of us had lost relatives in the city bombing in Germany, so we sympathised. Some of the French also hated General De Gaulle, who they described as a traitor and a coward. De Gaulle and his gang were our enemy too, so we had that in common. After the war, I was amazed that De Gaulle became the president of France!

Why do you think the French hated De Gaulle so much?

I said *some* of the French hated him. I think it was because De Gaulle threw in his chances with the English, and some of the French detested the English. Honestly, to listen to some of those French farmers cursing the old 'Anglo-Saxons!' It was 'Anglo-Saxon' this and that – terrible French swear words, too. Some of those French hated the English more than we Germans did, I tell you that for a fact.

But many other French people had no understanding of the world at all, no more than if they were farmers in Russia or Poland. I am not criticising them for this – I'm sure that country people in Germany were equally ignorant. And in America or Britain, too.

I myself was from Berlin, and I liked to hear about world events and discuss them with my comrades. I considered myself well-informed at that time, even though I was only a Gefreiter *(Private First Class.)*

Did the Germans ever form relationships with the French women?

Of course, this happened. Why do you ask that question?

It is a subject that is not spoken of today.

Oh, well then, let's speak about it. Do you want to know the facts?

Yes, please. That's my purpose.

Well…since you ask, I'll tell you what went on. The truth is that sometimes the French ladies in our sector would get pregnant by German soldiers, and when that happened they went to a house in the inland zone, a house that was run by Catholic nuns, to have the babies. This house, which was known to everyone as 'The Children's House,' became a kind of orphanage for French-German children; there were many of them being looked after there. If you can imagine the situation, we Germans in 1944 had been in France for four years, almost exactly four years, and so the orphanage was much needed.

By the way, I have relatives who were in the German army in France in the 1914 war, and they tell me that the same thing happened in those days.

But there is a very sad story connected with that Children's House, in fact, and the things that happened when the Allies invaded.

How was this orphanage affected by the invasion?

It was caught up in the events, as everything and everyone was caught up.

One of our men in the bunkers on the dunes was rumoured to have fathered a child that was now in the Children's House, being brought up by the nuns there. When the Allies bombed inland, which they did very heavily, the Children's House was hit badly...I don't know the details, but some of the children were killed. Our comrade in the dunes was said to have lost his child in that attack. I don't know if this was true, but the man in question certainly became fanatical about killing the enemy after that. He blamed the Americans, because they were supposed to be the ones who bombed the Children's House.

That's a sad story, indeed.
Did you yourself have any personal dislike of the Americans or the English?

I had lost several relatives in the daylight and night bombing of Berlin, and so I was angry about this, yes; I was very bitter. Many of my comrades felt the same way. The frustration for us was that we were not fighting the war against the Western powers, really. Our real war was with the Soviet Union and the threat that we believed they posed to us in the East. Today, of course, we in West Germany all understand that this belief was mistaken, but ten years ago the feeling against the East was very strong. And this added, you see, to our anger against the Americans and the English Empire, because they were diverting our strength, our forces, away from the battles in the Eastern Front.

What a foolish thing that war was, when you think about it. The Americans had so much space in their prairies and mountains, and the English had India and all those places in Africa. And yet they wanted to take France from us, and stop us fighting the Reds. All of us there on that area of sand dunes, me in my concrete panzer, and the PAK gun, and the little two-man bunkers, we all should really have been in the East, fighting the real enemy of Europe over there. But the Western Allies insisted on threatening us in France.

That is what we thought at the time.

For you in the dunes, in that isolated place,
how did June 6ᵗʰ develop for you?

That terrible day…I hate to remember it, and at the same time all the events are still very clear in my mind here.

I and my young loader, we went into our concrete panzer at midnight, replacing the other crew who went off to sleep in the fortified houses. There was a lot of rumbling of aircraft in the air, but we couldn't see anything up there…we thought this was an especially heavy bombing raid.

The concrete panzer was pretty comfortable, because it was all stripped out inside and there was plenty of room. The turret had a 50mm gun, and in addition to the telescopic gunsight it was fitted with periscope binoculars which could focus on the sea immediately beyond the dunes. On this night, there was moonlight, but all I could make out was clouds over the horizon of the sea.

But then we never saw much happening on the sea at all.

You never saw much on the sea between England
and France? In 1944? Are you sure?

Yes, there was never much activity out there. It is strange, isn't it? Despite all this massive war going on, the sea during the night and

156

the day was quite empty of ships; it was rare to observe one of our S-Boats (*gun boats*) and we only occasionally glimpsed a proper warship, which of course was always British or American, as the Kriegsmarine *(German Navy)* did not operate big warships between France and England.

Anyway, on that night of the 5th, there was aircraft noise and heavy bombing inland, but being in the panzer we couldn't see what was happening out there. All our watching and waiting went on for hours, until sometime around five am, when everything changed.

First, our officer came to us on horseback (he had been a cavalry commander in the first war, and he prided himself on his Austrian horse.) He told us that there was suspicious activity to the East, involving gliders and such things, and to be completely vigilant. Therefore, we checked over the gun, and I went out to see if anything was happening around us.

There were flares in the sky, I don't know where from, and they lit up the underside of the clouds, and I could see many planes moving through the clouds, which worried me. Our only Flak was a single 20mm gun behind us, near the fortress houses, and this remained silent. I had a very bad feeling now, and I felt very exposed out there, even with our concrete shell. I suppose that all the other crews in the bunkers around me were thinking the same thing *'What the devil is happening?'*

First light came at about five fifteen or five thirty, I think, and I noticed that the sea was still empty as far as I could make out into the distance. All I saw was a series of flashes on the horizon, which I thought might be more flares. Then there was a horrific noise in the air, which was a long crashing sound, and we began to be hit by huge explosions. These explosions were incredibly powerful...they made the whole concrete box around the panzer move and rattle.

I figured out that these were naval shells coming from out on the sea, something which had never happened before in my experience. I could actually see the flames of the warship guns firing, that was what the flashes were out on the sea. After several of these explosions, which landed randomly around us, the air was full of sand, smoke and dust, and it was hard to see anything through the periscopes at all.

The intensity of that bombardment was more than anything I had known on the Eastern Front. When one of these naval shells exploded near us, the shock wave came through the ground and travelled through the panzer, which felt like a punch in the stomach. These blows came again and again, every time a kick in the belly, and making my ears ring horribly.

The Czechoslovakian lad who was my loader got down on the floor of the panzer and began sobbing, the poor idiot. He was not very bright, as I told you. I told him to shut up, but he was only seventeen, and had not been in action before. What a way to start!

After that, I think we were bombed by aircraft, but I'm not sure. I couldn't hear properly, but I felt a lot more explosions, which seemed to be some distance away. A few of these bombs came close, and bits of shrapnel came crashing off the turret, and a lot of smoke was coming in through the air vents. I braced myself and closed my eyes, that was all I could do. When the bombing finally paused, the explosions seemed to fall behind us, in the inland zone. I opened the side hatch of the turret a tiny bit and looked out. What a sight that was.

One of the small concrete bunkers was destroyed, and the concrete was in pieces all over the dunes. There were huge craters in the sand everywhere around us, and in places the sand was on fire from the explosive. The PAK gun near us was in one piece, and the crew there signalled to me with a green signal flag that we used (we had no phone or radio, of course, and I was deafened anyway, I could hear nothing at all.)

That particular PAK gun was commanded by the man I told you about, the fellow who had lost his child in the Children's House bombing.

The light was fully up, and a drizzle was coming down, which damped down all the smoke and dust. I wiped my eyes and tried to look out at the sea through the periscope binocular. And so, at that moment, like thousands of other German soldiers, I saw the number of ships that the Allies were bringing against us. I was staggered at the sight, even though I could only see it dimly. I was absolutely stunned, and also very angry.

What did you see? Why were you angry at this point?

Out on the sea…well, the horizon was like a solid wall of ships. As if someone had put a steel curtain across the horizon, that's how many there were. The warships that were firing on us were lighting up the whole array of ships with the flash of their guns. I looked up out of the hatch, and saw that overhead there were vast numbers of planes, which I couldn't hear because my ears were deafened, but I could feel the vibrations of their engines in the air…probably nobody can understand that sensation unless they have been under an air fleet like that, not with the modern jet engines, but the propellers from those days. The air itself was vibrating around us.

But why were you angry?

Because of the senseless waste of all this. All these planes, these ships, were crewed by men who were the same as us, from the same civilization and race as us, and yet they were launching this attack against our Europe, while all the time the Soviets were massing their armies against Europe in the East. It was such a waste, so unnecessary.

But soldiers are not allowed any moments to reflect on such grand matters, are they? By now the light was quite clear, and with the light came the Allied aircraft. A large number appeared over the fleet of ships, I can't be sure but I would say a hundred planes, at different altitudes and speeds. I saw several of these approach our area at very high speed, almost as if they were diving on us…I sealed the hatches again, and soon I heard the impact of cannon shells on the turret. These aircraft cannon were very powerful, and they partly split open the armour plate around the cupola. If they had come round again, they might have destroyed my turret completely, but I heard them go off to the south.

Through my periscopes, it was difficult now to see anything because of smoke outside; whether this was a smokescreen the Allies had put down with their shells, I don't know. I managed to get my young loader off the floor of the panzer, and we got ourselves into some kind of fighting shape, ready for whatever was to be thrown at us.

What was your feeling at this stage?

I was determined to hold the resistance point. I still felt angry about the whole situation, furious even. I was also puzzled as to how the attackers thought they could climb the cliff that led off the beach onto the dunes. There was a low sea wall there, and then a sand cliff of several metres which was strung with mines. It was a low obstacle, but very hard to climb for men or panzers. At times, the sea wind blew the smoke clear, and I could see large numbers of craft on the sea, coming closer. These were boats with high front walls, vertical walls, which I later realised were ramps. Again I had the feeling of a wall of steel coming towards us...an absolute wall.

By the way, the approach of these craft was not rapid, but quite slow. I saw several explosions when a craft hit a Belgian gate with a mine, and the detonation blew big pieces of steel from the hull. I saw one craft in which the front ramp was blown off completely, and inside were a large number of men, all of them scrambling around as the craft tipped over and sank. Several of these craft were on fire in one place or another. I saw many bodies in the sea, even before the craft landed.

Then a bombardment began again, which blew up the sand all around us and blinded us with smoke and dust, and we had no way of knowing what was happening. We were there, just me and this scared boy, in our concrete panzer, as this great army came slowly towards us.

After that, there was a long, long period of time where there was just smoke, explosions and firing from the beach direction. We had resistance points in the headland there, looking down onto the beach, and I could see flashes and clouds of smoke coming again and again. I was in a state of real anxiety, not knowing what was happening. Of course, there was a terrible battle going on at the beach while the Americans were coming ashore, but at the time I didn't know what was going on. This went on for hours, I think, with us in the concrete panzer not knowing if we were winning or losing or what the enemy were up to.

I knew that a lot of the troops on the beach front itself were from the Eastern Regiments; these were Russians who had changed over to our side. I felt sorry for them, because they were miserable men, who had no real heart for fighting alongside us at all, but there they were, in the middle of it all. We had thousands of these Russians up and down the coast, and nobody today knows or cares what happened to them after the invasion...I can tell you something about that later, though.

I would like to hear that. But when did you first see the enemy on the land, on the dunes?

It was much later. I saw explosions down at the edge of the dunes, where the low cliff was. These were big flashes that threw sand a great distance into the air. The noise during all this time was unbearable, with the huge impacts coming again and again. I primed the turret gun and tried to see through the gun sight, but all I could see were some of our own troops, or maybe the Eastern troops, running back from the cliff. These men were caught by a shell blast and thrown in pieces across the sand, which was a horrible sight. I dreaded the thought of dying like that.

Then I saw some kind of explosion on the edge of the dunes. This explosion ran left and right in a line, and I suppose it was an explosive cord for clearing the barbed wire there, or something like that. A few seconds later there was a cloud of sand and an American panzer came up over the top of it, onto the dunes.

This was a great shock to me, as I didn't think it was possible for the attackers to come off the beach, but I fired on that panzer immediately. It was a Sherman class panzer, which was very high in profile, and made an easy target - especially with the big, white star they had painted on the front. I aimed straight at the star, but my shell bounced off the armour and went off over the beach behind. This Sherman fired on me very quickly, and I imagine that the crew had studied plans or photographs of our positions, because they seemed to know their way around the plateau.

They shot me in the front of my gun mantle, which dislocated my gunsight and dazed me with the impact. When I managed to look out through the cupola, I saw that the Sherman was firing on the PAK gun behind the metal shield near me too. There were other Shermans coming up this path onto the dunes; one of them hit a mine, I think, and started to burn up in flames very brightly.

I tried to fire again, but with our damage there was no way to aim our gun. We were hit again, and this round came into the turret itself. It was a nightmarish moment, because the Sherman's warhead came through the turret front plate, and hit my loader fully in the chest where he stood. It shattered his whole chest at once, and passed straight through him, and ricocheted around on the floor of the hull without hitting me. The bulk of his body had slowed the shell down, just enough to stop it bouncing off the walls and hitting me, I think.

So this poor boy, who barely needed to shave his chin, saved my life in that way. He died instantly, standing next to me. That was the end of the concrete panzer as far as I was concerned.

What did you do? Did you try to surrender?

I tried to get out of the panzer, without really knowing what I was trying to do out there. I slid out of the turret side hatch and got behind the turret, sheltering there. The situation on the dunes was appalling. There were bits of bodies on the ground, and huge craters, and dust and smoke everywhere. That Sherman which was on fire was burning like one of those flame torches that metal welders use, you know the ones I mean? Like an oxyacetylene flame. It was burning like that, sending up a very tall, blue flame, going up many metres into the air.

To my side, I could see our PAK gun in its metal shield, a few hundred metres from me, and it was still firing. That was the gun commanded by the man who hated the Americans. That gun kept firing, firing, even though it was being hit by rounds from the Shermans.

The Shermans were coming onto the dunes in numbers now, I think there were three or four…they fired very rapidly, with their gun barrels depressed down to aim at that PAK. In a minute, that PAK stopped firing, but the men in there kept firing with a machine gun. I could only crouch and peer out from behind my turret.

In a few minutes, American infantry began coming up onto the dunes, and the Shermans were shooting away at that machine gun behind the PAK shield. One of the American infantry had a flame-thrower, and he got close enough to use it on the PAK. The flames were enormous and they shot out very fast, like a fire hose but full of burning liquid. The whole PAK position was covered in these flames; the burning stuff was dripping off it and making a pool of fire on the sand.

At that moment, something awful took place…it was almost like a sign from God that we were doing wrong. A strange, circular wind blew up on the dunes, some kind of small tornado, and it whirled around and it fanned the fires from the burning Sherman and the burning PAK…there was chaos all around me in this whirlwind. Ammunition was exploding, men were screaming, both German and American and in Russian too. All the time, the planes were racing over us through the smoke, firing their cannons inland. It was absolute hell on that sand. Absolute hell.

How did this battle end for you?

I wish I could say that I was a hero, but I was drained and finished by all of this. I remained crouching behind the concrete panzer turret, and when those American soldiers began running past me towards the inland area, I didn't do anything to attract attention. It was only when the first dozen troops had charged right past me that a soldier noticed me there. He hit me in the face with his rifle stock...those American rifles were much heavier than ours. He had a bayonet fixed on it, and he was going to stab me with it, I think, but an explosion close by diverted his attention.

Other Americans ran up, and threw grenades into the concrete panzer. The poor panzer, with the boy's body inside, exploded with all the ammunition. I remember that these soldiers were dripping wet from the sea, and steam was coming off their limbs. One of them pointed back to the beach and sent me off running down there with a kick to my backside. I ran to the beach, and other Americans halted me and put me in handcuffs under the edge of the dunes. There were a few other German men there in manacles, and several wounded and unconscious. I noticed that the Americans had separated the Russians who had surrendered from the Germans. The Russians were being taken away separately, that was clear.

On the beach itself, I was shocked to see the remains of that battle. It was a sight that would make the bravest man very mournful. There were bodies all along the sand, some still in the water and many just piled up on the sand. These were all American dead, as far as I could see along the sand. All the way along the beach, one after the other, into the distance. Closer to us there were German corpses, men who had fallen out of their points on the sea wall, and they were very burned. We German prisoners were all mute, just looking at this.

As the minutes went by, I began to think more about what was going on at the beach, and I was amazed at the amount of ships and vehicles the Americans had available. There were landing barges lined up on the sand for hundreds of metres, and huge numbers of jeeps and armoured vehicles moving around. They had machines there which I didn't even know the name for…trucks which drove on the water and then came up onto the land, and flat rafts which carried stores and jeeps. There were metal ramps lying around which maybe they had used to get up onto the dunes, and armoured bulldozers with enormous blades which were digging out a bigger exit lane from the beach.

I recently spoke to another German veteran who mentioned that he was surprised that the Allies had brought no horses with them for the invasion.

Yes, that *was* a surprise to us. We commented on it. If that had been a German army, even in 1944, there would have been a lot of horses and wagons there, in the supply element, because of the lack of fuel and trucks. In fact, one of our men stupidly asked one of the American guards, 'But where are your horses?' The Americans just laughed at this and gave him a cigarette.

I remember that there were lots of the barges and boats on fire, too. I think this was from artillery, because the posts with mines and the Belgian gates were all still there, although some of them were flattened. Everywhere there was activity and machinery, and there were clouds of smoke and sand drifting past us. The new American troops coming onto the beach ran right past me. Some of them looked scared, but most of them looked very eager to get into France…I remember that very clearly. Those troops *wanted* to attack and conquer France. They were very highly motivated.

How were you treated as a prisoner?

I was taken on a ship that same night to somewhere in England, on the coast. By the way, there were no Russian prisoners on that ship, not one. We got off the ship at about eight in the morning, and we had to walk from the docks to a rail station in the town. There were lots of English civilians about, all old men and women, and they all stopped and stared at us going past in our ragged German uniforms. That was a strange moment, when we came face to face with the English women. I must say that none of them shouted at us or cursed us - not that I could hear, anyway. Maybe I didn't understand what they said. I didn't see any of them spit at us or throw stones, anyway. But I remember that the eyes of these women were very bright, they were very proud, to see us trudging away in our defeat. We were a pitiful sight, in our rags and bandages.

I suppose that a scene like that has been repeated many times in human history, hasn't it? Captured prisoners trudging past the women folk.

But to answer your question, we were treated well in England. Our camp was visited regularly in 1944 and 45 by Red Cross inspectors...some of these Red Cross folks were from neutral countries in South America, which we found fascinating.

Also, the English army doctor in our camp was very interested in me because of my frostbite injuries from the Eastern front. He brought other army doctors to examine me, and they asked a lot of questions about how I lost my fingers and nose, and what treatment I received, and what happened to other German frostbite sufferers. I told them what I knew, because it was hardly a military secret. I got the impression that nobody in the British Army had ever suffered frostbite!

After May 1945, after we surrendered, I got to know this English doctor well, and I worked as a basic assistant for him, so we often talked. He was fascinated, I think, by my stories about the Russian front and what went on there. I think that the English had almost no understanding of the Russian front. To them, the whole war was North Africa and Italy and Normandy, but of course the war in the East was fifty times the size of that, maybe a hundred times the size.

That reminds me, talking of Russia, I can tell you something you should write down for sure. I once asked this English army doctor, who was a very pleasant man, what the hell happened to all the Russians who were in the German forces in Normandy.

This was what you were going to tell me about the Russian defectors?

Yes. There were thousands and thousands of those Russians and Eastern Europeans in the Wehrmacht along those Atlantic Wall beaches, and we German prisoners often wondered what the devil became of them after the invasion. They must have surrendered in big numbers, because they had no stomach for fighting in France – why should they? But there were none of them in the prisoner of war camps, that was for sure. It was as if they were separated from us, and then they just vanished. So where did they all go? What happened to them all?

What did this doctor tell you about the fate of the Russians in Normandy?

I shall tell you something strange and worrying now, Herr Eckhertz, although you may not believe what I say. The Englishman told me, after we had been drinking, that he knew what happened. He said that when the Allies invaded Normandy, there were representatives from the Soviet Union among them. Yes, it's true. Among the American and English troops, there were commissars from the Red Army, who were there specifically to search for the Russian defector troops. And when these Russian defectors were taken prisoner, they were immediately separated off and handed over to the Russian commissars, right there on the beaches. They were put on ships from Normandy and sent back to Russia via the Baltic, back to the Soviet Union. And when they got back, they were all immediately shot as traitors. There was no Geneva Convention for them.

The Americans and English didn't want them executed in France, because it would have been hard to explain after the war. So they handed them over to their deaths.

Do you believe this is true?

If it is not true, then where *are* the Russians from Normandy? There must have been ten thousand of them or more, some of us figured out. Did they all just disappear? Where are their graves?

Well...talking to you has given me a lot to think about. You have brought home to me some new dimensions of the tragedy of Normandy...what you said about the Children's House, and the fate of the Russian defectors.

These were terrible events, but they need to be remembered.

—

THE LUFTWAFFE PILOT

**Thomas Beike was a Leutnant (Pilot Officer) attached
to Jagdabschnittführer 5 (Leading Fighter Group
5) in the area North of Évreux, Normandy.**

*Herr Beike, you are the only Luftwaffe veteran that I have
met as part of my project of interviews about June 6th. I am
fascinated to learn of your experiences on June 6th, and to
learn, for instance, if you flew a sortie on that day?*

Well, that isn't a very good start to our conversation, Herr Eckhertz.
Your tone of voice is really rather ironic. I hope you don't subscribe
to the *'Luftwaffe did nothing'* school of opinion, which holds the
Luftwaffe partly responsible for the German defeat in Normandy.

*It was not my intention to be ironic, Herr Beike. My purpose
is purely to set down the experiences of Germans during June
1944, and not to push any particular point of view.*

I see. Well, perhaps I was hasty in my remarks to you just now. But
the fact is that we who were in the Luftwaffe are accustomed to
being told that we 'did nothing' or 'disappeared from the skies' in
June and July 1944. The wretched Allied journalists and movie mak-
ers have simply encouraged this version of events. The fact is that

we in the Luftwaffe were facing enormous difficulties even before the invasion began. This was despite our situation appearing to be excellent, superficially.

Can you explain your situation? In what way did
it appear to be excellent, as you say?

You see, our section's small airbase, which was in the Evreux-Lisieux sector was one of several in that area positioned quite near to the coast. The base was on a plain belonging to a country estate of some kind, and the chateau had been requisitioned to provide accommodation for the pilots and senior officers. So I went from bedding down in a frozen hut, as I did in my posting on the Eastern Front, to sleeping in a proper bed with a staff servant to attend to meals and the polishing of boots and other necessities.

This chateau had a wine cellar which was very well stocked, and the quality of food available locally was remarkable. We did not barter for food with the local civilians in the way that the Heer *(German Army)* did, but nevertheless we ate well. We regularly tried to send parcels of French food home to our relatives in Germany, where the diet was very restricted. Our families were under instructions from us not to mention this in their neighbourhoods, because of course it made the Reich seem inefficient. The parcels often went missing anyway.

What else can I say about our life? As you are a man of the world, sir, you can also appreciate that we pilots were popular fellows with the French ladies. We were officially forbidden from having anything more than a passing relationship, if you understand me, with French women, but in many cases the pilots and the ground crews, the Flak crews and so on formed quite affectionate bonds with some of these girls. The ladies were extremely astute, I remember, and in many ways they ran the local villages and towns in the absence of their menfolk, who were often in the labour force or the internment system.

So, all in all, on the surface, you could say that our situation appeared excellent, on the face of things.

But below the surface, how did things stand?

In a number of ways, things were in a bad way; a desperately bad way. The simple fact was that we in the fighter groups could not live up to the expectations that people had for us. We could not live up to the image or the legend of the Luftwaffe as it had been from 1939 to about 1942, which was when the very large bombing raids started over the Reich. Let me explain the problems for you, as you are evidently interested.

The basic issue was that the command echelons of the Luftwaffe could not supply us with enough aircraft, spares, fuel and fresh pilots to be an effective force, compared to the colossal resources of the Allied air fleets. To keep a fighter aircraft in service, you need a great deal of spare parts, oil, coolant, lubricants and so on, and all of these were in short supply in 1944. It was quite common for a fighter to be waiting in its hangar, fully armed, pilot ready, fuelled, but unable to take off because coolant could not be found for the engine. Or, when the coolant arrived, the special air filters could not be replaced, and so on, with endless combinations of things that were missing or could not be repaired. This meant that units took off below strength, meaning that yet more planes were lost when they ran up against the big Allied formations.

As for the pilots, we simply did not have enough good quality, fresh pilots to replace those lost in the air. You cannot just take any fellow and press him into service as a pilot, and an experienced pilot cannot be made to fly combat missions around the clock – the mind and body cannot cope with that. The end result of all this was that our units were under strength and each individual man was badly over-stretched, with all the mental stress that is a result. So each Luftwaffe pilot, living in his chateau with his polished boots and so on, was under the surface a somewhat tormented individual.

How did the pilots try to cope with these pressures?

Some were able to cope through mental strength. Religion was a comfort to others, and our Luftwaffe chaplains became psychologists in some ways, offering counsel and advice. On the other hand, some of us found distractions with the women...while some others turned to alcohol, which was freely available, or even to certain drugs which were used, such as mixtures of amphetamine, and chemicals such as cocaine.

At the time there was the well-known branded stimulant product called Heroin, made by the Bayer company, and this was used as well. It was no secret that Hermann Goering, our supreme commander of the Luftwaffe, was extremely fond of this Heroin stuff too. But all these stimulants only made matters worse after their initial impact was used up.

On that subject, Herr Beike, I sometimes hear from Heer (German Army) veterans the stories of our men taking drugs, especially amphetamines, to keep them going at certain times during the war. Are you saying that this was widespread in the Luftwaffe also?

I can only say that it certainly happened. We have to remember that the use of stimulating drugs was more common in the 1930's and 40's, and much less frowned upon, than it is today in the 1950's.

Let's remember that Bayer, which I think is probably still the largest German pharmaceutical company, they invented their two wonder drugs in the 1930s, Aspirin and Heroin. They were intended to go hand in hand, if you remember back then *(Aspirin = Hope, Heroin = Heroism.)* You could get Heroin very easily from a pharmacist, just like Aspirin.

Today there is talk of banning Heroin and preventing its sale, which personally I would support. I knew several officers who used that unpleasant product during the war, and a couple of them became quite addicted to its use. It's said that Goering himself died from a Heroin overdose before he was due to be hanged at the Nuremberg trials.

But we have strayed from the subject in hand, haven't we?

Forgive me, but the question of drug use in the Third Reich interests me... and I have never heard such a frank description. But yes, you were talking about the reasons for the Luftwaffe's decline after 1942.

Exactly. And all the time, you see, as our strength was sapped, the massive Allied air fleets, funded by their international finance backers, became bigger and more powerful. And all of this was brought out into the open when the Normandy attack happened in June 1944. All of this was exposed brutally, as if a strong light was shone onto a festering wound, when suddenly you could see all the problems clearly. That is what happened in France that time.

You say that the Allied forces had 'international finance backers.' What was your view of the international situation at the time?

My view during the war was that we were engaged in a conflict which was ideological in origin, the conflict between our German National Socialism, which had finally unified Europe after all its centuries of conflict, and the vested interests of International Socialism, represented by the Bolsheviks. I took a great interest in these political matters, you see.

The conflict that we had with the Western Allies was incidental to this primary struggle between the two competing and fundamentally opposed forms of socialism: *National* and *International.* We had no great argument with the Americans or the English, but the fact was that the Western countries were pooling their resources with the Russians, and the three Allied powers were drawing on all the accumulated wealth of their banking and finance agents. I was convinced of this at the time.

Since the war, I have realised that this view was partially mistaken. I had underestimated the animosity between the Anglo-Americans and the Soviets, which we see openly displayed today. At the time, that mutual dislike was concealed well, and they put on a united front. But the fact remains that the British Empire, the American banks and the Soviet command were pooling their resources. Why else, on the Eastern front, would we sometimes see Russians driving American panzers and trucks? Or Russians flying British planes?

And all of this pooling of resources was brought to bear on the beaches of Normandy, which became a kind of anvil, I suppose, on which the Allies hammered and hammered with all their strength, above all with their massive aerial power from above.

The Allies were very active in the air in the build-up to the invasion, weren't they?

They were extremely active. The British RAF came over at night, and they caused huge destruction to the French railways, road junctions and that kind of thing. My Geschwader *(squadron)* was not equipped for night-fighting, but we regularly caught RAF aircraft around dawn if they were returning over France. The Americans carried out raids in the daytime, and we were sent up against the American Jabo and twin-engined bombers frequently.

The problem was always the numbers and the airframes. Some of our group were kitted with new aircraft, and the latest designs, but in my squadron we would go up in aircraft that were two years old, with refitted engines and equipment. When you saw the American planes, it was obvious they were new from the factory. Just before the invasion, I saw inside one American plane, a Mustang, which crash-landed in a field near the coast. That plane was completely new, without even scratches on its canopy. All the pedals in the cockpit were unmarked. And our planes creaked and let in rain water. But you mustn't think I'm complaining; I'm just telling you what I experienced.

By the way, I spoke to the American pilot of that Mustang before he was taken away, in my very poor English, and I told him he was a lucky bastard to have such a fine plane. He answered me in excellent, very old-fashioned German! It was very strange. I heard from the interrogators that this pilot had a German surname, and they believed that he was from a German-speaking farming town in the USA.

All this Allied air activity... did you get the impression from all this activity that an invasion was coming?

Well, all this Allied bombing escalated in May, and there was a definite feeling that 'something' was on the way. The tonnage of bombs they were using was enormous, even on small targets. When they bombed the rail yards at Rouen, which I think was in early April that year, it was astonishing. I flew over there a few days later, and I saw they had bombed the yards into dust, from one end to another, including all the civilian houses along the tracks. Everything was flattened, and of course the French had no air raid shelters in the way that we in Germany did, or the English in London had. I heard that five hundred French civilians died in that one attack alone. And attacks like that took place daily.

As for us, our air field was bombed repeatedly, and it was only because we had strong blast walls around the planes that they stayed intact. The shelters for the aircrew were very thin slit trenches, and half a dozen of us would jump into these things while the Lightnings and Thunderbolts bombed our runways. Even before they left, our engineers would be out there in the open again, getting ready to repair the damage. But while the craters can be filled in if you have the workers and the tools, if your stock of engine oil is destroyed, or the new shipment of hydraulic tubes, which has only just arrived after a long delay, is set on fire...all these things make it so hard to put aircraft into the air.

I imagine that you were in the air on June 6th itself?

I did get up there, yes.

Our pilots' sleeping accommodation had been moved from the chateau to a farmhouse, because the chateau was too obvious as a target. This meant we were several kilometres from the airfield itself, and had to go back and forth by car. On the 5th, it was the birthday of one of the other pilots, and we had a small gathering at the farmhouse to mark this event. I won't say 'celebration,' you understand, because the war was no time to be celebrating anything like that.

What form did this gathering take on the evening of the 5th June?

Well, there were six of us pilot officers, and two senior officers, one of whom attended with his wife, who was visiting the base from Germany. You may look surprised, Herr Eckhertz, but this was quite acceptable in our section. At about nine pm, the senior attendees departed, leaving only us pilots. We were joined after that by several French ladies, who were well-connected locally and were excellent company.

In what role did the French ladies attend this gathering?

In what role? As guests. I am sure you can understand that if one is in France, it is inevitable that such ladies will find their way into the company of pilots.

Are you saying that these ladies were your girlfriends?

I really wish that I hadn't mentioned this matter. It is sufficient to say that these women were present as our guests, and we appreciated their company over the wine that we drank to mark our comrade's birthday. And all of this went perfectly well until late in the evening, about midnight, when there was a great build-up of aircraft overhead.

We went out to see what was happening; the noise was from the North, over the sea. The ladies, I must say, were very upset at this display of air power that the Allies were making over France. We could tell that these were Allied aircraft from their engine tone, which was level, whereas our large aircraft had a rise-and-fall tone to the engines. We stood in the darkness listening to all this going on in the air. The ladies made remarks such as 'You must save us from those *salauds Anglaises*' (*English bastards*) and similar things. For them, it was very upsetting, this threatening force, and we sent a squadron car to return them to their homes.

We did not know what the situation was, but we opted to get some few hours' sleep, as it seemed likely we would be needed in the daylight. Pilots must be reasonably fresh, you see, because of the demands of eyesight and reflexes, and those few hours of rest were the best contribution we could make to the war at that moment.

How did you sleep?

Badly, to be frank. Being an airman, I could not help listening intently to all the aircraft, and the sounds of our Flak firing at them, and estimating their altitude, numbers, direction and so on. I knew that there were very few night fighters located so far West in France; most were over the narrower part of the Manche (*English Channel*) and Holland to the East, to counter the bomber streams going into the Reich itself. I asked myself who would be up there to meet these Allied intruders, and what were these Allied planes doing? Of course, I know now that I was probably listening to the airborne infantry transport planes which caused so many problems for us on the day itself, but at the time I didn't know this.

Ultimately, my orderly woke me before first light, and we pilots drove to the airfield just as the grey light came up.

Strangely, almost all the aircraft had now stopped. There were some individual planes overhead, but it was nothing like the swarms of the night itself…this sudden silence all seemed very ominous to us. As we neared the airfield, we saw a peculiar sight, so baffling that we stopped and stared. This was an Allied glider which had crashed into one of the meadows, and it was just sitting there on its belly, apparently abandoned. In retrospect, this must have been a single glider which had drifted inland from the attacks on the coast, but the sight of it alarmed us. Some of our troops were nearby, searching for the occupants, and they told us to beware of paratroopers and glider troops.

When we got into the base, we were briefed on the situation, which appeared to be an airborne landing around Carentan to the West. That is all we were told at that point.

Troop reinforcements were arriving to guard our site, which was obviously a potential target, and our ground crews were under orders to blow up the buildings if the Allies tried to capture them. Breakfast was eaten in some excitement, I remember. When the light was full, a wave of enemy fast bombers came over, but fortunately they attacked the nearby decoy airfield.

What was this decoy?

Oh, because of all the bombing, we had created a structure near to our base which, from the air, resembled a runway and buildings, while our real facilities were heavily camouflaged with nets which, and all our plane dispersal points were concealed by false trees. So these enemy planes, which were the USA Lightning type of bomber, hit the dummy airfield. They flew off, no doubt congratulating themselves on their attack. But the issue for us was: how to make ourselves useful?

What aircraft were you equipped with?

The Messerschmitt 109, type Gustav, which was based on the original design from the 1930s, but with a new supercharged engine. It was still a formidable aircraft. You're probably aware that the designers had made the 109 as fast as possible by making it as small as possible, which meant that the fuel tank was very limited. But otherwise, in experienced hands, it was still probably as good as a Mustang or even the new version of the Spitfire. *'Probably as good'* – that sums up our problem!

We got into the cockpits at about six thirty that morning, still under all the camouflage, and we simply sat there and waited. We were kept informed, because a runner would come up and give a verbal communique, or bring a note of the latest understanding of the situation. But still there were no orders!

What were your feelings as you sat in the cockpit?

Frustration, nerves, excitement, and anxiety of course. Any pilot who waits in his plane on such a day and doesn't feel fear, I would say he is not telling the truth. I felt many things mixed together. I knew that this was a big effort by the Allies, whether a complete invasion or some other kind of attack, and I couldn't imagine what we would find when we got up among the enemy.

I could see a lot of planes going overhead. It was a rather grey, damp morning that day, and the enemy planes' exhausts stood out very bright in the murky light. The runner came finally with an order for us to intercept enemy aircraft over the coastal area. Priority was to be given to attacking troop transports and bombers, of course. This was at about nine am, and just after that the order was rescinded, and we turned off the engines again. To do justice to our commanders, it must have been very difficult to make sense of the situation, and to take a decision on where to allocate the fighters.

In the end, in the mid-morning, three of us were ordered to take off and fly to the coast near Caen as an armed reconnaissance patrol. So we were to be reconnaissance pilots! This was hardly a promotion, but it finally got me into the air.

Was the Messerschmitt suitable as a reconnaissance plane?

No, it was completely unsuitable. Visibility was very limited forward, because the engine cowling was right here, under your chin. You were meant to dive on things to be able to see them. We could see nothing behind, with no bubble canopy, and even to the sides the wings obstructed the view. But you must improvise in such times, and we were determined to see whatever we could. One problem was that our planes had no radio connection to our base...in the air, we could only speak to each other. So we would have to observe, see what we could, and then return to base at speed without being shot down, to make our report.

As my ground crew were closing my canopy, my commander stepped up on the ladder and shouted to me that this was a vital mission, that the aerial information we could bring back was essential to the task of driving the enemy back to the sea. He gave me his personal Leica aviation camera, in the hope that I could take aerial photos with it; obviously, the chances of using a hand camera in such a situation are almost zero, but the act underscored his urgency. I put the camera inside my seat harness, but in the situation that followed I completely forgot about it.

I was the second plane to take off, and we began to climb in a staggered formation of three, separated by altitude and latitude heading to the North West to Caen. As soon as we levelled out, we were hit by a pair of Mustangs that came down from the 120 degree point, on our rear quadrant. The tore right through us before we got our wits together...damn, I blush with shame when I remember that, to be attacked so quickly and in such a basic fashion.

What was your armament in the Messerschmitt?

We had 20mm cannon in each wing, two machine guns over the engine cowling and another cannon firing through the propeller. This was a far better armament than the Allied fighters, because the 20mm was very powerful, and completely accurate, with one being inside the propeller. The Mustangs at that time had, if I remember right, six machine guns. These Mustangs that caught us...with their speed, they were past us and already banking before we could evade.

I wasn't hit, but one of my comrades was, and he began to make a lot of grey smoke as he turned away. As he banked below me, I remember that an orange glow began to spread from his engine. I remember that I groaned, knowing what this meant, and in a few moments his cowling flew off in pieces and flames shot back over his cockpit. I could not look properly, because the air was full of these damned Mustangs, but I remember seeing him with his arms over his face, like this…and then he was simply lost in all the flames. This was the pilot whose birthday we celebrated the night before; he was twenty-five years old. I doubt if he has a grave or a headstone of any sort in France.

I gained height and accelerated, faster, always faster. My task was to observe the beach head, not to engage enemy fighters. I saw my remaining comrade in his Messerschmitt, ahead of me, making for the coast as well. My rear visibility was so limited, I twisted around trying to see those planes, and Flak tracer was coming up as well, which must have been German fire, as we were still inland. Those Flak gunners were in a panic and shooting at anything, it seemed. I crossed over the rail lines near Caen, and still couldn't see those Mustangs, so I went in a straight line for the coast. There's a river inlet with docks near there, and I went over it at maximum speed, which was over 600 kmh. The coast itself just leapt up at me at that speed, and from that height I could then see a massive line of ships out at sea, about three kilometres from the shore. This just happened like that, in the blink of an eye…my canopy glass was just full of these ships.

I was astonished at this sight. I wondered if I was hallucinating, or if this was a delirium of some kind. I had never seen such an assembly of ships, and I'm sure nobody will ever see such a thing again, perhaps not in human history. The sea was absolutely solid with metal, that is no exaggeration.

After a couple of seconds, no more, I turned to fly West along the coast, so that I could see down to the right, and I banked my wings to give a view of the shoreline. These were the beaches that the English and Canadians attacked, I forget the code names they used for them.

West of Caen, this would be the Gold and Juno beaches.

Gold and Juno? Well, for us this was the Caen sector. I saw that the beaches were crammed with vehicles, moving in on transport barges, and even tanks were being unloaded like that. The thought came to me, 'So this is the big invasion, this is it.' No other explanation was possible. Throughout the beaches, there were fires burning, vehicles and boats on fire, and explosions from artillery. I saw flamethrowers being used inland, very powerful ones, and the flames lit up a wide area down there.

The enemy were driving a bridgehead inland, that was clear to see, and they had enormous resources building up on the sand waiting to move off. I could see flashes of bombs and shells all over the inland area. I remember that some of the fields were flooded, and the exploding shells sent out a concentric shock wave through the water that was very noticeable.

I took all this in within a matter of seconds, but for that time I was stunned by the sight. Of course, there were many Allied aircraft in that sector too. There was a low umbrella of fighters over the beach, and they came straight for me. There were three coming after me. I went down to minimum height and maximum speed, which was safe because the land is so flat there, and the German Flak would be less likely to misidentify me, I hoped. I thought that if I could move away from the beach head, the Mustangs would turn back to protect their sector. So I used a huge amount of fuel accelerating to the South West.

I went west as far as Saint Lo, and I couldn't see the Americans behind me, so I turned East and followed the forest back towards Evreux. That was the extent of my mission, there was nothing further I could do. I tried, in my mind, to estimate the number of ships on the sea, but I couldn't do it. It was thousands, surely. Do you know what the figure was?

Actually, I don't know the number. It must be thousands, I agree.

I must be one of very few Germans who saw that from the air. Going over the land on my return to the airbase, which only took a couple of minutes, I saw lines of our armoured vehicles on the roads, and many more dispersed in the fields. Fortunately my plane's yellow nose and black crosses must have been clear for them to see, and nobody fired up at me.

When I came to put down again at the airstrip, I saw on the runway the burning outline of our third Messerschmitt. I found out later that he had returned with an engine fire, and blown up as he came in. I was the only one to survive of us three, you see. The smoke from this burning plane was a beacon to the American planes, who came back just like a pack of wolves. I landed as they were strafing again, and I had to jump straight into a slit trench on top of the ground crew. The enemy realised then, I think, that they had originally bombed the decoy airfield, and they came back repeatedly with new bombers. In between the bomb bursts, I ran to the main shelter and gave my report, with more bombs exploding around us. We were kept in those shelters like prisoners for several hours, which was the Allies' intention, of course.

Did you fly again on the 6th?

The air field was too badly damaged, and the orders were still contradictory for several hours. They ordered us to strafe the beaches, and then No, leave the base and take the planes inland, and then No, wait for orders…each time our heads span a bit more. It was only on the 7th and 8th that we got into the air again, but I did not penetrate as far as the coast after that, the fighter screen up there was too heavy. Then we were moved to an airfield further to the South East, and we were tasked with low-level strafing of opportunity targets, which is not a good use of a valuable aircraft, and we were tasked also with intercepting the attacking planes to keep them away from our armour concentrations around Caen-Rouen.

Did you have success in the strafing role after June 6th?

We were so few in number, and at the new airfield the problems of supplies and maintenance were even worse. As for pilots, to replace the two men we lost on June 6th, we received a novice with minimal hours flying experience and a forty year-old training instructor. The novice was shot down by a Spitfire over Rouen on his first sortie with us, and he crashed near the bridge. That new version of the Spitfire was an absolute freak of a plane; it was faster even than our latest Focke-Wulf, it was said. There were rumours that it was supersonic, but of course that was impossible in those days.

But you asked about the strafing; well...I am not proud of it, but I personally shot up a row of Churchill tank men in that week after the invasion. They were dispersed behind trees in the bocage *(hedgerow country)*, and they had made only basic attempts at camouflage. We got this information about their position from a local French civilian, in fact, who was passing us intelligence about the Allied locations.

You see, we couldn't go up, patrol around for targets and then attack them, as the Allied pilots did. We were so outnumbered that we would have been brought down immediately. But if we had reliable, specific information that a certain target was at a certain location, we could race over in one pass and hit them and then go for home, with no need for a second run at them.

The French who sympathised with us, and there were many, often gave us this kind of target information, through channels that our people had set up as we retreated.

The French gave you information about Allied panzer positions?

Absolutely, yes. I know this for a fact. Remember, please, that the French were in two minds about the invasion at first: would it succeed, or would it fail? In the first days and weeks, it was by no means certain that the landings were a permanent lodgement, or that they would develop into a full invasion even if they were. Everyone remembered the peculiar attack on Dieppe, when the Canadians invaded but then left after a few hours. Was this going to be a repeat of that, but on a bigger scale? So, because of this uncertainty, many of the French in the Allied zone put their bets on both horses, if you see what I mean, and they played up to the Allied invaders while secretly passing information to us.

A certain contact gave us excellent information, and this particular alert about a group of the Churchill tanks came from her. I went up and set myself on a direct course for the location, knowing I would only have one pass before having to break for my base again. As soon as I saw the copse of trees, I saw the outline of the Churchills, which were stationary with no attempt to break up their outlines with foliage or nets. I also saw the crews assembled in a large group, in a meadow to the rear. Perhaps they were having some kind of briefing there. In my one pass, I came down on them while they were starting to scatter, and fired everything into the middle of them. Just one second, like this. It felled them like skittles, I have to say. I was gone from there before they stopped rolling. It was very precise.

*Do you know what happened to the French informants
when the Germans withdrew from the sector?*

I don't know what happened to this particular one, or even who she was. I mean, I *assume* it was a woman. The fact is that many such people came to Germany with our forces when we retreated from France. This is a part of the war that is not discussed today at all, Herr Eckhertz. The fact was that quite a number of the French followed us out of France, rather than be paraded as 'collaborators' and the like by the Allies and the French patriots who sprang up all over the place after the invasion. Such French helpers were welcomed into the Reich, even though they gave us more mouths to feed.

Did you yourself manage to get out of France before it was lost to the Allies?

No, I was taken prisoner after the massacre of our forces at Argentan, which the Allied newspapers called the 'Falaise Gap,' I believe.

I had been injured in a crash landing in July, and I was hospitalised at a field treatment centre near to Alencon. I should have been returned to Germany for recuperation, but the policy was to have recuperating pilots near their bases so that they could be pressed back into service. The hospital was overrun by the Americans very early one morning. We heard engines, and suddenly there were Jeeps in the courtyard, and these huge American fellows, like giants, with their Thompson guns over their shoulders, were already making friends with our nurses. I don't know whether the Americans put their tallest men in the front line, or if this was by coincidence, but these fellows were close to two metres tall, all of them.

There was nothing we could do to avoid capture. We were put in trucks and driven to the West, and our route took us past the Argentan-Falaise area where the massacre had taken place. I saw some terrible things on that journey.

I'm sorry, Herr Beike, but you have said 'the massacre'
twice now. Can you explain what you mean?

I am referring to the large number of German personnel who were killed by air attacks as they were retreating from the battlefield between Falaise and Argentan. Huge numbers of our forces built up in that bottleneck, and the Allied aircraft, the jabos above all, simply flew over and massacred those men. Some were armed combatants, you see, but many were unarmed rear echelon men, drivers and engineers and the like.

On those prisoner trucks, I'm sure that we were quite deliberately taken past some of the worst destruction. I remember that we were driven slowly, with repeated halts and delays, on a road which went between some fields where some of these bombing attacks had happened. The bombing was probably only a day previous, because we could still smell the burning, and the wreckage and bodies were not yet cleared away. The things we saw in those fields were shocking, even for the most experienced men among us on the trucks.

On one side, I remember that a row of our panzers had been bombed, beautiful Panther tanks too. There were six of these panzers, all with their turrets blown off, or their wheels blown off, and the metal tracks lying around everywhere.

Between them were many dead horses still attached to carts and wagons, and many motorcycles and cars, dozens of cars. The bodies of the men that had been killed were lying around everywhere, still in the open, covered in flies. There must have been two or three hundred bodies in that field alone, all black with soot and horribly torn up. And this went on for kilometres, field after field. It was a place of endless destruction.

We also passed a group of our soldiers who had survived the bombing, but who had been driven insane by the experience. These men were being kept in a stockade in the open, acting just like helpless lunatics in an old-fashioned asylum. And these were men from the elite Divisions, and SS men among them too, all reduced to this pitiable state.

I swear to you that in one of these dreadful meadows, I saw a line of our Hitler Youth boys, the lads who were sixteen or seventeen, that had been stupidly sent to fight with the Waffen SS. They were all dead, these boys, lined up as if on parade, all shot one after the other. What the devil was the explanation for that act, I do not know.

And we were shown all this deliberately, you realise, in order to have an effect on us. We were all crushed by the sights, and we remained virtually silent for days afterwards. This is why I call the events at Falaise and Argentan a massacre.

I have read in the newspapers that General Patton visited those fields at Falaise, and he said that, if he wanted to, he could have walked for hundreds of metres on the dead German bodies that he saw, without ever touching the ground. That's a strange choice of words for a General. But I have to ask, Herr Beike, how is this diffeent from what we in the German forces did to our enemies? This was the nature of the war, was it not?

I cannot say what was or was not the nature of the war...it is too big a question. I would rather not talk about this entire situation anymore now. I appreciated the opportunity to tell you about the Luftwaffe, and my mission on June 6th...I am glad we spoke about that. But this conversation has brought back to me the memory of those dead bodies. I would prefer to stop our discussion at this point.

Thank you for the account you have given. It has opened my mind to some aspects of the conflict that I had not considered before.

—

THE TROOPS IN THE
OBSERVATION POINT

**Heinrich Runder was a Grenadier (Rifleman) with
the German 709ᵗʰ Static Infantry Division, manning defences on the Cotentin Peninsula.**

*Herr Runder, I believe that you were in a position to witness part
of the assault on Utah beach from a location to the West.*

Yes, I was posted in a Widerstandsnest *(resistance point)* on the coast
to the East of Valognes. This was on the Western edge of what the
Americans called their Utah beach. Why they called it Utah, I don't
know to this day.

What was your resistance point like?

It was a fortified position on ground overlooking the beach itself.
The position was very basic in construction, being made of logs
rammed into the sides of a trench in the earth. The soil was very
sandy, you see, and the logs were needed to hold the walls up. We
were on dunes behind the low sea wall, and our task was to fire on
any attackers who appeared in front of us, and to defend a PAK *(anti-
tank)* bunker and a concrete observation post which were nearby.

We were a Static Infantry unit, which other units jokingly
called 'the belly army' because of the age of our troops. This was

misleading, because while some of our men were aged forty or over, others were much younger. But many of our men had been classed as physically unfit, or they were considered otherwise unsuitable for service in the mobile combat divisions.

When you say that they were 'otherwise unsuitable,' what does that mean?

Let's be honest, Herr Eckhertz; any conscript army will contain men who are rather slow-witted, or men who are unable to think like front-line soldiers. Now, such men cannot stay at home, they must play their part, and a Static Infantry role is a good way for them to serve. I am sure that those men acquitted themselves well when they were called on to fight. It was not lack of bravery on their part, but lack of mental faculty.

I can say categorically that there were also men in the Static Divisions who had previously suffered mental problems as a result of being in combat, especially on the Eastern front. You know what I mean – mental breakdowns and this kind of reaction to fighting. Such unhappy men were often transferred to the Static Divisions, in France and elsewhere.

This is an aspect of the Static Divisions that I had not considered up to now. Can you think of specific examples of these troops who had mental problems?

Well, my own cousin was one such example. He was in a dreadful battle in the East, at Kharkov, and he was awarded the Ritterkreuz *(Knight's Cross.)* Despite his bravery, he had a mental collapse. In the earlier part of the war, you know, such men would have been treated harshly for their symptoms, but by 1943-44 we were so short of manpower that he was transferred to the Atlantic Wall, which was a kindness at first. I can think of other examples, other stories that I heard, and I'm sure this situation was common. Of course, France was a good place to send such unfortunate men. The life in France was without combat, and they could recuperate to some extent while still serving in the forces.

But we all knew that an invasion would come, sooner or later.

You expected an invasion in June 1944?

Personally, yes, I did. We were told by our officers that an attempt at invading France by sea might be made at any time, and logically this had to be in the summer because of the rough seas in the fall and winter. My comrades and I would often sit at night in our barracks in April and May that year and say, 'Will they come tomorrow? When will they come? When?'

On the day that they came, what was your experience?

On that day before the invasion itself, we started to be aware during the night that the Allies were mounting some kind of operation. This was the Monday night, the 5th June. I think that nightfall came at around ten pm, and exactly as soon as darkness fell the air seemed to absolutely come alive with the sound of aircraft. I remember this very clearly: large numbers of planes began to pass overhead precisely as the air went dark. The timing of this was remarkable: they must have calculated their approach exactly so that they came over France literally the very moment that night fell.

I was on duty in our trench, and I recall listening to the engine noises, and exchanging glances with my comrades. None of us knew wanted to guess at was going to happen, but this was not the normal night-time bombing activity, which was itself very heavy by then.

At the same time, we could see and hear bombing to the south, and we received a telephone call from our Leutnant telling us to watch for paratroopers and glider troops. The Leutnant himself wasn't shirking; he was moving between the trenches and bunkers in our sector and maintaining contact with all the men.

The night was quite wet, and it was impossible to make out details of what was happening overhead. We had no searchlight, and the nearest one was at a Flak battery guarding a larger bunker complex about two kilometres inland. Those guns fired on and off, into the early hours.

What was in your mind during the night?

I was very apprehensive. I had been in action before, in Tunisia, where I received a head injury from a shell burst, and I dreaded being in action again. To be frank, some men excel in combat, and others manage to somehow struggle through, and I was in the latter group. By the way, I did not really understand the political ideals of the Hitler regime, but still I was convinced that I was in France to do my duty as a soldier and to protect Germany from attack.

You saw your role as protecting Germany?

Our training had impressed this on us. The idea was that the Western Allies were in the pay of the Bolsheviks in the East, who were orchestrating world events against us. I remember that phrase clearly from some of the officers: '*They are orchestrating world events.*' To us, this meant that the Reds were closing in on Germany in the East, and their partners the Americans and the English were trying to crush us in a pincer from the West, by attacking through France. This is another phrase I recall: '*We are in a clamp, and Germany is caught between the Anglo-Americans and the Slavic races.*'

We had no great understanding of politics, my fellow Landsers *(foot soldiers)* and myself, but we understood the idea of the clamp closing on us. We all believed that we were in France to stop the American-English clamp from crushing our homeland from the West.

Well, we did not actually speak about all this as we were standing there in the dark with all these unseen planes passing overhead, but I am sure that it was in all our minds in one way or another. Then,

I think it was at about one am, the cloud cover overhead cleared a little bit and we could start to see what was up there. The moon was almost full, I think, and there were fires to the South which shed some light upward onto the clouds remaining.

To the South East, we could see very large numbers of aircraft moving at medium altitude. When I say large numbers, I mean literally scores of planes going over at any one time. And as soon as these planes moved away, another twenty came to follow them. It was a dreadful sight for us, because these could only be Allied planes, coming from the North; but at the same time many of us grudgingly admired the Allies for their organisation. The formations of those planes were perfect, even in the dark, and this impressed us greatly.

We saw no signs of air combat, apart from the very sporadic Flak aimed up at the planes. I remember that one of these aircraft was hit by Flak, and it began to leave a trail of fire in the sky as it descended. It made a large red ball to the South where it crashed. At this point, our officer rode up to us again, and directed us all to man our guns and be vigilant for airborne troops. I remember that his voice was strained, and he was a bit confused in his orders; to see our experienced and trusted officer in a state of confusion was worrying for us.

How did the morning of June 6th unfold for you?

You see, we were right at the southern point of our Valognes sector, where the peninsula starts to widen out down towards, I think, Saint Mairie. This meant that we were on the upper edge of the zone that the Allies chose to attack on June 6th. To our East was the Dunes area, which I now know that the Americans called Utah beach, and then across the bay of the Virc was Colleville and those places which they called Omaha. I know these American names from reading magazines since the war ended, but during that night, obviously, I had no concept of what was happening from one minute to the next.

I've heard since the war that the attack on the Utah beach zone drifted to the East of its planned assault point because of the tides or the wind or something, and that may be why my particular sector was spared the initial assault. I often think about what might have happened to me if, by chance, the tides had not been so strong that day. Would I be speaking to you at all today? Would I still be alive?

I also have such thoughts about the war. But here we are, speaking today, the fortunate ones. Do you consider yourself lucky to be alive?

Yes...in the sense that I was not a natural soldier. When I said to you that some men excel in combat, those are the men who thrive on such uncertainty, because they have type of mind that can adapt to changing circumstances and exploit the changes. I do not have that type of mind, because I prefer things to be predictable. One might say that I am a simple man, and this may be true, but the Static Infantry divisions had huge numbers of men such as me, and frankly we were not natural soldiers.

All in all, the night of the 5th was a time of great anxiety for us.

At times, we saw flashes to the South, maybe somewhere around Saint Mairie, and shapes in the sky which we thought might be parachutes. But in the darkness and drizzle it was difficult to make anything out clearly.

When did you first become aware of the scale of the invasion?

Oh, my God, this was at first light on the 6th, when we could make out the sea more clearly, and also the light rain stopped falling. I remember that the sky was overcast above the sea in front of us, but a bit brighter over to the East. When the light came up, some of our men at the end of our trench shouted to the rest to come and see what was happening.

When I looked over the trench at that side, onto the sea to the East, I can tell you that my throat went dry, painfully dry, and my hands began to shake. I was not the only person to be affected in this way; one of the very young lads began to retch as if he was going to be sick. It was the effect of pure fear, to be honest with you, but it passed.

What could you see on the water over there?

A vast number of ships. Absolutely vast. We were looking from the side onto the flank of the formation, as the ships came towards France from the horizon. We had a pair of binoculars that we shared, and using these I could see a line of ships which was literally endless, it simply stretched off into the distance. And behind that first line there was a massive formation of ships going back for many kilometres. It is impossible to give you an impression of that formation unless you saw it yourself.

There were many kinds of ships, some large battleships which were clear to see, and many small craft, some of them with anti-aircraft balloons attached. I remember that the bodies of these balloons were a kind of pearl-grey colour in the light. Above all this, there was an absolute hive of aircraft moving overhead.

But the strangest thing about this sight, now that I think back, is that, apart from the planes, there was no noise! The enemy warships were not firing their guns, and from the coast, from our positions, I did not hear a single gun being fired. I think that if you ask other veterans of that day, they will confirm this: that many of our bunkers simply did not fire at this formation as it came closer. Of course, the range would have been too far for any but our most powerful guns, but the silence along our coast was very strange to experience.

I remember also that in front of this fleet, between the beaches and the invaders, there were a couple of small fishing boats, local French boats. These boats remained static for some time, then they slowly raised their sails and they tacked away from the formation. Very slowly they moved away, up towards Cherbourg. What must have been their thoughts, I cannot imagine. In our trench, we were making ourselves ready for what might happen.

*You mentioned that the invasion on Utah did not initially
land on your particular beach. Were you observers, or
did you come into contact with the enemy?*

We were strafed by enemy aircraft before the invasion ships began
to approach the shoreline. I think that the first ones were Mustang
type fighters, and they came upon us very quickly from the West.
The intention was, I suppose, to keep us with our heads down under
cover, so that we could not observe the landings to the East.

These planes came along the beach and shot down at us. I
remember that the bullets went along the parapet of the trench and
made explosions of sand. One man was blinded by a deflected bullet. This was a large calibre bullet, and it smashed open the whole
side of his face; he sat down slowly, with the blood coming out of
his eye and cheek. Another man had a bullet pass directly through
his hand, right there in the palm, so that he could not do anything
more as a fighter. Both men were bundled off to the rear behind
the sand dunes, although the nearest field treatment station was
several kilometres away, I think.

In the middle of all this confusion, the thought came to me that
those Mustang aircraft were very handsome machines. They were
polished metal, and the metal caught the light from the East as they
flew off. I was envious that the Allies had such superb machines. We
could see on their wings the American star, and one of our young
lads shouted out that these planes had flown across the ocean from
America. We cursed him for being so stupid, but it shows you how
simple-minded some of our troops were, that they could think this
was possible. And all the time, the formation of ships came closer to
the shore, until the warships began bombarding.

You saw this bombardment?

There was mist on the sea, but we saw all the flashes from the guns
of the bigger warships which were a long way back behind the leading craft. These flashes were enormous, and even when the sound

came to us it was very loud. We saw explosions on the shoreline which raised large plumes of dust and smoke. This was a terrible sight – because we knew who the men were down there on that shoreline, and we felt sorry for them, even though many of them were Russians.

The men were Russians?

Yes, that was a zone which was manned by Russian units that were working for the German army, troops who had changed sides when they were captured in Russia. There was a whole company of them dotted around down there; we called it 'Little Russia' sometimes. God only knows what the Americans thought of them when they found them all there, or maybe the Americans knew about them in advance…maybe that's why the Americans chose to attack that sector? I wonder if that's possible. Well, we felt pity for them, anyway. We knew also that if the battleships turned their guns onto us, we would get the same treatment as those Russians.

The Allies, of course, had no intention of just letting us stand and watch this. We were bombarded next with rockets which shot out from smaller ships on the edges of the formation. The sun had not yet come up completely, and the rocket trails were very bright as they came towards us. What we saw was a great network of these bright trails in the sky, coming towards us at incredibly high speed. They were stabbing towards us, if you can understand what I'm trying to say. They stabbed at us, and they exploded on the sea wall area below our trench.

The explosions were very powerful, and we threw ourselves to the bottom of the trench. I could feel the blasts, which made my ears ring and made my nose bleed. The shock waves blew sand over us, and some of the trench walls collapsed behind the logs. Some of our men were blinded with sand being blasted into their eyes, and other men refused to get up from the floor of the trench. These rockets came again and again, and they kept exploding into the ground below our point and around us.

From where I was crouching, I could see the large bunker behind us, which was a concrete bunker mounting a PAK gun. One of the rockets struck the bunker, and simply blew it to pieces. The walls and roof of the structure all flew apart, and the gun itself crashed down near our trench.

This destruction went on for a long time, it seemed to me. I think in reality it was about thirty minutes, but if you are on the floor of a trench, time is hard to follow. My watch stopped working, which I believe often happens in a bombardment. When I thought that things could get no worse, a huge piece of one of these rockets crashed right into our trench. This was the tailfin unit from the back end of a rocket, and it flew along the trench hitting the men randomly. I remember that one man was hit in the arm, which was almost torn off by the fins, and other men were caught in their bodies and faces. This fin assembly ended up sticking into the end of the trench, throwing out flames and smoke. I thought that if the bombardment went on for many more minutes, we would all be carved to pieces in our trench.

After some time, the rockets became less frequent, and we were able to organise ourselves and get back into our proper positions. I looked over the top of the trench, and towards the South, I could see a huge number of small craft on the sea, between the main fleet of ships and the shore. There was a lot of smoke in the air, and it was difficult to make out fully, but in the end, as the sea breeze blew the smoke away, I saw many of these craft going quite slowly towards the beaches down there.

How did your commanders, your officers respond to this event?

Everything was in confusion for some time.

We were still being bombarded at intervals by rockets, which were coming from the ships on the edge of the fleet out there. These explosions made us take cover frequently, and made it difficult for us to see what was happening. That was the purpose of the rockets, I suppose. The sun came up, and we could hear explosions from the Southern beaches, and see a lot of movement of vessels between the beaches and the fleet. That fleet kept growing bigger all the time – it simply astonished us to see so many ships all in one place. And still no German ships, no German aircraft! No German response except for us in our trench.

Our Leutnant came into our trench, very out of breath, and told us that this must be the main invasion of France taking place to the South. He was very agitated and he seemed unsure what to do. I think he wasn't being kept informed by his superiors, and he had no information to give us about what to expect. We all just assumed that our position would be attacked at some point very soon.

How did the day progress? How did the men in your trench react?

Well, for one thing, rumours began to spread – all kinds of crazy rumours and stories. This is the way with troops who are not kept informed, I think, they begin to repeat rumours and things get distorted in the retelling.

A soldier came to our trench bringing ammunition, and another man to replace a telephone cable. Both these men said that the Americans were landing on the shore to the South, using amazing machines and weapons, machines that the German defenders could not understand. They said the American panzers were suddenly appearing five or six kilometres inland. There were rumours about American panzers landing from the air, or coming out of special submarines – all kinds of absurd, wild exaggerations. But of course, as nobody was telling us what was happening, what else could we believe? How else could American panzers suddenly arrive in that peaceful part of France?

This horrible waiting went on for some hours.

Around midday, I think, our Leutnant came back and said that Americans were storming along the high ground above the beaches to our South. He ordered us to defend our position to the last man, the last bullet, and all that kind of thing. We could still see the huge fleet sitting on the water out there, and the warships were still firing, shooting inland. We saw a Luftwaffe fighter, a Messerschmitt, go over our beach very fast, and then it turned inland and it just disappeared without shooting. That was the only German plane I saw on that day. Meanwhile, the sky over the Southern beaches was absolutely full of Allied planes. We ate our midday ration watching these planes.

You ate at such a time?

It's better to eat something before a battle. We had our rations there, so we ate them. Because this was France, our army food was supplemented with very good sausage and cheese, and our officer allowed us to drink some schnapps. It may sound strange, but I actually have a good memory of that meal, because we were all there together, relying on each other and encouraging each other, and knowing that the day could only get more difficult for us. We knew that many of us would probably be among the fallen by sunset, but there was nothing we could do to avoid this destiny. It was better to accept it.

Of course, this strange phase of inactivity could not last. In the afternoon, we were strafed again by Jabo *(fighter-bomber)* planes of the Thunderbolt class, I think, which fired out rockets from under their wings.

These rockets exploded when they landed and threw out a liquid which exploded with a very bright, red flame. The first group of these rockets flew over us, thank God, and burst open in the fields behind us. There was a very strong smell of burning tar or rubber, and we could feel the heat from the flames even in the trench. After that, we heard another of these Jabo planes diving down on us...that wait seemed to go on for ever; we stared at each other in the trench and listened to this screaming engine getting louder. That pilot sent his rockets all along our defences, and one of them exploded right there at the end of my trench.

The next few moments were complete hell and chaos. I still struggle to make sense of it all. The burning liquid blew up in a great ball which spurted out along our trench; I mean that it poured along the trench with a horrible force. Have you seen a big water pipe that has burst in the street, and the water comes flying out into the air for four metres, five metres, under great pressure? That is the way this burning liquid flew along the trench, splashing out everywhere. I can still see this today in my mind: there were half a dozen men lined up along the trench between me and where the rocket burst, and each one of them was covered in this burning spray that came towards us. And the liquid was sickening in the way it worked; it was some kind of gasoline fuel mixed with rubber or nylon, or something like that. It stuck to everything like glue, to the men's uniforms and skin, and their hair and bodies. It splashed in front of me, and I ran like a madman, I'm not ashamed to say, and I got away from it.

When I turned to look back, many of our men – who a few minutes before were eating their last meal – were completely on fire. One by one, those men fell to their knees and gave up their struggle, or they simply fell back into the flames and disappeared from my sight.

How did you react to this event?

The few of us who survived, we ran down the communication channel into the next trench. We were stopped there by the Leutnant who had his pistol drawn, and he ordered us back to the trench despite our reluctance, saying that he would come with us. I remember that as he did this, one of the American planes came over again, very low. This plane shot all along the trench lines with machine gun fire, but the worst thing was that the slipstream, the wind from his wings and engine, this wind fanned up the incendiary flames even more, as if it was fanning a bonfire. We could hear the flames becoming like a furnace in the trench we had just left.

The Leutnant was a good officer, and he did not force us to do something that he himself could not do, and he clearly could not bring himself to go into that trench. Instead, he told us to go and man the observation bunker nearby.

What kind of bunker was this?

We called it a bunker, but in fact it was just a small concrete dome big enough for a handful of men, with firing points. It was in a position close to the sea wall, so it had an excellent view along the beaches to the South. It was intended as an observation post, not a defensive position, but logically the enemy could not leave it undamaged, because it had such a strong view of the landing zone. When we got into this bunker, we found only two soldiers, who were observing through binoculars and giving commentaries into a field telephone. Who was on the other end of this phone, I don't know; I suppose it was our artillery. The bunker was defended with a single machine gun, a 34 type, and we manned this.

I was trained on the 34, and I became the gunner, aiming it along the beach. The observer soldiers told us that the Americans were moving along the headland, along the top of the higher ground, and knocking out the defensive points all along there. In fact, there were not many manned points along that stretch at all, and when we looked through the firing slits we could see Americans already moving towards us on foot.

That was my first sight of the enemy as individuals in France.

How did the Americans appear to you?

It is strange, the thoughts that come into your mind at such a moment. Their green uniforms stood out quite strongly against the sand and earth of the top of the cliffs, I remember. I was surprised that their assault troops didn't have camouflage uniforms, as our top units of Panzergrenadiers had. My head was spinning, I was dazed, and this thought came to me.

Well, this was my time to fight. I primed the gun and fired on them from about six hundred metres away. I had one of their men in the ring sight, and as soon as I started firing, I moved it along their line and shot the men behind him.

What manner of emotions did you have when you did this?

I was too dazed and shocked to have emotions. I could still smell the burning incendiary fires, and my eyes were streaming with tears from all the acrid smoke, and I only wanted to do my duty as well as I could. I was not in a state to think about things at all. The gun was well-maintained and it fired perfectly – I remember thinking that.

There was a short battle, between our observation post and these Americans. Some of them got down into the rocks and fired on us from there. The wounded American men crawled into the rocks also, and I chose not to fire on them. But of course, all that we were achieving was to draw attention to our position, and inevitably the Americans brought up heavier weapons to use against us.

What weapon did they use?

I think it was the Panzerschrek *(bazooka)* type weapon. I saw a white flash come out from between the rocks, and this thing shot straight towards us and exploded on the outside of the bunker. The rocket didn't penetrate into the bunker, but it did make a huge blast and smoke which blinded us for a few seconds. I aimed the 34 at the rocks and fired all over that area; again and again I fired, until the ammunition belt ran out. The observation soldiers were firing too with their rifles through the slits.

The Americans fired that bazooka on us again, and this time it exploded close to one of the slits. This sent fragments of stone and concrete inside the bunker, which flew around and hit us. It was like being hit with a hammer as these stones smashed into us. I was hit in the face, which broke my cheekbone, as I learned later, and knocked my front teeth out. I was stunned by that injury, and one of the other men took over the gun.

I do not remember the other events very clearly after that, because of my injury.

I recall that I left the observation bunker, seeking medical help, and I went away along the trench. I had no gun, and I had blood pouring down onto my chest from my mouth. I was very confused. I remember looking around, and seeing behind me an American soldier climbing on top of the bunker roof, onto the dome itself, and throwing grenades inside. I realised that there were these American men everywhere suddenly. They were standing on the top of the trench, looking down at me. There was a lot of shooting and yelling, all happening at once.

Of course, what happened was that while we were firing on one group, another unit had come around and overrun our position from the side. The observation bunker gave out a lot of smoke, and I knew that it was all finished in there.

Did you surrender?

I was so dazed, that I just stood there. The Americans were shouting at each other; I think they were having some kind of argument. One of them jumped down into the trench and hit me in the chest with his rifle butt, which knocked me over. The next thing that I recall, I was being taken in handcuffs down to a point lower down in the dunes, where a lot of our men were lined up under an armed guard.

This was much later in the day, towards evening. The dunes were full of equipment that our men had thrown away, and some of the Americans were going through all this stuff, all the haversacks and coats and so on. They were very pleased if they found a bayonet or an officer's cap; I suppose these items were souvenirs for them. An American officer who spoke German told us that France was being liberated from Germany now, and that we would be treated well provided that we followed orders.

How did the German troops respond to being prisoners?

There were a couple of us who said they wanted to organise an escape and then get back to German lines, and that kind of idea.

Such a thing would have been completely impossible, obviously. The amount of men and vehicles that the Americans had, just in that small part of the beach, was astonishing for us to see. There were many jeeps and trucks, and piles of stores. Inland there were loud explosions and flashes, and columns of smoke rising up. There was no way that any of us could have escaped through the lines. The vast majority of us accepted the situation. I had no more desire to fight or resist, I can tell you that.

We were very quickly put on a ship and taken back to England overnight. We were filmed by newsreel cameramen when we arrived. We had to file off the ship and go marching away across the docks under guard, with the cameramen taking a record of everything. If you see the newsreel films of German prisoners landing after June 6th, I am probably in there, with a bandage around my head, and my teeth missing.

But to answer your question, most of us were relieved to survive that day, and to be taken prisoner. I think that many of us felt in some way privileged to survive the day, when so many others had not lived through it. Inside the ship, we sat in silence, with very little speaking...and so we went into captivity.

Were you held by the Americans or the English?

At first we were in a large camp run by Americans. After a month, we were dispersed, and I was sent to a smaller camp in the North of England.

Did you notice differences between the Americans and the English? Or were they quite similar in their behaviour?

There were differences. The English were quite similar to us Germans, because they liked repairing things. If a machine stopped working, an English person would enjoy trying to fix it, and other English would gather round and give suggestions, or tell him he was doing it wrong. Then the man who repaired it would tell his friends,

'You know that generator in hut seven? Well, this is how I fixed it. First...' and so on. This was actually quite like us Germans.

But the Americans wanted everything done quickly, whatever the expense. So if a generator failed, it was *'Get me a new generator, damn it,'* and it had to be done at once. This was not our way, because we had so few resources, and we thought that making repairs was the right thing to do.

Regarding the camp conditions, I can say that the Americans and the English followed the Geneva Convention very strictly, and we could not complain about our conditions. I was given medical treatment throughout my imprisonment.

By the way, I remember that near my camp in the North of England, there were huge camps of Italian prisoners who had surrendered in North Africa in 1941...these Italians were now very comfortable in England, working on farms and speaking English. I wouldn't be surprised if some of them are still there.

I myself was repatriated to West Germany in 1946, on a ship from Felixstowe.

Looking back on June 6ᵗʰ, do you think that the day could have had a different outcome?

I really don't see how that would be possible on the 6ᵗʰ of June itself. If you had witnessed that attacking fleet on the sea, the sheer number of ships they had available. I think it was inevitable that on the day itself, the Allies would gain a foothold in France, some kind of bridgehead.

The other side of the coin, of course, is why, immediately after that happened, our German forces could not have wiped out this bridgehead. With all our panzers, our Luftwaffe, the wonder weapons which we had, how could we not take back these few square kilometres of land that the Allies took on the day itself?

Men such as me, we could not have held back the enemy forces with our machine guns firing from our bunkers. But the inland troops were supposed to be our very best, all the panzer units and the Waffen SS men and those others. Still today, when I think about it, that is a puzzle for me. Why did our elite troops not push the Allies back at once?

But the whole thing is over, it's all done with, and there's no point in dwelling on that question today. We have to try to look ahead, we who survived that day.

I would like to thank you, Herr Runder, for giving
such a complete account of your experiences.

—

THE MILITARY POLICE

**Niklaus Lange was a Feldgendarme (Military Police Officer)
attached for security and traffic control to the 21st Panzer
Division near Caen, inland from the Juno and Sword beaches.**

*Herr Lange, I think that we might have met before. When I was
in Normandy in early 1944, I was escorted in the Caen area by a
number of military policemen, and I think you were one of them.*

That is correct, Herr Eckhertz. I was on a superb Zundapp motorcycle, if you recall. I used to wear my goggles up on my helmet all
the time. I remember escorting you near to that big emplacement
at Bayeux where you interviewed some of the troops. I loved that
Zundapp motorcycle, I must say.

*I wonder what you can tell me of your experiences
of the build-up to June 6th in Normandy?*

With that question, my mood turns from the light to the dark in
some ways. But you are right to ask the question, because those of
us who were involved surely witnessed a unique event in human
history, and it would be folly if these experiences weren't collected
and set down in some way.

I was assigned at that time to the headquarters of the 21st
Panzers. My role was to ensure traffic control if the panzers or

command units were using the civilian roads. The Division as a whole was involved in very urgent preparations for a possible attack throughout early and mid-1944. In that whole Caen area, there was a large amount of construction work on anti-tank obstacles, beach obstacles and resistance points, stretching all along the coast.

What form did you think a possible attack would take?

There were many ideas about how this might happen. They might come from the sea, or using paratroopers. There was a particular concern that the Allies would try to capture airfields in the region, and use them to land troops. Other people thought the French themselves would join some kind of uprising against us. The effect on us was that we saw everything as a threat: the sea, the skies and the local people.

Some other veterans that I have spoken with have said that relations with the local French civilians were very good. What was your experience?

My experience was that the civilians simply could not be trusted. Of course, we should have been in control of them, as we were the dominant partner in our partnership with France, but the French civilians found so many ways to undermine us.

If I may ask: you use the phrase 'our partnership with France.' What did that mean?

Well, the 'partnership' was what the French government called the presence of our German troops in France. I know that the Allied press call the French wartime government the 'Vichy Regime' or something like that, but we never used that term. We called them 'the French government' or 'the French authority.' They put out a large amount of information to the civilians explaining why we, the Germans, were there.

What reasons did they give?

The main reason was that we were a protection force, a kind of guard, against all the bad things in the world which might harm the French. These bad things were Communism, secret societies such as Freemasons, and of course the Americans and the English who wanted to occupy France and use up all its resources for their own people. The French were very aware of how lucky they were to have such a fertile country, so rich in farming and industry, and they were very defensive about foreigners taking their produce. The French government played on this fear a lot, I remember.

My God, if you went to the local cinema, which we were allowed to do, their newsreels had these endless information films from the French Government, explaining this over and over again. *Partnership – protection - prosperity*, it was really drummed into them.

And yet, you see, for every ten French civilians who went home from the cinema grateful for our presence, I would say there were two or three who were planning against us.

That is interesting, because some of the other veterans I have spoken to have implied that the level of French resistance activity was actually lower than we see in popular portrayals today, in films and books and so on.

But the armed Resistance was only part of it. You had the theft, the rackets, the gathering of intelligence which the French passed back to the Allies.

What does this mean? Can you explain the thefts, the rackets?

Well, don't forget that French society was very corrupt, extremely corrupt. I'm sorry if that is an unfashionable thing to say, but it is a fact. Damn it, but I was also in France in the first war, in 1918. I saw how the French population made money out of the war. They did the same in the second war.

211

*This picture of France in 1944 which you are
portraying is very controversial.*

But it is the reality that I knew. You asked to come here to talk about
the reality, didn't you? Well, then. I am sorry if I seem angry, Herr
Eckhertz, or agitated. But I saw a side of France on that day that you
are interested in, that day of June 6th, which is not widely known.

*Maybe we can come back to this.
What can you tell me of your experience on
June 6th? How did it begin for you?*

It began, as I remember so clearly, on the night before, on the 5th. On
that evening, which was cool and rainy, I was tasked with escorting a
number of officers in an armoured car convoy to a command centre
near to Janville. As a military police man, my task was to ride ahead on
my motorcycle and ensure the roads were secure, holding back other
traffic as necessary, and stopping civilians from taking an interest.

The memory of that night...talking to you brings it back. There
was a light rain. The asphalt road was wet and it reflected the flashes
of bombs exploding to the North. Everyone was on edge, because
the bombing was intensifying all the time.

Oh, and I remember at one point, there was a gap in the
clouds and an aircraft appeared right above us. It just appeared,
and floated over us, and then swooped away. This was an English
Mosquito bomber, the thing which had two Spitfire engines on a
cheap plywood body...I recognised it at once, from its profile, and
so did the officers in the cars. Everyone stood up to watch this hideous thing go swooping over us...it was like a vision of death. It was
like a vampire bat floating over us. And the worst thing was that we
recognised it, and we knew it was made out of cheap wood, just plywood and timber...and in our hearts, we knew that our engineers
could not build an aircraft like that, not even in German metal. The
sight of that wretched plane was offensive to us. Even the officers
shouted out and cursed it.

Who were these officers that you were escorting?

These were officers of the panzers, I think they were logistics people. Their role was to decide on supply dumps, the best routes and
roads for the different types of panzer to use, and so on. They were
important people. The presence of officers like that had to be handled carefully, because they were likely to be attacked by partisans,
terrorists and that kind of operator. In the Caen-Bayeux area, we
had lost several of these officers to terrorist incidents.

What form did these 'terrorist incidents' take?

I mean that the officers were assassinated by local partisans. In one
case, an officer was machine-gunned from a fast car. It was not difficult to identify the terrorists involved, because so few of the French
had access to cars that worked on gasoline. In another incident, a
bomb exploded under a wooden bridge that our men were crossing. Their Kubelwagen (*VW jeep*) was blown into the river and they
drowned like that.

So there was an atmosphere of tension, you understand, and we
all knew that the threat was all around us.

Would you still, today, describe these attacks as 'terrorist' attacks? Or
as 'resistance attacks,' which is how the French would describe them?

I can't answer that. That's not for me to say. I am not thinking about
the present day, but about the ways things were ten years ago. In
those days, these attacks were definitely terrorist attacks; that was
how we in the Wehrmacht described them. I was only a military
policeman, not a great thinker at all. The important thing was that
we were alert to the threat, and we guarded the officers carefully,
with our lives. That was our job.

On this evening, the night before the invasion, after that
Mosquito bomber went overhead, the area was bombed heavily.
I think the bombers were trying to destroy the road junction just

North of us, because there were big impacts from there, and we could feel the blast waves. We halted the armoured cars in a sunken road, and I went on ahead to see the damage. That was my job, to secure the transit through the road system.

That junction was badly hit. There were fires in all the houses on the corners, and a lot of wounded French civilians coming away from the buildings. Some of these were pushing injured people in wheelbarrows and handcarts, and very distressed. The road itself was full of craters. The danger was that there were bombs on delayed fuses, which was something the British and American bombers used all the time.

Did the Allies use delayed fuses on their aerial bombs a lot?

Definitely. I had seen areas where the bombs, which were buried underground or buried in buildings, went off one after the other at precise one hour intervals for twelve hours. You could have set your watch by those bombs, they were so accurately timed. This was all done to keep people away from the area, to prevent repairs.

Well, we are talking about the Monday night…by this time it was after midnight, so it was the 6th itself, I suppose, and the whole damned sky was full of the noise of these bomber planes going over, doing as they wished. When I got back to the armoured car column, there was a buzz of activity around the radio car, because reports were being made about airborne attacks. Everything was confused, and the planes were going over, making the cars rattle with their noise…it felt as if something big was happening.

The officers began to look on the map for somewhere to halt in the darkness, away from the roads. One of them suggested a house nearby which functioned as a hotel and was often used by German officers. This house was a small mansion, with its own generator and kitchens. It was very secure and comfortable, a good choice.

And so we went to this hotel, this French house.

We pulled up outside there before one am, and we requisitioned the dining room for the officers to set up their radio sets and maps. The room became a command centre, if you like, for these panzer logistics men. I made myself useful and stood guard at the door outside, and I could hear them discussing the different attacks that seemed to be taking place. The staff of this house, this hotel, brought food and drinks to the officers in the dining room. I was jealous of that, because I had eaten no meal since lunchtime, but duty is duty.

How did the night unfold?

The amount of aircraft above reached a peak at around one am, I think. I was standing outside the garden doors of the room, with my machine pistol across my chest. I had a good view of the sky, and there were obviously lots of planes up there, but also clouds. There were big bursts of flak exploding at times.

I saw one plane explode, and this lit up the whole sky for several seconds. In the orange flames, I could see a whole mass of other planes moving South East. I couldn't count them all! Then, as the burning plane fell to the ground, those other planes faded back into the dark sky again. I thought, 'My God, what is all this?'

Did you think of the word 'Invasion' then?

Yes, I did. There were so many planes up there, it had to be an invasion. I reported this sight of the planes to the officers at once, and they added it to their reports, I think.

And now the night became worse for me, more full of threats... what happened was that as I was standing there, on duty, one of the serving women, the waitresses, from the hotel, came out and offered me a tray of coffee and bread rolls. It was real coffee as well, not our ersatz German coffee, and she told me that it was from a supply from before the war. Well, I could not refuse. I was grateful to her, you understand. She went in and offered the same to the officers. One of the officers, a Hauptmann (*Captain*) came out and stood watching the sky with me. I expected to be criticised for eating on guard duty, which of course was an offence, but the Hauptmann told me to eat well, because the next day would be a long one for us all. He could feel what was happening too, you see.

The waitress stood near us, with her tray, ready to serve the officer. He was very smart in his uniform, very professional. He told the waitress, in French, not to be alarmed by all the planes, because the German army would protect France from the Allied aggression. The waitress then offered to show the officer to a room for some rest. She said, 'I see you are tired, monsieur. We have rooms where you can rest for an hour or so, and return refreshed.'

This is an odd thing for you to remember happening
in the middle of all this activity.

You will see why I remember this. Personally, I did not approve of the officer going off with this French lady, but it was not my job to think about why he did this. But some time later, the other officers came out to look for the Hauptmann, and demanded to know where he was. I went into the house to find this room where they had gone to.

I found that the hotel staff had disappeared; there was not one of them to be found in the whole place. Bombs were falling nearby, so I thought they had gone to find shelter. After looking in the bedrooms, I found the Hauptmann. And this is why I remember this so well, and also why I say that we could not trust the French, you see.

Why? What happened?

The Hauptmann was dead. He had been shot in the side of the head, at very close range, and the bullet had made a terrible mess when it came out of the front of his skull. He was face down on the white sheets of the bed in there, and there was his blood and his brains all over the bed and the wall.

This was a disaster for me, as I was meant to be guarding him, but he had left and gone with this serving woman deliberately.

Do you mean that she had shot him?

Well, close to the body, we found a Browning assassination pistol, so she must have been responsible; her or one of the others in the hotel.

What is a Browning assassination pistol?

Have you not heard of these damned pistols? They were very common in France at that time. The assassination pistol was a simplified version of the American 9mm handgun, but it was smaller and it only held one bullet. There was no magazine, as there was on the normal pistol.

The Allies made thousands of these evil little guns, and they dropped them into France for the terrorists to use in exactly these situations. The idea was that the victim would be unaware of the killer's intent, for example sitting at a table in a restaurant or on a train, or indeed in a bedroom. The killer would move from behind and put the pistol to the victim's head and fire the single bullet. The pistol wasn't made for fighting with, in fact once it was fired, the empty cartridge couldn't even be removed from the chamber, you would have to lever it out with a knife or something.

And that is how I found this pistol, by the bed, still with the cartridge in it. She had dropped it and escaped.

You say these pistols were very common?

There were thousands of them in circulation. Once, we caught a parachute drop that the British RAF made near Bayeux. There was a canister with a hundred of these guns inside, and other canisters in the zone had been removed by the partisans already.

I suppose the idea was to make every French civilian into a possible assassin, just waiting for the moment to kill a German. I can tell you that hundreds of our personnel in France were killed by these things, in cafes, hotels and so on.

Now, if you ask me about the Normandy invasion, my own view is that a directive went out from the Allies on that night before the invasion, saying, '*Shoot an officer. Find a German officer and just kill him with a single-shot Browning pistol.*'

That way the Allies could disrupt our command system and cause confusion at such a critical time. I believe that on that night, the 5th of June, these pistols were being used all over Northern France. It was a very ruthless way to run a war, wasn't it?

But what were the consequences for the civilians who used these pistols?

They would be executed if they were caught, naturally. Murder is murder, after all. But in all the disorder caused by the invasion, there were chances for them to get away. There was great upheaval in the area, with the bombing in the night and the alert about the beach landings in the morning.

In our case, the Hauptmann's body was taken away to Divisional command, and our military police tried to investigate, but in all the confusion this did not progress. In fact, the area around the hotel was captured by the Allies the following day, the 6th of June, which gives you some idea of how close to the coast it was. So the whole situation was lost in the fighting in that sector. I don't know, of course, what happened to the killer herself, and the others from the hotel; I suppose they hid themselves until the Allies took over and then emerged as 'patriots' or whatever the designation was.

I can still see that little bedroom and the blood on the walls.

I see that this event had a deep impression on you.

I would like to take a break from this discussion…no, I am not saying stop the interview, but I am stressed.

Why? Because it is a shock, to see an officer of panzers assassinated in that way. That very calculated and cynical way. The damned

English must have been behind that act; that cynical way was the way that the English fought that war. We saw that at St Nazaire, and also when the British destroyed the French fleet in Algeria, and on so many other occasions. The British are the most calculating and cynical people on earth, that is my view. I make no apologies for stating it. I would rather deal with Americans, at least they are basically honest.

Can you explain why St Nazaire and Algeria are still in your mind when it comes to the British?

Why? At St Nazaire, those British laid a trap for our men, using a time bomb, and killed many unarmed Germans and French civilians, for no reason. In Algeria in 1940, the British Navy sank the entire French fleet in the harbour at Oran, before breakfast I believe, with no warning at all. The British killed two thousand French battleship sailors just like that, with no warning or anything. And these were the French sailors who were on the British side a few weeks before. I ask you, imagine if the German navy had done that. What would the reaction be? And yet today, nobody talks about the French fleet in Algeria. We are all too polite to remember it.

What was your experience of June 6th itself, the day of the invasion?

Let me get my thoughts collected…I would like to take a schnapps, Herrr Eckhertz, if you don't mind.

I would not wish this interview to distress you any further.

It is fine if I have a drink…like many veteran soldiers, I often drink when I recollect the things I have seen. This is perfectly normal, I believe.

You asked me about the 6th of June itself. I remember that after the killing at the hotel, the officer group moved its base to a camp in woodland towards the coast, and a new Hauptmann took over. I left them at that point, which was around four or five am, and I was assigned to traffic control at a crossroads about two kilometres inland. The light was just becoming grey, and we could see the sky overhead.

The amount of aircraft going over that sector was enormous, and all kinds of planes, too: transports, fighters and bombers. I could hear and feel explosions from the beach sector, and there was a lot of smoke in the sky over the sea. It was a damp kind of dawn on that day, with low clouds, and if you watched the horizon towards the coast you could see the low clouds actually flickering with the blast waves of all the detonations. Do you see what I mean? The clouds were actually moving with the energy of the explosions.

I remember thinking, 'My God, if even the clouds are affected, and if I can feel it through my boots from here, what is it like for those unlucky men on the beaches?'

You were thinking of the German soldiers? Not the Allied troops?

I was thinking of our men, yes.

But after about an hour of this, a lot of traffic began to stream back down the road from the coast. There were our trucks and wagons, and our soldiers driving civilian cars, and many of them on foot or on horses. It was a full retreat, I can tell you. I kept the crossroads open as well as I could, but of course those Allied planes came over very low, and bombed the whole road. There was nothing we could do except to throw ourselves in the ditches and hold on tight.

Those planes, I think they were the Thunderbolts, the ones with the big bodies…they dropped a horrible kind of bomb on the road. These bombs fell down from the air, and then they split open, like grenades. They were packed with metal fragments like ball bearings, and these metal things were screaming all over the place. If they hit a car, they would just rip it to pieces; I saw them blow up one of our armoured half-tracks, which was a superb vehicle, and the half-track was cut in half in a moment, like a toy. God help any man who was caught in that explosion. Even the horses were caught up in it, and there were pieces of horse flesh all over that road. I remember at that point, as I was looking out of the ditch, a squad of Russians came running down the road, shouting and yelling in Russian. It was chaos.

Who were these Russians?

These were the type of Russians that had come over to work for us, to serve in the German forces. I think they were mostly Ukrainians, and they were very anti-Stalin and anti-Polish in their views. I saw some of them in training before the invasion, and they were big fellows, but this bombing had panicked them completely. They were charging down this road, throwing away their guns, and arguing with each other about what to do. Some of them were wounded, and they were hobbling or limping along towards the crossroads.

Well, another one of these planes came over and used these bombs again with the ball bearings inside...most of those Russian fellows were cut to pieces in front of me, in the middle of the crossroads. One moment they were there, and the next minute I looked out of the ditch, and there were only clothes and bits of men with smoke coming from the pieces. It was like a butcher's slab, that road. The ones who survived ran like madmen, there was nothing I could do to hold them back.

Have you ever been under bombardment, Herr Eckhertz?

Yes, in the first war in France, against the French. But in the second war, I was never in combat, except being in the air raids on the cities.

Well, then you have seen something of it. It is a terrible thing to witness such destruction of human beings. For me, it was all the worse, because I had been in the first war in France, in 1918, when I was seventeen years old. What I saw on that crossroads was worse than anything I saw in the first war, believe me. Everyone who came through that crossroads was affected; men vomited and wept unashamedly. Women too, there were some of our female nurses and female logistical staff retreating through there in trucks. And with every minute, those planes came back and added more bodies, more smoke. It was only about nine or ten o'clock, and our infantry left the area in numbers, all moving to the South. I joined them, as there was nothing I could do any further.

I felt very helpless in all this; first because of the dead Hauptmann, and then because of all this bombing and the piles of dead. In the afternoon, I rejoined my field police unit, and we were pulled back behind a defensive line further inland.

What was your role there?

It was chiefly catching our stragglers, the men who were moving around without orders or having 'mislaid' their units. Some of these men were genuine, if you know what I mean, and they had been cut off from their units or misdirected. Others were trying to escape combat by going back to the rear, or they were trying to lie low and then surrender later on.

When an army is retreating, you get this big mixture of people, the front line troops, and rear echelon men, cooks, drivers, medics and all the rest of them, all churning around together in a mess. Some men take advantage of this and avoid their duties. We had to kick down the doors of barns and houses and pull these idlers out, and send them up to the front line. Most of them went, too, because very few wanted to face a field court martial.

Is that what happened to the men who didn't want to go?

A few of them refused to go to the line, and they were handed over to the command. It would have been better for them to take their chances with the Allies, frankly. The courts martial were held in a farm building nearby, and we could hear shooting in the courtyard at intervals, which meant the firing squads. Remember, this was still done under the original Wehrmacht punishment system, where there was a trial, or at least a hearing. After that summer, it changed to a 'mobile court martial' system where the field police officers could pick up anyone and have them shot immediately, without any kind of discussion.

This went on for all that day, and into the night, and all the time the shelling and bombing went on, and there was this constant flood of men and vehicles going into the line and coming out. On the second day, the Wednesday, some stronger units came up from inland and stabilised the line in that zone. We were withdrawn to the rear, and we slept like dead men in a barn full of straw. That was the deepest, longest sleep I have ever known.

May I go back to something you said, which is that you had already fought in the first war, in 1918. I would guess that you are a similar age to myself.

I was born in 1901, so I was seventeen when I fought in the first war, and forty-three in the second war at the time of the invasion. I didn't serve between the wars, of course; I was a civilian policeman until 1939.

What proportion of the combat troops on June 6th were aged in their forties?

It's difficult to say. I would guess about half were over forty years of age, or under eighteen. But that's a very rough guess. I'm talking there about the Static Divisions who were on the coast and took the weight of the first day. The inland units were made up of men of a more normal military age.

Among the men, like you, who had served in the first war, what was their attitude to serving again in the second war, do you think?

It was our duty to serve again. Our generation was not accustomed to hesitate over matters of duty, as you probably know. If the authorities said 'This is your duty,' then it had to be done. Of course, the regime took advantage of that willingness to serve, and, as we now know, the minds of many people, especially the young, were turned to evil things.

But while we are on the subject of that, don't forget that many French people served the German regime in this way as well; there were many young French in the Waffen SS, and the French civilian police worked closely with the German authority right up until the fall of France, as I saw myself on many occasions.

I realise now that in this respect, the second war was different from the first war. In the second war, the governments of Germany and France were more united, more closely linked.

That is a very controversial point to make. You say that Germany and France were 'united' in the Second World War?

No, I said that they were *more united than in the first war*. That is obvious, surely, if you think about the matter.

In the First World War, the government and the state of France remained at war with Germany for four years up until the 1918 armistice. In the Second World War, on the other hand, there was a very short period of nine months at the beginning, from September 1939 to July 1940, and then another nine month period at the end, after August 1944, in which the government and state of France was at war with us.

Do you understand? I am pointing out that from July 1940 to August 1944, which is almost the entire war, really, the French government supported and cooperated with Germany in all areas. And not just the French government, but the French state: the police, the civil service, the factories, the transports and all the rest of it.

This was why I said to you at the beginning that we were so suspicious and distrustful of the French civilians, because although their government was completely on our side, we knew from experience that the French people had minds of their own and did not always do as they were ordered. That is what happened in the hotel, and that is how our officer of panzers met his death in that hotel room…which I can still see today in my mind.

Herr Lange, it seems to me that the war has affected you deeply, and you seem to be angry about it still.

That's a polite way of telling me I shouldn't drink schnapps in the morning. I can see why you were a propaganda writer, you have a good way of putting things. But I am surely not the only person who drinks because of the war, am I? And I saw only a small part of the war, a tiny part. My God, what was it like for the others?

Your account has been very valuable for me to hear.

—

The Infantry in the Houses

**Helmut Voigt was a Grenadier (Rifleman) with
the 716ᵗʰ Static Infantry Division, based in the
Saint Aubin area, inland of Juno Beach.**

*Herr Voigt, you said to me that you were posted in the Normandy-Calvados
area at the time of the invasion. I remember visiting that zone in April
1944, and I saw many of the strong points dotted around there.*

I was fortunate enough, as I originally thought, to be assigned to
Normandy, yes.

At first, this seemed a piece of good fortune?

Of course. I felt very fortunate to be posted there. To be honest, my
friends mocked me and said it was because of my father, who was
very senior in a large German bank at the time. The fact was that
my father made loans available to German officers, or some kind
of affair like that. When I say 'officer,' I don't mean a Hauptmann
(*Captain*) but someone at General rank. But I'm sure that this had
no influence on my posting to France. I was classed as medically
unsuitable due to my eyesight and flat feet, and I was assigned to the
Static Infantry Divisions in France when I was seventeen. I arrived
in January 1944.

I felt rather guilty about this, because some of the boys my age who had similar physical shortcomings were sent to the front line in Italy or the Eastern Front. My mother would write and tell me, 'Do you remember so-and-so from the school, well, he has been killed in Italy.' And I would think, 'My God, I remember him from the school yard. That could have been me.'

Was it possible for German parents during the war to influence their sons' military postings at all?

No, I don't believe that was possible. Even Ribbentrop, that damned foreign minister of ours, the one who got us into the war, his son was on the Eastern front in a panzer, wasn't he? So I felt very lucky to be in France, and also a little guilty. But fate was being patient with me, of course, and my time to experience the war was approaching fast.

May I ask, what was your personal view of the war, its reasons and your role in it? What was your thinking at the time?

My father, being in the banking profession, had affected my thinking about the war completely. My father was very sympathetic to the National Socialist (*Nazi Party*) view of the world. In this view, a United Europe was trying to assert its independence and its very right to exist, against certain powerful international forces. America and the English were in an unholy alliance with the Bolsheviks, and it was these Russians who were orchestrating world events from Moscow. Moscow – that word! During the war, so many bad things were explained by saying that 'Moscow arranged it' or 'Moscow has done this to us.' Even when the Americans and the English bombed our cities, when they began destroying whole towns, the newspapers would often say this was done 'at the command of Moscow.'

From an economic perspective, my father said this was all connected to international finance, and the way that Moscow and the American banks wanted to take over the world. In 1944, I considered myself to be far more educated in these matters than my comrades, and I would sometimes give them small lectures about this angle, which they found interesting.

Since the war has ended, of course, I have come to believe the opposite of this, and I suspect that the Soviets actually had very little influence over the Western allies. Certainly, when you think how quickly the Americans and the Soviets became enemies, which happened within months of the end of the fighting in Europe, it is hard to believe that the Americans were interested in helping the Soviets at all. If they were, they surely could have bombed our German armies on the Eastern front as heavily as they bombed our cities – but they didn't do this.

Today, I think the reality was that the Americans and the English were *competing* with the Russians for control of Europe. The Normandy invasion, if you think about it like this, was the American and English way of keeping the Russians out of Western Europe! It was a way of stopping the Russians reaching the English Channel, which they certainly could have done with their huge armies. Russia could have started at Calais. Anyway, that is my personal view now.

Did you expect the Normandy invasion to come when it did?

There was no doubt in our minds, I think, that the Anglo-Americans and the De Gaulle French, who called themselves the Free French, would try to invade Western Europe while the summer weather lasted that year. And when I saw the very intensive preparations being made along our part of the Atlantic Wall in the early months of 1944, all the fortifications and the defences, it was clear that our leadership certainly expected an attack to come soon.

Having said that, the atmosphere was in some ways rather unreal in early 1944 in Normandy. Everything was so pleasant, the landscape and the weather and so on, that the war seemed unrelated to it. But as the weeks went by, and we built more fortifications, minefields, anti-tank traps and everything else that we were creating, we all felt that war was coming.

What was your role?

I was the loader in an anti-tank turret which was fixed onto a bunker in a fortified village, inland of the beaches near Saint Aubin. The village had been emptied of civilians before I arrived, and the houses were strengthened with concrete and extra brickwork, plus logs and earth mounds. These houses were quite hefty farmhouse buildings, with stone walls and narrow windows, and so they were very suitable to being adapted for defences. When I arrived, in January, there was a large team of International Workers pouring concrete into moulds to reinforce the ground floor walls, and digging several anti-tank ditches to the North of the place.

Who were the 'International Workers?'

Well, these were conscripted labourers who came from the Eastern countries. I think that a lot of them were Hungarian or Polish. I certainly did not envy them their task, as they dug and worked constantly, literally around the clock. In fact, the first deaths that I saw in the war were several of these men who unfortunately died while they were working, and they were buried in the bottom of an anti-tank ditch. That unsettled me greatly, seeing that human bodies could be disposed of in that way, but later in the war I saw that this was not limited to the labourers. German troops, too, were often buried in craters or trenches.

Who labelled them 'International Workers?'

The officers called them that. We also called them 'helpers' or 'Eastern Helpers,' I remember. But by February, these fellows were all taken away, and we occupied the fortified houses.

The idea of the houses was that the anti-tank ditches and minefields North of us, towards the beaches, would force any attacking tanks to come within range of our buildings. We would then fire on them with PAK guns sited in the ground floor of the houses, and with the tank turret on my bunker.

Your bunker with the tank turret was not a house?

No, it stood slightly back from the houses. It was an earth mound with a hollow concrete block inside it, reached through a doorway at the rear, and on top of this block was a tank turret. The turret was very, very old; I think it came from a pre-war Italian tank. It had a 50mm gun, which was quite weak, but the range was intended to be very short.

My role was to stand inside the hollow block and reload the gun. The shells were not heavy, I must say. The gunner was a Gefreiter (*Private First Class*) who was aged about forty and had a lot of experience with PAK guns.

The fortified houses had a 75mm gun and a 37mm gun on wheeled carriages aiming through slits in the ground floors. The houses also had two platoons of infantry who had to fire guns and Panzerfausts (*disposable anti-tank rockets*) through loop holes in the walls. It was a good design, because I could understand the way that the enemy tanks would have to steer away from the obstacles and come onto our guns.

Our area was part of the 'Satan's Garden,' which was what we called the beach and coast defences. I felt quite confident that we could hold back enemy armour for long enough to allow the inland panzer reserves to come up and counterattack against the enemy. This was the idea, that we were a way of holding back an advance, to give our own forces time to move up behind us and push them out of France.

What kind of training did you have?

We were well trained on the guns, and on small arms and use of the Panzerfausts. We were all trained on the different guns, in case we had to change roles, and we were taught in theory how to defeat tanks at close range with grenades and gasoline bombs, although we had no practical experience of this.

At the same time, work was going on all around us, with the minefields being extended and more ditches being dug so that the whole 'Satan' area was strongly fortified. We were very proud to be part of the famous Atlantic Wall, which was being featured very strongly in newsreels and in the press at the time, of course – as you yourself know so well. When I had a few days leave at home, my little sister asked me, 'How high is this wall? How long is it?' As if it was the Great Chinese Wall! Of course, I was forbidden from explaining to her any details, and so I told her it was a very high wall indeed.

And what was your involvement in the events
of June 6th? How did it begin?

It started on the night of the 5th, which I think was quite humid and damp. Yes, it was a bit rainy, I recall that well. We were woken and moved at about four am from our sleeping barracks, in one of the houses, to take up our gunnery positions. The soldiers we were replacing weren't allowed to sleep, they were sent off to man slit trenches nearby.

The officer told us that an attack was expected, either from the coast or even from inland. This rather worried us, because all our training was based on shooting at tanks coming from the coastal zone. We had not practised shooting behind us, into the inland zone. In fact, I'm not sure that the turret on the bunker even rotated all the way around.

There was a huge amount of bombing happening to the South West, and a lot of noise of planes overhead. I only had a brief impression of this, because I went quickly down into the bunker when the other crew came out, and I prepared the gun with the gunner. The noise was a bit muffled in there, and to light our work we had an electric torch with a red bulb. The red bulb was so that it would not affect our night vision if we went outside at night into the dark. That worked well; you could have the red torch on in the bunker, and then go out into the dark, and you could see in the dark.

When it got towards dawn, there began to be heavy bombing or shelling close to us, to the North. These explosions were big enough to shake the ground under the bunker. I had not been under attack before, and so this was very alarming for me. I knew that my turret bunker was the most secure of the fortifications in our strong point, and so I felt sorry also for the men in the fortified houses.

My gunner, who was a professional man and very calm, urged me to concentrate on having the ammunition to hand. He told me that he could see flashes and explosions for a long distance in front. Truly, to be confined in that concrete box, unable to see out, feeling these huge impacts close to us, that was a frightening time for me. At about six am, the explosions grew closer, and began striking very close. I think that these were shells from warships at sea, because there was a rushing noise, not a whistling noise like aerial bombs. This rushing sound would come, and then the whole bunker would shake and move. I could actually hear debris crashing into the tank turret; this made a sound like hammers striking the steel.

In my mind, I had always imagined shrapnel as small pieces of metal, but some of these impacts were enormous. That turret rang almost like a bell, making a ringing sound that hurt my ears painfully. Again and again these hammer blows came, and even the gunner was silent and tense, and he began praying in between the blasts. Just as he finished a prayer, we were hit directly on the bunker. This was a shock which stunned me. Pieces of concrete fell on me, and I am not embarrassed to say that I threw myself on the bunker floor and covered my head. I had trouble breathing, because the blast wave had knocked the air from my lungs, even through the walls of the bunker. I stayed like that for some time. My ears were affected, and all the sounds were like being underwater.

I looked up to see if the gunner was alright, and to my amazement the whole turret was gone. The complete steel structure had been blown off the concrete, with the gun and the gunner himself. There was just the hole, open to the sky. Up in the sky, I could see red flashes and white explosions which looked like stars. Everything was exploding, everything. I waited in the ruins of the bunker while all this went on above me, on the ground up there.

What were your thoughts in the bunker?

Well, I had my carbine, and I had intentions of going out to help the men in the houses, which was my task if the bunker was knocked out. But it was impossible to venture out with all the explosions. Then a large piece of shrapnel came into the bunker, through the rear door, and hit the wall behind me. This metal was red hot, and I threw fire-sand on it to stop it setting off all the ammunition. This made me think that in fact I was sitting on a gigantic bomb, and if a piece of debris did fly in and blow up a shell, I would be finished anyway. So I crawled out of the bunker door with my helmet and carbine.

Outside, I saw the turret upside down about twenty metres away, and the body of my gunner near it. He was horribly shattered, even today it distresses me to remember the state of him. He was broken like a doll. I was sick at this sight, and I ran around the bunker to the front, to the houses. By now it was daylight, I think it was about six thirty am, but my watch wasn't working. I saw that one of the fortified houses was destroyed, but the other one was still standing. The bombardment was lessening, and I ran into the house to offer help. This was the house with the 37mm PAK gun. The men in there were crouching by the firing slits and watching the coastal zone. There was a telephone, but it wasn't working.

The most senior man there was a Feldwebel (*Sergeant*) and we followed his orders. We aimed our guns through the slits, and we waited for any enemies to approach from the coast, in the area between the ditches. Some of us were shaking, and the Feldwebel kept up a constant stream of encouraging words to sustain us. We waited like that, very tense and anxious, for what seemed like ages. The light came up, and it got well into the morning, and all we could see between us and the beaches was smoke and flashes of explosions…the waiting was awful. One of our men lost his nerve completely, and began shouting that he wanted to leave the house, and the Feldwebel was ordering him to shut his mouth. Just as he was speaking, there was a great roar overhead, and that whole house seemed to explode around us.

I saw that planes were passing over head, and they were dropping small bombs onto us from under their wings. I think these were Hurricane class planes, but they moved so quickly that I couldn't see properly. The bombs which they dropped as they came towards us flew out from under their wings and came skidding towards our house across the fields. I saw five or six of these bombs bouncing towards us and tumbling over in the air as they came. There was no time for any of us to react.

The bombs hit the house, and they exploded on the stone walls. The noise and shock wave was devastating; more powerful than the shelling, I think. Part of the house collapsed and buried some of the men at one end. I could see some of them moving under the rubble, but there was nothing we could do to help them. I looked around for the Feldwebel, and saw that he had been killed by a large wooden splinter, which had gone through his eye and into his head. We pulled his body out of the way – there was nothing else to do.

The PAK gun was still working, being behind the reinforced concrete slabs, and the gun crew had it ready again in minutes. We had been told that when a bombardment stops, the enemy are very close, and this was the case, as the men said that they could hear tank sounds from beyond the fields. I myself could not hear this, as my hearing was damaged, and in fact with my poor eyesight I was not much of a soldier. But I helped the gun crew have the Stielgranate (*explosive cap*) ready for the 37mm.

What was the explosive cap?

These were large projectiles that fitted onto the front of the gun barrel and were driven by a shell fired from the breech. The projectiles had a Panzerfaust type of warhead, and they were said to be highly effective against tanks, as they had a shaped charge. Do you know what that means?

It is a type of warhead which flattens itself against a tank's armour, in the manner of a Panzerfaust or the American bazooka.

That's right. So all you had to do with this weapon was to hit the enemy tank at some point on its surface, and the shaped charge would send a shock wave through the steel plate and blast pieces of the metal off the other side, into the tank. This was the idea. We did not have long to wait to see if it worked, in fact. We could hear a lot of shooting and detonations from the coast, and shortly we saw a Sherman class panzer come through the target area. This happened just as we had been told it would.

What was your feeling on seeing this enemy tank?

I was very surprised at its appearance. It was wet, and dripping with water, and steam was coming off it, I suppose from the hot engine. I could not understand why it was dripping wet, but afterwards I learned that the Allies used amphibious tanks on that beach. Frankly, if someone had asked me before that day, 'Is it possible to make a heavy tank float and swim, and then climb onto land and start fighting?' I would have laughed at the idea. I had no concept that this was even possible. This is why I was puzzled at the sight of this Sherman.

At the same time, I began to shake with excitement and fear, and I am not ashamed to confess that my bladder was weak for a moment. I cannot be the only soldier in history to have had that experience, I am sure.

I can assure you, Herr Voigt, I have spoken to many other veterans who had similar experiences in action.

Well, so it is normal, then. Such is the experience of the infantryman, who is a fragile human being under his uniform. But this

Sherman advanced on us very quickly, perhaps believing that our house was completely knocked out.

In an instant, the PAK gunner fired off the projectile, and we saw this large, bulbous warhead fly off to the tank. It hit the tank straight on the front plate, low down, and it exploded. It was just as we had been trained to do. The Sherman gave a great jolt and lurched from side to side. I was astonished that it was so simple to knock out the famous Sherman tank. I began to have wild thoughts that we could knock out many more, perhaps dozens of them...The Sherman began to emit smoke, and the turret hatches opened. Two men came out, and they appeared to be badly wounded and covered in soot.

I am sorry to say that one of our men shot them with machine gun fire from a MG42, which was a very accurate and powerful gun. This caused an argument among us, because some of our boys shouted that this was the wrong thing to do, and others were shouting that we must kill all the enemy troops in whatever way possible. This argument did not help the two Sherman crew men, because they were lying dead on top of their tank as it caught fire.

The speed at which that Sherman burned was remarkable, within a minute or so, there was an absolute column of fire coming up from the back of it. It shook from side to side, which I suppose was all the ammunition exploding within the hull. Barely two minutes after we had fired on it, the whole machine was invisible inside a wall of flames. However, we had provoked the enemy, and revealed our position to them, and they responded quickly.

We began to take high explosive strikes, which I think came from tanks beyond the ditches which we could not see through the flames and smoke. Most of these shells went wide, but several hit our house, and began to knock it to pieces around us. The strengthening of this house was all on the walls, not the ceilings, and so there was nothing to stop the shrapnel and masonry crashing down onto us below. Several men were crushed by falling blocks of stone, as if this was a medieval battle. If anyone was wounded, there was nothing to be done for them, nothing at all. They just lay there on the floor, crying out.

Was there any leadership or direction?

No; the Feldwebel was dead, and we were all basic soldiers. We also had no way of communicating with our company command, which was to our rear, so we were completely isolated. When the shelling paused, a few of our men jumped out through the firing slits and raised their hands in surrender, shouting that they did not want to fight any more. These men were blown up with a high explosive shell; I don't know whether this was a deliberate shot to kill men as they surrendered, or just bad luck. But the rest of us then resolved *not* to surrender, as we saw the bodies of those men lying literally in front of us, with smoke coming from their skin.

We saw no more tanks approaching us, but we heard the sounds of tanks moving to our East. This seemed to indicate that the enemy advance was going around our position, and moving inland that way. The morning continued, with a constant mass of aircraft going overhead, and explosions in the fields around us, but our fortified house seemed to be forgotten by both sides.

It was only at about midday that an officer, a Leutnant from the Company command, came over to us with a handful of fresh troops. He told us that we were now in a pocket which was almost surrounded by the Allies, and that similar pockets existed all along the coast, because the enemy was deliberately bypassing resistance points that were not a threat to the direction they wanted to take. He said that these pockets were steadily being 'mopped up' by the supporting Allied tanks and infantry.

He was a very professional officer, we trusted him, and he ordered us to remain defending our house. We thought that he would then leave, but he stayed with us in the PAK position, and he had a field telephone on a cable reel that his men unwound, so we could see that he was in contact with the command. This gave us reassurance that we were not forgotten. His men also brought some rations, ammunition and medical kits.

How long did you remain defending this house?

This strange phase went on for about another hour. I say strange, because we could hear the Allies overhead and hear their tanks, but nobody came to fight with us. The Leutnant told us to be ready for action at any moment, because surely the enemy would deal with us soon.

Sure enough, around one pm, we were bombed again by the enemy Jabos. They bombed us in the same way, making their little bombs skid towards us across the fields. But these bombs were not explosive, they were filled with an incendiary material which burned with a very bright, pale flame and expanded in the air. These bursts of fire exploded on all the houses, and on our house some of this burning stuff shot in through the apertures and loopholes. This burning chemical was a horrible weapon, an absolute nightmare.

This was the incendiary that used phosphorous or magnesium?

Yes, I found out from some of our medics later that this was a phosphorous weapon. Our medics found it very difficult to treat people who were burned with this chemical, because the stuff ate its way through their flesh and entered their bones and internal organs. It was like an acid in that way, like a corrosive acid. I didn't know this when the bombs exploded; all I saw was a very bright flash, as bright as a flash bulb on a camera but much longer lasting.

I saw lines of this white material fly in through the loophole slits where some of the men had set up their rifles. This stuff was like a burning powder, it is difficult to describe it exactly…I jumped back, but several of the men at the loopholes were caught by it. As soon as it touched them, it set their uniforms on fire. Some men were hit in the face as well, and they went around in a terrible way, clutching their faces, and screaming. It was a terrible scene, and we did not know how to stop this stuff burning. Even when the men rolled on the floor, or if we tipped sand over them from the sandbags, even then the stuff kept burning inside their skin. Some of these men were on fire inside their bodies.

I must pause for a moment, Herr Eckhertz, because this memory distresses me, and I have not spoken about this to anyone until now, not even to my wife.

Would it be better to leave this part? We could go on to a later part of the day. Or we could stop the interview; perhaps that would be better.

No, now that I have started to describe this, I want to tell you what happened.

The fact is that this phosphorous chemical went inside some of the men's bodies, I think because they inhaled it as they struggled around. This stuff was burning them from inside, in their throat and lungs. It was actually setting fire to them from inside.

The shrieks and cries that these men gave out were unbelievable, and there was nothing to be done for them. One man was absolutely convulsing in pain, and his mouth and nose were exhaling a white smoke as the chemical burned him up. The Leutnant took a rifle and smashed him on the back of the head with the stock, to knock him unconscious. That was a merciful thing to do, because the poor man then died in a state of unconsciousness.

While all this was going on, we were in chaos inside the house, and we didn't see the situation outside. Finally, someone shouted, 'Panzers out there!' The Allies had sent three tanks up to our house to finish us off, and these tanks were now surrounding us. These were Sherman type tanks. The PAK crew fired on them with the explosive cap round, but the one they fired did not hit the Sherman properly, it deflected off the edge of the hull and went flying off into one of the other wrecked houses. Just a moment after that, the Shermans began firing on our house with high-explosive rounds. They had their gun barrels lowered right down, and they just stood there, about fifty metres away, and fired down into the house. The PAK gun was blown up straight away. I was hit by shrapnel from this explosion, and my uniform was ripped off my chest so that I was partly naked.

This was the end of the resistance point in that house, as you can imagine.

Did the men try to fight back?

It was not really possible. The house was on fire, and we only had four men still able to fight, including me and the Leutnant. One of the troops had the MG42, and he fired this from an aperture; he was shouting out that there were enemy troops approaching outside. He was a brave man, that man with the machine gun, because he stayed there firing on the enemy even though the house was being blown up around him. One of the panzers fired directly on him, I think, because the walls around him exploded, and he was thrown back onto us in the house. He literally landed on top of us, and he was completely shattered from the explosion. We had to get out from under all the parts of his body, which were all over us. Even the Leutnant was shaken by this, and he ordered us to leave through the rear door.

Were you planning to surrender, or to escape?

My intention was just to get away from the enemy. I was not sure what would happen if we tried to surrender. So we charged out through the back exit and ran out into the rear area, which was an open yard fortified with earth and sandbags. As soon as we came out, we rushed straight into a squad of enemy soldiers who were jumping in over the earth walls. This was a great shock to me, as it meant we were surrounded and completely cut off.

What was your impression of the enemy troops, face to face?

To be honest, they terrified me.

They were very large men, powerfully built, and their faces were completely emotionless. I saw, I think, half a dozen of these men taking aim at us with the sub machine guns called Sten guns. They had brown uniforms, and from that I thought they were English, although it turned out that they were Canadians. I recall their faces now, I can still see them in front of me, just as I can see you, Herr Eckhertz. They were very calm, not at all excited, just as if they were doing a job. Of course, this *was* their job, but the way they acted was very methodical, very cool. The Leutnant, who was next to me, raised his machine pistol at them, and they shot him down immediately.

That was it as far as I was concerned. I dropped down my rifle and raised my hands. One of the other German men was slow to do this, and they shot him down as well. The way they did this was also very methodical – not in anger or fury, if you understand me, but purely in a mechanical way. Shooting us meant nothing to them, it was just a job.

The end result was that the house behind us simply collapsed, and I was taken prisoner together with one remaining comrade, whose name I did not even know.

Was this the end of your fighting on June 6th?

That terrible day, which was so full of shocks and dangers, was not over for me at all. The time was about one pm or later. The situation around the houses was very confused. Although our resistance point was destroyed, we could hear a lot of shooting and firing from the South, where I knew there were other points. The Canadians who captured us went on in this direction, following their tanks. We two surviving Germans were left under guard of two Canadian troops who kept us with our hands on our heads, facing away from them. They did give us a drink of water and a cigarette, though. All around there were noises of vehicles and men shouting in English. I do not speak English, and I did not understand what they were planning to do with us. This went on for five or ten minutes.

Then there was a huge burst of firing from nearby. I could hear bullets flying through the air, and there were explosions of grenades or small bombs. I thought, 'What the devil is happening now? Will this never end?'

I thought that by surrendering I would be out of the battle, but I realised that it does not work so smoothly! I was still on the battle-field, but now without a gun. I crouched down to protect myself, and I looked around at our guards.

To my horror – and I do mean that I felt horror – the two guards had been hit by the gunfire. One was obviously dead, and one was wounded and unable to move.

I don't know where these bullets came from, or even if they were German or Allied in origin. But now my German comrade and I were terrified of being discovered with these two shot men, in case we were accused of having somehow killed them. What were we to do? We discussed it quickly, and my comrade urged me to join him in running off to the German positions to the South. He said that he was going with me or without me, and he took the machine pistol from the dead Leutnant and began to run off towards the South.

Well, I decided to go with him, because he seemed a capable man and I thought that if I was found alone with the two Canadians things would go badly for me. In retrospect, what I should have done was to stay with the Canadians and tend to the wounded one, by giving him first aid and finding him some morphine and so on. I should have done that, because it would have shown the Canadians that I was a humane person. But my head was spinning with all these experiences, I was scared of being alone there, and so I took a German rifle and followed my comrade to the South.

This must have been a dangerous journey for you.

It was a foolish journey to make. Everything in that zone was in disorder and confusion. We realised that the fighting was certainly not over, because we could see Sherman tanks firing and lines of Canadian troops following them. We took cover beside a hedge-row along a road that led South, and we ran along there towards our lines. We aimed for a point that was South, but away from the

Shermans. I knew this area well, and I knew that we had a resistance point with a dug-in panzer on a ridge down there, which was connected by sunken paths to the inland German forces.

I had the idea that we could get to those paths and get into the German zone again. But there was a great deal of firing all around, and Jabo planes coming over very low, firing towards the German lines.

At one point, we took cover in a ditch, and we found two other Germans who were equally lost, who had escaped from a bunker on the coast itself. These men were full of stories about the amazing weapons that the Allies were using: swimming tanks, and tanks that carried bridges, and battleships that could come onto the land, and that kind of thing. They were quite hysterical about all of this; the assault had affected them mentally very badly. They had rifles, but they refused to move and they were waiting for the battle to die down.

We left them, but we were very worried about these wonder weapons that the Allies had invented. Why hadn't the German army developed these machines? We were still muttering about this when we came in sight of the dug-in panzer on the ridge.

What kind of panzer was this?

This was some old French panzer, the type we captured early in the war. It was embedded in an emplacement, protected by mines and infantry in trenches. It was there to stop the enemy using the ridge to observe the area inland. I can only think that the Allies had such air superiority that they did not need to capture this position in the first hours of their attack, but they opted to push past it, relying on aircraft reconnaissance. Or possibly the ridge was too small as a feature to be important to them. Whatever the reason, the panzer emplacement was still there, and as we squinted at it (it was about one kilometre away) it seemed to be undamaged.

We took shelter under the hedgerow and observed it for a minute. We formed the impression that the area to one side of it was still in German hands, and so it marked the boundary, if you see what I mean, of the Allied invasion at that point. If we could get to it and enter the German lines, we would be among our friends again. The problem was – how to get to it? The area in front of it was mined, and if we showed ourselves out of the hedgerow, we were likely to be shot in all the confusion by both the Allies and the Germans.

As the minutes went past, we were joined by another German soldier, an engineer, who had retreated from a point near our fortified houses. We were also joined by a French civilian man, who was simply an ordinary farmer who had been caught in the open by the attack and was scared to leave the hedgerow for fear of being shot. This fellow was aged in his fifties, and he seemed close to collapse from all the anxiety he was suffering. We really didn't know what to do with him or where he should go.

The engineer soldier had a flare pistol, and he said that by firing a green flare this would alert the Germans at the panzer emplacement that we were on their side; green smoke was the sign at that point for friendly forces. I pointed out that this would only attract attention to us and draw the Allies onto our location.

While we were debating this, the fields were strafed by Typhoon Jabo aircraft that were firing cannon. These cannon shells were devastating; they tore up big clods of earth from the ground and dug deep holes. The thought of those shells hitting your body - that was awful. We could only lie flat under the hedge and watch the planes going over us. The noise was terrible, with the screaming sound of the engines and the exploding noise of the shells hitting the earth. I don't know if the Typhoon had some kind of air siren, as the old Stuka originally did, for psychological effect. It certainly sounded like that to me. Maybe it was just the engine noise, but it was very intimidating, very frightening. I feel sorry for anyone who had to experience a Stuka attack, I can say that from my heart.

After that, another wave of Typhoons came in. The sheer number of planes that the Allies had available was incredible to us. There seemed to be no end to these planes, and still we had seen no Luftwaffe planes at all. This second wave of planes fired rockets, and they fired them down at the panzer emplacement. The rockets streaked down right above us, and exploded all along the ridge where the emplacement was. They kept exploding, and I could hear shrapnel flying around even at a distance of a kilometre. The shrapnel made a hissing and buzzing sound as it flew out.

That old panzer was completely knocked to pieces by the rockets. It just disappeared in all the explosions, and there was nothing left except smoke. In all this noise and shooting, I am sorry to relate that the French civilian collapsed died there where he lay. I imagine that he suffered a heart attack or some similar condition. It is impossible for civilians to be under such a bombardment, simply impossible.

What did you do with the body of this man?

There was nothing to be done; we left him where he was. That was the way of things in the war, I am sorry to say.

Did you manage to get back to German lines that day?

We waited until the late afternoon. There was constant firing and shooting, and many more aircraft going overhead. Our intention was to run out after dark, and try to make it to the paths behind the ridge which led to our inland forces. We still wanted to rejoin our army, and the risk in surrendering seemed very great. We only had a little water in our canteens, and as we lay there I personally felt feverish, I think from all the things I had seen and experienced. I was trembling a lot. Finally we crept up to the end of the hedgerow, near to the destroyed panzer. The engineer who was now with us said that he knew a path around the edge of the minefield, and we should take this track just as the light faded.

When it was deep dusk, the sky was still lit up with flares and flashes of explosions, and a very heavy gun, perhaps from a naval ship, was firing over us towards the inland zone. Those shells going overhead made a roaring sound. All the light and noise made us confused, I think, and the engineer, who was guiding us, took the wrong way into the minefield and was blown up by a land mine. It was one of our anti-personnel mines, which were a very nasty device because they injured the lower body but often did not kill the person outright.

That was a terrible moment. The engineer had his legs blasted away, but he was still alive and conscious. He was unable to move, and he tried to call out to us not to follow him into the minefield. He was lying on his back, with his legs missing, and although the light from the flares was not like day, I could see that the ground all around him was dark with blood. His clothing was giving off smoke from the explosion. I saw that he tried to pull out his pistol, possibly to shoot himself, but he did not complete this action. He slowly went still in front of us. That was the end of that man, who had tried to help us.

Now my comrade and I were completely trapped. We could not get through the minefield, and there were Canadians all around us. We decided to surrender, and we stayed still with our hands up in the air. The mine explosion must have got their attention, because in a few minutes a vehicle appeared near the hedgerow. This was the small, tracked vehicle which the British used. They were everywhere, these little things, all the time.

They called it the Universal Transporter or something like that.

Was that its name? Well, it was a very good vehicle. This transporter came up, with two soldiers in it. They fired a machine gun over our heads, and we shouted in German that we wanted to surrender. They took us on the transporter down to the coastal area, and handed us over to their Military Police. That was the end of things for us.

How were you treated as prisoners of war?

The Canadians were always very professional. If I was going to recruit soldiers today, I would start with Canadians. We were put into a house under guard and we were given water and biscuits, which we consumed ravenously, as we hadn't eaten all day.

This house was full of German prisoners: artillery men, drivers, infantry and all kinds of administrative troops. The Canadians were holding prisoners in there before interrogating them and leading them away.

When I was interrogated, the officer asked me about the battle at the fortified house and what I knew about it. I was very worried about this, because those two guards had been shot, and possibly the Canadians were going to link me to the shooting, especially as I had escaped because of that, even though I didn't even see them being shot. I began to deny being at the house at all, but in my bewildered state I made a very poor liar, I think, and I began to shake and stammer.

The Canadian officer who was interrogating me stood up and pointed his pistol at my head. He placed it right here, on my forehead, and he was closer to me than you are now, Herr Eckhertz. He told me to tell him the facts, and so I broke down and told him what happened, very quickly.

That night, they put me in a cellar room under a guard, and in the room next to mine I could hear some poor German fellow being beaten up by the interrogators. They were really pounding him, I can tell you. I think he was a Waffen SS man, and they were demanding to know about the SS locations, and this went on for a long time.

In the morning, they took me in front of that officer again, and he had with him one of the men who had guarded me when I surrendered at the fortified house. This was the man who had been wounded, and he was there to identify me. I could not follow their conversation, but the Canadian man spoke to the officer and it seemed that the officer was satisfied with my explanation, because I had been honest about the events.

I have no doubt that those Canadians would have killed me right there and then if they thought I was lying. I'm sure they would have shot me.

And yet you said that you admired the Canadians,
that you would recruit them yourself?

Yes, of course. They knew how to use violence, when to start it and stop it. I was impressed by all this. They were always very professional. To be quite frank with you, having been a prisoner of the Canadians, I would like one day to live in Canada. Of course, that will never be possible for me now. But it is just the way I feel.

Were you a prisoner of the Canadians for long?

I was transferred to American custody, and eventually they put me on one of their ships. I was on this ship for several weeks, firstly in harbour in England, and then going across the Atlantic to America to be held as a prisoner there. This ship was very cramped, and we were all very sick, as none of us had been on the ocean before. That voyage went on for about ten or twelve days in the end. I ended up in a prisoner of war camp in Idaho.

How were you treated?

This is very strange to recall...the fact is that we were all astonished at how well we were treated. The food was superb. Every day there was corn, bread rolls, tinned meat and potatoes. Every day, Herr Eckhertz! I don't mean on Sunday, you understand. And this was in 1944. And we were prisoners...it was almost madness. Every mouthful I ate in the USA was a guilty privilege, if you know what I mean. So many other people were going hungry, or were starving.

I thought all the time of my parents, who I knew were living on almost nothing in the Reich; and since the war ended I have read about the poor people in Holland who were almost starved because of the Allies cutting them off in the war.

Were you treated well in other respects?

The Americans who guarded the camp were friendly. They gave us this excellent food, and they let us organise ourselves, by groups and ranks. But we were not allowed to work, as I believe prisoners in England were allowed to work.

We offered to work. We offered to repair things in the nearest town, and work on civilian machinery, but we were not allowed to. The strange thing was that many people in that town were of German descent. We knew this because some of our men went there to get medical treatment, and they saw store fronts with German names and newspapers with German-sounding names in the articles. But we were never allowed to help in that town.

*Why did you want to help? Did the Americans
really need assistance in the local town?*

Oh, no…it was because of the boredom we suffered, because of the boredom of being behind the wire all the time. And, to be frank, many of our men had hopes of being allowed to settle in America after the war, because by the end of 1944, early 1945, we all knew the war must be ending soon. Many of us hoped that the authorities would let us assimilate into America.

But that changed when the films came across the Atlantic and were shown everywhere. The films changed many things.

The films? What films are these?

I mean, the newsreel films of the camps, the concentration camps.

You have seen these films, just as we all have. I remember when the films arrived, we were brought into the mess hall one morning, this was in May 1945, just after the war ended, and we had to watch the film. I think it was called '*This Was Your Germany*' or '*This Was Germany.*' It was specifically made to be shown to German people. They were showing it all over Germany, in every town and village. It went on for about thirty minutes, all the things from Dachau and Belsen and those camps.

When the film ended, the American guards refused to speak to us, or even to *look* at us. Even the guards who had been friendly and helpful, they refused to look at us. They just shouted commands and locked us in the camp with the food. There was some kind of regulation that said we had to be given food, and they could not break this regulation, apparently.

> *What emotion did you experience on see-*
> *ing the films of the concentration camps?*

Some of us said that it was a hoax. Most of us knew, I think, deep down, that it was true, and that this was what the regime of the Third Reich was capable of doing.

One man, who had also been in Normandy, said to me, 'Is that why we fought, then?' That was the question. Was that why we fought all those years?

Because we were soldiers being ordered to do our duty, and our duty was for nothing if it was to defend all of that in the films. It left us very confused, and also very betrayed. And all of the time, the Americans, who now refused to speak to us, kept giving us more food than we could eat, because of their regulations. We had no appetite, but the Americans kept giving us food.

That was a strange time, and a time which showed us more than ever the resources which the Allies had.

> *Herr Voigt, thank you for being so candid in*
> *your account to me of your experience.*

You know very well that I was one of the lucky ones. We should ask God that our children will not have these experiences.

THE AIRBORNE TROOPS

Gert Hoffmann was a Festungswerkmeister (Fortification Development Officer) attached to the 352nd Artillery Regiment, 352nd Infantry Division, in the sector of Carentan on the Southern Cotentin peninsula, inland from the American Omaha beach.

Herr Hoffmann, when we spoke on the telephone last week, you told me that you had encountered the first American airborne troops on June 6th itself. I am very keen to hear of your experience. But can you explain what your role was in the Atlantic Wall?

Listen…if you want to take away a completely accurate and factual account of what I saw, I must first clarify that the phrase 'Atlantic Wall' is itself rather misleading. There certainly was a 'wall' along the North East coast of France, around the Pas de Calais, where there were enormous concrete bunkers and gun emplacements, the kind that featured regularly in the articles that you and your colleagues used to write. If you go to Calais today, you will still see our bunkers above the town. Most of those bunkers were overrun from the rear, from inland, of course, as the Allies spread out in that direction.

But the further West you went, the less substantial the fortifications became, because the Western area, including Normandy and Brittany, was not originally considered a likely site for an invasion. Up until the autumn of 1943, the Normandy defences were quite simple, being mostly small bunkers, minefields, anti-tank barricades and so on, with a few larger concrete emplacements. Many of the smaller bunkers were actually civilian stone barns or houses, which had been reinforced and fortified, not at all like those massive concrete blockhouses of the Pas de Calais zone.

It was when General Rommel was put in charge of the Atlantic Wall that the Normandy area began to be more heavily reinforced with more barricades, anti-tank ditches, much bigger bunker structures and so on. But this process was not finished when the invasion came, which was very fortunate for the Allies. We had many other plans for the Normandy coast which were only just coming to fruition.

I understand from your remarks that you were
involved in the construction of the defences?

Yes. I was a Fortress Officer of the Divisional artillery. Our role was vitally important, although today it is largely forgotten. We humble Wehrmacht engineers and builders have been eclipsed by the panzer men and the infantry and all the rest.

I spoke a few weeks ago to a Wehrmacht engineer who was in
the Courselles sector. He gave me a very interesting description
of his attempts to use a 'Goliath' type machine on the beach
there. Were you involved in similar programmes?

Not with the Goliath system. My role was in the creation of zones of fire on a large scale. This meant that we found ways of altering the landscape of the battlefield, using mounds, ditches and other means, in order to influence the way that an enemy attack, especially an armoured attack, would progress inland.

We have to be honest today and say that the function of the coastal defences, I mean the emplacements on the shoreline itself, on the sea wall, was only to slow down an attack and give time for the alert to be sounded and a counterattack to be implemented. Of course, the infantry men inside those sea wall emplacements didn't know this! On the contrary, they were told repeatedly that their mission was to drive the enemy back into the sea, to prevent them moving off the beaches, that not one enemy boot must step past the shore line, and so on. But this was purely to motivate them. We could hardly tell those boys on the sand, 'You're only there to slow the Allies down.'

It was expected that, at least in the first few hours, a determined Allied attack using armour would progress inland. In fact, it would be better if it *did* progress some small distance: this would bring large volumes of troops and armour into a prepared zone where they could be surrounded and ground down. This would destroy the enemy's capability and also, very importantly, deter future attacks.

Was this the official strategy?

Of course it was, at least from spring 1944 onwards. If anyone tells you, '*The Wehrmacht expected to defeat the invasion on the beaches, the Germans expected to halt the Allies right there on the sand*' – don't believe them, please. That would be a foolish objective for a defending army to have. We in the Wehrmacht were not foolish. My God, we had learned from our own mistakes by then.

You see, this was a bitter lesson which we learned in several places, but above all at the battle of Kursk in Russia in 1943. You may know the story of Kursk? Well, at Kursk we made the dreadful mistake of allowing the Soviets enough time to prepare a *defence in depth* against our panzer formations. Those Russian engineers took over a zone of ten thousand square kilometres, and they built a huge series of traps for our armour, with endless ditches, forts, traps, minefields and so on.

None of these defences was insurmountable by itself, and over several days they were finally overcome, but the cumulative effect was to bog down our panzers, and turn them from a thrusting attack force into a slow or static target.

The Russians showed us how to defeat an armoured attack properly! Not with a single line of fortifications, as the French tried to do with their absurd Maginot Line in 1940, but by taking a whole geographic zone and making it into a swamp for panzer forces, a swamp for men and vehicles. Making the entire landscape into a swamp for the invaders. That was what we planned to do in Normandy, in the absence of a true shoreline 'Atlantic Wall.'

It was very fortunate for the invaders that they came in early June; if they had waited until late June, we would have had these defences in a much stronger state to entangle them.

Can you give an example of how you planned to 'alter the landscape' as you said, to build defences?

Yes, this was more complex than it might sound. You could not make these defensive systems too simple; for example, you could not place two minefields with a narrow lane between them, and hope that the enemy would come charging through the safe lane, because the enemy would very obviously suspect a trap. It was more that we had to change the topography of the land to influence their advance, to manipulate their progress.

An example...yes, an example would be the landscape we created around the base of the Cotentin Peninsula. There, we opened the canal sluices and we flooded a wide area of fields to a depth of two metres, which panzers cannot cope with. Then, we placed a series of incendiary barges along one side; these were river craft fitted with burning material which would explode as the enemy approached, deterring them from trying to ford the water. We created a lane around one side which could be used to cross the floods, defended lightly so that the enemy would think they were fighting their way through.

As the enemy came out of this, they would be faced with an anti-tank ramp system camouflaged by nets, which would hold up their panzers as they broke through. Onto this zone, we had Nebelwerfer (*rocket mortar*) batteries calibrated to fire on the stranded vehicles. Any panzers that finally crossed the ramps would become caught up in a system of bunkers armed with PAK guns, firing down a slope. And so on, and so on.

The enemy would find himself with a long, thinly spread spearhead of armour which grew less powerful with each phase, very vulnerable to being isolated and ground down. This was all very closely based on what the Russians had done to us at Kursk. Now, if you multiply this by the dozens of such traps that we were preparing over hundreds of square kilometres, you see how difficult it would be for the invaders to advance. They would become bogged down and trapped within their initial bridgehead.

Finally, an armoured counterattack using our fresh mobile forces would sweep through the remnants of the enemy and demolish the threat. That was the plan, anyway.

You mentioned anti-tank ramps and also anti-tank ditches. These were different structures?

Yes, the ditches were designed to deter a panzer from trying to cross, because the vehicles would be trapped inside the gap.

The ramps were the opposite; they were preformed concrete obstacles, which were poured into moulds on site. They were high, concave shaped ramps, hollow inside, which would deter a panzer commander from trying to climb up over them. They also prevented the panzer crews from seeing what was on the other side. If a brave panzer tried to climb, it would get stuck on the inside curved face and burn its engine out, or it would shed its tracks as it tried to get a grip on the concrete. The interior of these ramps could be fitted with mines or incendiary bombs, to destroy the trapped panzer. The cost of these ramps was very low, and they could be assembled quickly by conscripted labour directed by our engineers.

What conscripted labour was this?

The International Workers. They were men from Eastern Europe or elsewhere who were working under our command. I regret that we needed to use such labour, but our manpower was so limited we had no choice. So the cost of these anti-tank ramps was the food for the workers, plus the concrete, which was sourced locally. Given enough workers, we could put up many kilometres of these ramps, in addition to the anti-tank ditches, throughout our zone. But we were only at the very early stages of this programme when the invasion came.

And yet, when the invasion happened, you found yourself facing not panzers but American airborne troops. How did this happen?

Battles do not go according to plan for anybody, neither for the victor or the defeated. In my case, in the first week of June, I was encamped near to La Madeleine, where we were planning to build a belt of the concrete ramps and fit them with incendiaries.

By the way, this was part of a defensive landscape which comprised the local river, which we flooded, and a series of low hills which we were fortifying with concrete resistance points. The resistance points were a combination of PAK emplacements and two-man concrete box points. These were to be manned by the Static Divisions, so we put great emphasis on making the advance of the enemy predictable, so that the Static boys would know where to shoot.

The Static infantry were not expected to move quickly between firing points and fight improvised engagements, this was not manageable for them physically or mentally. So the anti-tank ramps would manipulate the enemy's advance onto the firing arcs of the Static guns. But all that we had completed by June 6th, though, was to flood the land around the river. This meant flooding a number of civilian houses, and their upper windows were still visible. The area became unhealthy due to the floods, with many insects and bugs… it was an unpleasant place to be. I was certainly glad of that cool rain which came on the 5th, on the day before the beach invasion.

How close were you to the beaches?

About twelve kilometres. I was billeted in an empty civilian house, with two men to assist me. One of these men spoke East European languages, to liaise with the International Workers who were due to build the ramps with concrete. The International squads contained some people who were quite skilled civil engineers, and it was worth communicating with them over the building process. The Internationals were not in the area yet, they were being held at a point further inland. So on that night, the 5th, I was with my two men in the billet.

Were you in a state of alert on the 5th?

The Static Divisions on the coast were alerted on the Friday before, I think. It was noticeable that patrols were increased and Flak searchlights were used more heavily over the weekend. That's what I remember.

How did you personally feel about the possibility of invasion?

I shouldn't say this, perhaps, but at the time I was an ambitious young man, and I was quite fascinated by the challenge. In the few months I had been in Normandy, we had built up the defences greatly, and although the job was far from finished I wanted to see how they would cope. I wanted another month or so for the defences to be truly finished, so in my arrogance I was praying for the Allies to come later, in July or August.

You say that you were praying?

Yes, Herr Eckhertz; misguided as I was, I was actually praying. Why is that strange?

I am a religious man, and I often had discussions with the Chaplains of the Infantry about our mission in France. In fact, just on that Sunday, which would be the 4th June, I had attended a chapel service in Carentan at which the German regimental chaplain addressed some two hundred of our troops on their duty. The chaplain was very clear that our duty was to drive out any potential invaders. He evoked the spirit of Charlemagne, who was the great Christian king of early Europe, who stood firm against the enemy barbarians.

Do you think that the infantry men in attendance
were religiously motivated?

Well, each man wore the Wehrmacht belt buckle that said 'Gott Mit Uns' (*'God With Us'*) which was the battle cry of Charlemagne himself. I think that most of our men had a fundamental belief in God, yes. Atheists must have been very rare in the Wehrmacht. I don't think I ever met an atheist in the German army.

We are going off the point, but what you say about atheism,
of course, applies only to the Wehrmacht...in the Waffen
SS, for example, most men were atheists, surely?

Were the Waffen SS atheists? I don't know about that. The *German* SS, I suppose – they didn't like their troops going to church, except to get married.

But you have to remember that by 1944, a lot of the Waffen SS men actually were non-German volunteers. The French and the Belgians in the Waffen SS, they were devout Catholics with their own chaplains who wore the SS insignia. The East Europeans in the Waffen SS, all the pro-German Ukrainians and that bunch, they were Greek Orthodox believers. People said that they would often go into action smelling of the incense from their priests' blessings.

And, of course, there was the Muslim SS, who I think were from Yugoslavia; it was known that they were very devout believers of their faith. Very devout indeed. I heard that they were very conscientious in their prayer times and fasting and so on. By the way, those Muslim SS men were considered very ruthless and effective troops indeed. We were glad to have them.

So you must not be surprised to hear of a German officer praying that the invasion would come later rather than sooner. In that sense, though, my prayers were not answered, and the invasion came sooner than we hoped.

And so it happened. You were describing the night of the 5th June, when you were in the flooded area around La Madeleine.

Yes. That was one of those long, damp twilights that you get in Northern France…the air was very tense. I did not have a telephone or radio set, and no orders were brought by courier, and so I was given no information. I admit that I had a supply of French wine in the billet, which I had acquired from a nearby wine cellar, and I got through a bottle of it as I stood watching the coast through my periscope binoculars. I had no immediate combat function, as I was an engineer, but I and my two men were armed with machine pistols.

I decided to get to sleep at about ten pm, as I wanted to be up well before first light in the morning. There was a lot of aircraft noise, but this seemed normal to me because of the recent bombing campaign. Foolishly, I allowed my two men to keep on playing cards in the kitchen of the house; that was something I would regret. Life in France made many of us lax and undisciplined, you see. We were becoming rather French in our behaviour. We would be punished for this casual attitude by the Allies.

I know that it was at three thirty am that I was awoken, because I checked the time immediately. I could hear planes in the sky, and there were flashes of Flak visible through the window. It was raining slightly. I kicked the wall of the adjoining room, where my men should be, but there was no response. I felt that something was wrong in the house.

I put on my uniform and boots and took my machine pistol, and I went to the kitchen…I saw one of the men at once, asleep at the table with his cards, the damned fool. There were beer bottles on the table, I remember that. I went out into the yard, and saw flashes in the sky all around; they were like flares, but lighting up quickly and then fading. I had not seen this before, and I was very alarmed.

261

What were these flashes?

I have never understood what they were, although other people who witnessed the landings also speak of them, I believe. Some flashes were green colour, and some were pure white. I think they were some kind of signalling system used by the Allies. It was a strange sight. But then, in the yard, I saw my second man; he was face down and completely still. I kicked him, but he didn't respond, and then I realised that he was dead. His throat had been cut, and there was a huge quantity of blood on the ground.

I stood very still, listening and watching. I wish I could tell you all the things I heard in that minute. There were Flak noises, plane engines, and various sounds of vehicles on the Carentan road. But closer to me, I heard sounds which I thought were men moving; it sounded like men in combat gear. There are metallic sounds and scrapes which are unmistakeable. I also heard voices, but I couldn't make out what they were saying, or even what language. I can tell you that my hair was standing up, and my heart was pounding hard, because I knew that the men out there might be observing me.

My other man now appeared behind me in the yard, apologising for being asleep, and before I could stop him he began speaking in a loud voice. The fool! He was shot immediately, through the chest.

The shots came from a wood beyond the yard. I jumped back into the kitchen, and my man tried to crawl after me, but he was shot again in the back. He made a lot of noise about that, which only stopped when they shot him again. I simply had no idea what forces were out there or what was happening.

Did you assume these were Allied troops?

They could just as well be French fighters, but the French were known to shout out slogans and threats when they attacked, whereas around the yard it was all silent now. So I thought this was some kind of commando raid by the English – that's what came into my mind.

262

I was determined not to be found, because the English commandos had a reputation for cruelty, which is one reason why they were classed as terrorists from, I think, 1943 onwards. I certainly did not want to fall into their hands.

Sorry to interrupt, but the British commandos were classed as terrorists?

Yes, exactly; this was decided in late 1943, I think. After that date, all English commandos were executed; I mean, their commandos who operated secretly behind the lines, rather than on a battlefield. This policy was well known to us at the time.

By the way, I knew someone who saw the result of a raid the English made on the Calais coast in 1943; the English commandos had used barbed wire as a garrotte to strangle and decapitate the German sentries. For this reason, they were called 'Churchill's Rats.' All of this was going through my mind while I sheltered in the kitchen of that damned house among the floods.

How did this situation at the house end?

Several aircraft were coming overhead, quite low down. The noise was very loud, and using this noise I ran over to the front of the house and went out of the main door. There was a road out there which led to the command of the regiment, and I planned to go directly to them to report the situation. There was no point delaying or hiding any more, and I was sure I would meet other Germans along the road.

I kept close beside a hedgerow and began to walk up this road. I didn't run, because I wanted to be quiet, and to listen. My heart, I can say honestly, was like a hammer in a barrel, slam-slam, like that. Just as I got away from the house, I came to the edge of the flooded area. There was a large, white shape in the water which puzzled me, and then I realised it was a parachute. I looked closer, despite all my haste, and I saw there was a dead man attached to it…I recognised an American type helmet. So they weren't English – they were Americans. He must have come down in the water and become entangled on his chute and drowned.

There were also various parachute canisters in the water; they seemed to be painted in luminous paint, or fitted with glowing lights of some kind, or possibly that was an optical illusion. I had to take all this in very quickly and then move on up the road.

In the middle of France, surrounded by great armies of hundreds of thousands of men, I felt like the last man on earth on that road! There was a silence, a lull that went on for several minutes while I walked alone along the road. That is my main memory of June 6th 1944, in fact. I remember walking quite alone, with my machine pistol, in a very strange silence that descended around four am. A terrible silence. It felt that the whole world was getting ready for the battle that we knew would come. It was close to dawn, and the rain stopped, and I remember that the roadside was full of flowers, but the air was full of smoke and explosive fumes. That is a strange, powerful memory for me: just those one or two minutes alone.

And then complete anarchy erupted on the road, and the peace of France was shattered forever. I believe that I had just lived through the final few minutes of peace that poor, innocent France would experience on that terrible day.

What happened on this road?

A group of six German soldiers came out onto the road from the hedgerow, and they challenged me. These were men of the Static Divisions, but very conscientious. They said that American parachutists were present all over the fields, and they requested orders. They wanted leadership in order to do their duty. I stopped to think about what to do with these soldiers, but as I stopped, other men broke through the hedgerows on either side of the road and attacked us.

There was a hideous, primitive fight in the middle of the road. I saw that these attackers were Americans, from their helmets, but I was completely unprepared for the aggression that they showed to us. The Americans cut the throats of two of the Germans immediately, without any request to surrender or put down their guns. The other Germans began to run, and the Americans jumped on them and broke their necks deliberately, like this…as you would do to an animal. They twisted and snapped their necks. Even on the Russian front, I had not seen such aggression. The sounds of such a fight are horrible, sickening. The rattling throats of the dying men, and the grunting of the attackers, the grunts of triumph they gave when they stabbed or twisted a man to death.

I came to my senses and shot at one of the Americans with my MP. My gun jammed, and the other Americans began to beat me up. I think that two of our men got away from there, into the fields, but I was beaten up, kicked and smashed in the head by their gun stocks. You can see here on my face the lines from the wounds they inflicted on me. I am not complaining, because many men in that war suffered far worse than me. But still, I was astonished at how violent they were. If they had asked us to surrender, we might have done so. I was shocked that the American troops were primed to kill in that way.

Why do you say that? Why were you shocked?

They came there to kill us, to do violence to us.

But this was the war, Herr Hoffmann. How can this have been a surprise, a shock to you?

It is hard to explain. I think that in my mind, I always had some idea that the Americans were civilised, but they were misguided, or they were misled. Now that you ask me the question, I try to understand my own feelings and it's difficult for me. I think that I had the belief, the subconscious belief, that the civilised Americans would not wish to disturb the peace of France. We in the German forces thought that we had gone to such lengths to protect France, to guard its people against harm. I think that deep down I could not believe that the Americans would shatter this peace we had achieved.

Of course, I was utterly wrong.

You were wrong about the Americans?

I was wrong about everything. I know today, ten years later, that everything I believed during the war was a mistake. I understand today that we Germans were not in France to protect the people, we were there only to exploit and persecute them. We should never have been in France, or Russia, Italy, any of those places. The things that we did were appalling…everything was wrong. Why would those Americans hate us so much? Why would they cut our throats and break our necks like animals, in the road, without a word? Well, because they knew the truth of what we were doing, that is why.

I see…Herr Hoffmann, when we began this interview, I thought that you would give me a very cool, clinical description of the engineering, the anti-tank ramps and so on. But now that you have told me your experience, I realise that out of all the veterans of June 6th whom I have interviewed, you are the only one, out of fifteen or sixteen men, who has shown such a complete understanding of his own mistaken beliefs and his own delusions during the war.

Is that correct? Well, but you must not be critical of the others. It is difficult for us, Herr Eckhertz. It is very hard for us…after everything that happened in the war years, for us to be brutally honest about ourselves, about our lives.

Would you like to halt this interview now?

Yes, I have told you everything that I have to say about June 6th.

Only…I would like to add that we in the Wehrmacht were only ordinary men, just as those Americans with their knives were ordinary men. We were not great thinkers, none of us were great psychologists or political experts. We were simple, ordinary men. And yet the other people hated us so much.

—

THE STUG CREW

Paul Breslau was the gunner of a Sturmgeschutz III self-propelled gun with the 200 Assault Gun Battalion, 21st Panzer Division, based in the Caen area south of Sword beach.

Herr Breslau, I have long been fascinated by the type of vehicle which you served in around the time of June 6th. Can you tell me about it?

Well, if you ask me that kind of question, I could talk to you all day...you see, the Stug III *(assault gun type III)* was the vehicle that kept the Wehrmacht fighting for those six long years of the war.

The story was that its inspiration came from General Guderian, who before the war pointed out to the panzer designers that, for five centuries, artillery guns have entered the battlefield pointing the wrong way! He challenged our engineers to create an artillery piece that is not towed behind horses or trucks, but faces forwards permanently, and is always elevated and ready to fire with its crew standing at the breech. With this simple idea, which was totally radical in those years of the 1930s, the Panzer Inspectorate came up with the Stug III.

It was a Panzer III chassis with a low superstructure, fitted with a fixed 75mm gun. By the time of the Normandy invasion, it had been improved and developed into a very fine machine. It was incredibly reliable, and gave reasonable protection with its armour plate. It was damned fast, too, if the crew fiddled with the governor arm on the engine, which we all did. The best thing about it was that it was so low and easy to conceal. If you stood next to it, the thing was not much higher than you. Of course, that meant that inside the compartment, you could not stand up, and you were permanently hunched over. But few men ever complained of this, I guarantee you. This concealment meant that it was perfectly suited to a defensive role as a Jagdpanzer (*tank destroyer*), as well as an assault role as a Sturmgeshutz (*assault gun.*)

May I read you something I wrote for 'Signal' magazine when I visited the Atlantic Wall in spring 1944? I wrote:

'In every field, our tank destroyers and assault guns lie in wait for any enemy who might be foolhardy enough to violate the peace of a United Europe under the guardianship of the Reich. Our gunners are crack shots, and all of them are members of the '1,000 Metre Club' – meaning that they can hit a target of one metre radius at a range of 1,000 metres with nine shots out of every ten that they fire. They train constantly, and they use the latest radio sets and telex devices to keep in touch with their command posts. Let us not fear a potential invader – but rather, let us pity him, for the onslaught that he will face at the hands of these cool operators.'
Well. Do you think that sums up those times?

It does. That's a good description, actually. I remember the '1,000 Metre Club' very well. It was a disgrace to lose your membership of that club.

On my visit to Normandy in the spring of 1944, I passed a group of three Stugs which were dug in around a village, I think it was Ranville. The vehicles were almost impossible to see from the road. I wonder if you were in one of those vehicles?

Ranville? Yes, it's possible that was me. We were based inland of Ouistreham, as part of the second line of defence, which meant that we were behind those poor boys in the Static Infantry Divisions on the beaches.

Why do you say they were 'those poor boys?'

I mean no insult in the phrase, but it is a fact that the Static Infantry were there to soak up any enemy attack, to slow it down and to alert us, the inland forces, of the danger. Nobody on earth expected the Static Divisions to defeat a serious landing, unless it was a very lightly-equipped raid. I'm sure you have met people from the Static Divisions, and I suppose that they told you that they were there because they were unfit, or for some other reason not allocated to be part of a mobile fighting unit.

It is true, many of the Static Infantry men have told me this. But I must pay tribute to their commitment and determination, whatever their level of fitness. I believe that they fought very hard.

Of course they did. I would never suggest otherwise.

But we must be realistic, and see the facts for what they are. It was accepted by everyone that if there was a real invasion on that coast, and not a commando type attack with a limited objective, then the beach forces, the coastal forces, would probably be overrun at first by a focussed assault. This was why a counterattack by our mobile armoured forces was so critical to any plan to defeat an invasion. *Counterattack is the surest form of defence* – that was the thinking of the Wehrmacht, and it was very true. In the end, of course, our full scale counterattack against the landings was late in being staged, and so the Allies had the chance to build up their strength in the coastal pockets that they captured on the first day. Even though my own Division, the 21st Panzer, did fight back at once.

I would be fascinated to hear your account of the counterattack phase. But can you tell me, what form did you expect an assault to take in the summer of 1944? Did you expect a massive invasion?

Our orders were to be ready for an invasion on that coast at any time. From about March 1944, that was the phrase: 'at any time.'

The question of how the Allies would invade was much argued over, of course. It seemed highly unlikely that the Allies would succeed if they attacked *only* on the coast. We knew they would have to use airborne forces, and we were trained to watch for these and to counterattack the possible landing zones in the area. We discussed endlessly, as you can imagine, what else the English and Americans would try to do to back up a seaborne invasion. We felt that they had to do something else; after all, they had invaded Italy with seaborne forces, and their progress there was extremely slow. Italy was a mincing machine for those Allied troops. Surely the Allies would not want to repeat that mistake in France, otherwise their war in Western Europe might continue for many, many years.

None of us in 1944 expected that the war would end as quickly as it did.

That's an interesting point…you, as a skilled German panzer man in summer 1944, how long did you think the war was going to last?

My God, a long time! We knew about the Reich 'Wonder Weapons,' but even so, we suspected that the Americans especially, with all their scientists, would have wonder weapons of their own. Among my comrades, most of us in 1944 felt that the whole war would continue until 1950 or some time such as that. We expected to be defending Europe on both sides, East and West, for at least another five years.

Were you really ready to fight on until 1949, or 1950?

Yes, we were. And beyond that, even after that, if it was necessary. Some of us expected the war to continue into the 1960s, imagining that it would reach a stalemate in the West and the East.

This is why we felt that the Allies would try to do something to prevent a stalemate, and accelerate their occupation of France as they had failed to do in Italy. We thought that they might set up a false government on French soil, maybe installing De Gaulle as their figurehead, and incite a mass uprising among the French population. We wondered what we would do if we had to fire on French civilians. Or would the French organise themselves into partisan brigades, as the Reds did in Russia? I knew from my own experience that a partisan was a dangerous enemy for a proper army to face.

Another view was that the Soviets might move one of their regular armies to the West, and invade France with Soviet troops. I see you are surprised at this idea, but many of us thought this was possible. The number of Divisions available to the Soviets was massive, we must remember. It would have been possible to move a Russian army to Iran, then North Africa, and then to launch them across the Mediterranean into the South of France. All of these possible combinations of events were in our minds, you see.

We often talked this over for hours on end, in our bivouacs when we were camped out beside our Stugs in March, April, May of 1944. It's so strange…that was only ten years ago, but it seems like another world…like the Middle Ages or something.

What was the life like for you, in that phase before
the landings? Physically and mentally?

Physically, everyone said that France was a paradise compared to the East, and this was undoubtedly true. We camped in bivouac tents beside our vehicles, and we spent all day maintaining the Stugs, travelling around the whole area to become completely familiar with the landscape, and practising firing and manoeuvres in the places where we expected we would have to fight.

I came to know the Caen area as if it was my home town. We knew where the ground was soft, where there were sunken roads with sides that could be climbed in a Stug, and which roadsides could not be climbed, and so on. We knew which copse had dense trees for concealing the vehicles, and where the rivers could be forded without bridges; all of this had to be known and memorised.

Of course, as this was France, we also quickly came to know which farms would exchange a few of our boiled sweets for a dozen eggs, or which houses would give us a chicken in return for some cigarettes. The French were crazy for our cigarettes and sweet rations, and prized them more highly than their own produce.

Physically, we were very well off, in fact you could say that we were living a healthy life. The exception to this was the Allied air campaign against us, which went on all through the spring and early summer. The air attacks wore us down psychologically, it has to be said. The explosive power of the small bombs which the Jabos dropped was horrible; for some reason, the English and American bombs seemed more powerful than ours or the Russian bombs. I don't know the technical reason for that.

The poor, helpless French suffered in this bombing as well, just as we did.

Can you think of an example of how the French
suffered from Allied bombing?

An example?

I recall very well one evening in May, this was early May and quite hot, when two of the English Typhoon aircraft came over without warning and dropped these small bombs on the road where we were. That Typhoon thing was a swine, a true bastard. We called it the 'Schreckliche Flugzeug' (*terror-plane*) and the French hated it too. The bombs that these two dropped went across the road, through a barn and straight into a farmhouse where a French family were sitting down to their supper. It did not damage our vehicles, because we had swerved off into the woods and we were hidden, but some of us went to look inside this farmhouse – my God. These six people, women, children, everybody, all laid out on the kitchen floor, lined up just like this, one after the other. All dead from the fragmentation shrapnel. Everything was wrecked in there, except for the pot of soup on the table, which was still steaming. Still steaming, yes.

I know for a fact that two young French lads in that village volunteered to join the Waffen SS French forces after that, so what did it achieve for the Allies? Today, when I see in the magazines and movies about how the English and Americans were greeted as heroes in Normandy, I am sure there's another side to those stories, and a side that will probably never be told. And all this daily bombing, these almost random, indiscriminate air attacks, they made us very jumpy.

How did June 6th unfold for you?

I remember that on the weekend just before, there was a big alert, and the Divisonal command put the alert code to the highest level. I don't know how they decided the levels, maybe due to intelligence or reconnaissance of shipping. So we actually expected an attack over the weekend. It was a warm weekend, and it seemed to go on forever, I remember that. But then on the Monday, the 5th, the weather broke and it rained, and the alert was reduced as well, and we thought, 'Well, we're ok again.'

On the Sunday, we had a big hare that we had caught, and we cooked that hare in French cider over a fire, I remember, which was excellent, and our mood was good. That's a good memory, that rabbit in cider!

But then, on the Monday night, absolute hell broke out in that sector. The world just changed like that, like throwing a switch.

I think it was just after midnight on the 5th, when this tidal wave of aircraft came overhead. That is how I would describe it, a tidal wave. We were camped under trees, and when we went out to the edge to look up, we could see the full moon, and lots of pale clouds, also many black clouds. Against these clouds were innumerable aircraft, all moving south in perfect formation. We stood and stared up at that. There was no Flak at first, no shooting, just these repeated formations going over, absolutely perfect in their alignment. It was like a damned air show.

Even when our Flak started, we saw that it brought down one or two planes, but it made little impact on those numbers. A plane crashed and exploded a few kilometres from us, somewhere near the river, and we discussed going to look at it, but our Feldwebels

(*Sergeants*) insisted we stay with our vehicles. This went on and on, and with all the planes above us there were also many of our motor-cycle couriers moving back and forth, and our reconnaissance teams moving around. The whole of France was awake that night, I can tell you. Don't believe anyone who says they were sleeping, and they didn't know what was happening! We were too expectant to be able to sleep, if you understand me.

Then, around three am I think, we were told that the enemy were landing paratroopers in the area, and that an aggressive para-chute raid was in progress against our area. We had not noticed any parachutes, but we heard fighting to the East, and in the moonlight we saw a convoy of our troops in trucks moving that way. Everything was very confused.

This was the phrase that was used? An 'aggressive parachute raid?'

Yes, that was what our company commander said. To do him justice, it was impossible for anyone to know at that stage what was going to happen. We all believed that the paratroopers would try to capture Ouistreham, where there's a harbour. That seemed the most likely explanation. Many of us referred to the Dieppe attack in 1942, saying, 'Oh, it's just Dieppe all over again.' This gave us optimism, because at Dieppe, of course, the whole business was a disaster for the English and Canadians. Some of our boys said, 'We'll get our handsome faces in the newsreels for the girls to admire,' and things like that. Because after Dieppe the attack was in the newsreels for months.

But still there was no order for us to actually do anything, and so we remained, waiting and guessing at events all the time, until first light. When the light came up, we began to see that this was a major event, whatever it was.

What did you see at first light?

The aircraft overhead were fully visible now. We saw many twin-engined and four-engined planes, and a large number of fighter planes of the American Mustang type. All of these aircraft had black and white checks or stripes on them. I can say that over the next few days we grew very sick of seeing those black and white markings everywhere. I think I saw them in my sleep at one stage.

The Mustang planes were coming over very low, as if they were spying on us, looking for us. We stayed under the trees. I did see a couple of Luftwaffe planes around that time, which were definitely the Focke-Wulf fighter type, and they were chasing several Mustangs North towards the coast.

You are the only veteran I have spoken to, Herr Breslau, who saw Luftwaffe planes that early on the 6th. What time was this?

About six am, probably. We saw them go up to the coast, but I didn't see either of them come back from there. That Focke-Wulf was such a beautiful plane, like a sports car for the air. But we forgot about them quickly, because in front of us, on the coast, there began to be a huge amount of explosions. We went to the edge of the woods and looked. We could not see the ocean itself, but we had a view down the escarpment, which was mined in places and had various resistance points built into it. It was about two kilometres down to the sea. In front of the escarpment, the poor old Static Infantry were in position. There were huge explosions down there, absolutely massive.

We could see spouts of dust and earth rising up as high as a church tower down there. We said, 'God, the men on the beach are taking a terrible beating.' All we could do was watch. There were lines of fire in the air as well, which looked rather like arrows, and I recognised these from Russia as the 'Stalin Organ' type of rockets. These rockets were coming up from the sea and falling on the headland area. It was a real storm down there, with smoke and dust and the flames from explosions. The noise was very loud. We knew that this meant something important was happening.

Slowly, this carpet of explosions began to move inland, up the escarpment towards us. I know today that this meant that the Allies were on the beach and were bombarding further inland, but at the time, of course, we didn't know that the Allies had actually landed. All we saw was this dreadful wall of explosions coming up the slope, getting closer to us.

How did you and your comrades react to this?

I felt very sick in the stomach. It looked to me as if the attackers – and we still didn't know who they were – as if these attackers simply wanted to blow up a pathway inland. As if they were just going to explode everything in their way. How could we fight against that? Also, we started to notice people running inland from the escarpment area; through binoculars, I could see infantry men in small groups or singly, running or riding on motorcycles and trucks, trying to get away from these explosions.

I don't mean to say that *all* of our infantry retreated like that, but I definitely saw quite a number escaping from in front of this bombardment. Of course, that was the worst thing they could do, because then the bombardment caught them in the open. I remember that a group of Landsers (*foot soldiers*) were riding on a civilian car which was hit by one of the big shell blasts. That car was blown into many, many pieces, it simply disappeared, along with all the men in it.

We went back to our Stugs and we started the engines, and we checked over the guns and ammunition in readiness. My role as the gunner required me to clean the optics on the gun sight perfectly, and I got the glass ready and applied a small amount of soap to the gun sight lens.

Sorry, but why was that? And why do you mention such a small act?

This soap was to prevent the optic from steaming up with all the heat and fumes inside the Stug compartment. It was quite effective. I mention it because this was a ritual of mine, in getting the gun ready for combat. Other soldiers will tell you that they have their own personal rituals, whether panzer men or infantry, or pilots, I suppose.

I see. Thank you for explaining that.

Such things are important to the mind, in the moments before a battle. And condensation on the optics was a real problem. Inside the Stug hull, it was so very cramped, with four sweaty men and all the hot machinery inside a box that wasn't much bigger than the cab on a truck, and the condensation got everywhere in the mechanisms.

We waited for some time with the engines running, while our commander was conferring with the Company command. Then, at last, we were told to move out of the wood and take up our prepared positions at the top of the escarpment. These positions were points where we had practised our arcs of fire, and where we calculated that enemy tanks would approach to avoid the minefields. Our driver emplaced us in our position; our other two Stugs were on either side of us. As soon as we halted, I set the gun sight range for the field of fire we expected.

Through my periscope, I also saw units of our infantry take up positions in slit trenches just in front of us, so we were firing over their heads. These were infantry of our own panzergrenadiers, and all this was our prepared plan for defending the sector. The infantry were well-armed with heavy machine guns and grenades and so on. My commander leaned out of the hatch and had a long discussion with an infantry Leutnant; that officer told us that there were tanks moving up from the shore and that the attack was on a large scale, with dozens of tanks being placed on the beach by barges.

When did you first see the enemy?

It was about eight am.

The first tank I saw was a remarkable sight! It was equipped with a rotating mechanism on the front, which was whirling around at an incredibly high speed. It was literally whipping up the ground on the escarpment, raising a big cloud of dust.

The range was about 1,500 metres, which for my 75mm gun was quite manageable. The spinning drum on that tank was setting off mines in the minefield, and that was a problem for our plans, because if the other enemy tanks moved onto us across the minefield, we would have to change our positions to fire.

Remember that the Stug was just a gun on tracks, it had no turret, and so aiming the gun had to be done chiefly by adjusting the direction of the hull left and right with the wheels, with the gunner only using a final few degrees at the end. As a defensive weapon it was excellent, like a PAK bunker, but moving the damned thing around was not ideal.

The mine-clearing tank, that you saw... that machine was called the Flail or Crab, I believe. Did you expect something like that?

Certainly not. I had no idea that such a machine had been invented. I found out after the war that the Allies had used it in Africa and Italy, but I had never seen such a thing on the Eastern Front. I must admit that I felt a kind of grudging admiration for the engineers who designed it, because it was an excellent idea. But all the same, I adjusted my optical gun sight onto the tank; that was my job.

It was a Sherman, and seemed to have no gun, and it was moving very slowly. My gun sight had a series of triangles inside the optic, depending on the range selected, and I used the hand controls to put the 1,500 metre triangle on this Sherman's turret. I can see the gun sight now as if it is still on my eye. And my hand on the firing lever, here. You squeezed it like this, you see.

Firing that 75mm gun always made my face jump off the gun sight, because of the recoil! When I looked again, after firing, I saw that I had shot off a big piece of the armour from the side of the Sherman's turret. This broken piece was rolling off across the land. The Sherman stopped, and then the drum and chains stopped turning. I shot again and I put the next round through the top of the hull. I saw this explode through the armour under the turret, because I could see a flash through the open part. Two of the Sherman crew came out of the hatches and tried to climb off. The Stug next to me shot them up with a high explosive shell. I personally found that unnecessary, but, there, it was done and that was the end of them.

I felt optimistic about turning back the enemy tanks now, because I thought the minefield was virtually impenetrable. It would take days to clear it properly, I knew that. Through the gun sight, I could see a number of other Shermans at the foot of the slope, and my commander fed me a commentary, telling me what was happening down there. The Shermans seemed to be hesitating, advancing and then moving back.

I put my triangle on one of them, and fired as he came forward, but the shell deflected off his front plate. That caused all the tanks there to reverse, and we fired several rounds of high explosive to encourage them. I saw our grenadiers in the slit trenches cheering us on for our shooting. Then a big puff of smoke appeared in front of us; it was grey-blue smoke, and this smoke began to rise up into the sky.

My Feldwebel cursed. He said this smoke was a marker flare, fired by one of the enemy tanks to mark our position. This meant that they had called for an air attack on us. He leaned out of the hatch and shouted to the infantry to extinguish the blue flare, but they were slow to respond, and other blue shells or flares burst close to us then. So this was how the Shermans did battle! They fired smoke shells to mark us out for the air force to attack.

My mood changed again, with that sick feeling in my belly, because I knew that we had no real defence against the Jabos. You know, those mood changes were so hard to take, the change from optimism to fear all the time. That is in the nature of battle, but it drained me, it exhausted me. Were we just going to sit and wait for the Jabos? If we left, we would be leaving the infantry to their fate. I heard my commander shout 'Air attack!' And then hell on earth came to us in Normandy.

What form did this attack take?

I did not even see the planes. All I could see was their shadows moving across the slope, incredibly fast. That was all I could see through the gun sight. Then I heard a series of explosions, very loud and rapid, and I felt the Stug rocking around in the blast wave. There was a loud noise of shrapnel or something hitting our hull, really smashing into our metal plate, again and again. There was nothing we could do except brace ourselves and wait for this to stop. Through the periscope, I could see that the infantry trenches were badly hit, with smoke coming out of them, but I didn't realise how bad it was at that stage.

I could also see several Shermans coming towards us behind the destroyed mine-clearing tank. One of these had another rotating drum machine on its front, and it was obviously going to try to clear a pathway through the mines again. I heard my commander trying to speak to the other two Stugs on his radio set, but there was no response from them. That's when I thought, 'Well, things are going badly for us now.'

Did you stay and fight with the Shermans?

We tried to, I promise you, but the situation was chaotic. The mine-clearing tank that we had destroyed was burning up fiercely, and throwing out a lot of smoke that obscured our view of the slopes. I saw the second mine-clearer come through this smoke, making a path around his destroyed friend and then go straightening up to steer towards us. I laid a shot on him, and fired, but the round didn't seem to penetrate the front of his hull. I think that the spinning chains on his drum were deflecting the trajectory of the shells. I don't know why that didn't happen with the first panzer, or maybe I was shooting poorly now, or possibly the gun bearings were damaged in the bombing.

I fired again onto his turret, but I took the shot too hurriedly, and it clipped the side of his turret and deflected off. It's very difficult under those conditions to lay a shot precisely, with smoke and all the dust and debris that was coming out of the ground from his rotating cylinder machine. I was setting another shot onto him, because I was determined to stop him, when he pulled over to one side suddenly. Behind him, there was a queue of these damned Shermans, lined up as if they were waiting for a bus. I think there were four of them, lined up in the lane that the mine-clearer had made. They couldn't advance, but they were at a range of about 900 metres now, and that made me nervous, because even their short guns would start to be effective at that sort of range.

Sure enough, the first one in line began firing at us, and the round deflected right off our sloping front armour. What a noise that made! The whole optic system shook, and I had to wait for it to steady before I could fire on him. I just got that shot away before he fired again, and I hit him low on the front plate.

My commander congratulated me on that shot, because we saw it go through the front and then come straight out again from the top of the hull. That sometimes happens, you see, if the warhead ricochets around inside the compartment and hits a roof hatch or something. That damned warhead is going at a thousand kilometres per hour, and it's a piece of tungsten about the size of a big pebble... my God, the things it can do to the men inside the hull. Nothing can stop it, you see, and sometimes it just bursts out of the panzer again.

So that Sherman ran off to one side, hit a mine and started burning. Nobody came out of it, the destruction was too great, I think. The mine explosion set it on fire completely. But of course, behind him was the next Sherman in line, and behind that one was another two or three. I remember thinking, 'How many do they have?' I also couldn't understand why our other two Stugs were not firing on these enemy panzers. We in my Stug seemed to be defending France all alone, single-handed.

Would it have been wise to reverse, retreat?

But that was the vehicle commander's decision, not mine. A gunner in the Wehrmacht panzer troops could not ask his commander to reverse the vehicle to safety, Herr Eckhertz! Such a thing was not possible. My commander told me to keep firing, keep firing...as we were fully stocked with ammunition, and our gun was obviously effective against the Shermans.

The next Sherman gunner, though – now, he was a good shot, an excellent shot. They should have made him the leading panzer, really. He fired and hit us exactly under the gun mantle, just between the mantle and the hull front. Our Stug had the 'Saukopf' (*pig's head*) type of mantle, which was a single piece of cast steel that deflected shots well. But there was a shot trap under the pig's head itself, which deflected an incoming round into the gun elevating system. All I felt was a huge crash as this Sherman round came right under where I was hunched on my seat. That was a moment of fear and panic, I can tell you. To be in a panzer when a round comes in is awful...sudden darkness, and smoke, the engine cuts out, and the crew men are shouting and cursing...it is a terrible few seconds after a panzer is hit. The fear of fire is always in your mind; should you open the hatch and jump, or is the panzer going to survive?

My commander was very cool, and he told me to check the gun. I found that the gun was dislocated from its mounting and could not be aimed at all. The driver reported that the engine would not restart. There was also a strong smell of gasoline building up in the compartment. The danger in a panzer is that the fumes will ignite without warning. I was desperately relieved when the commander opened the hatch and told us to leave the vehicle. Of course, the Sherman gunner took no pity on us, and fired again as we were climbing out. This round deflected off the cupola, but pieces of metal hit my commander in the legs. We helped him off the vehicle and took cover behind the raised wall of the emplacement.

That Sherman gunner systematically shot our Stug to pieces right in front of us. He shot rounds off the front plate, and then he blew it up with high explosive rounds. All the gasoline went up at once, so hot that it burned our skin and we had to run. The Sherman fired on us with his machine gun as we tried to run.

What was your personal reaction to this?

I could not blame the Sherman gunner. We had just destroyed two of his comrades. But my overriding emotion was to get away from the shooting. We were now effectively unarmed, of course, as we had only our pistols left. As we were carrying our commander away, I saw what the Jabo bombing had done to our defensive positions. The other two Stugs were badly damaged, because the shrapnel had exploded through their engine covers. The crews had left the scene completely.

I caught a glimpse of our infantry trenches, which were a sickening sight. The bombs had fallen inside the trenches, I think, or exploded just above them. There were many bodies of our troops inside there, all jumbled together. Some men were wounded and were trying to surrender. I saw several of them shot by the Sherman's machine gun. My crew managed to get down onto a slope behind us, facing inland, so that we had the ridge of the slope between us and the enemy.

I can tell you that on the other side of this ridge, on the sheltered side, there was what looked like half the German army, all pressed down on the ground, waiting for orders. There were our Stug crews, plus various infantry men, some clerks from headquarters, and many others, all sheltering from the attack. Nobody was in command there, it was as if we were all frozen. We could hear the Sherman tracks getting closer, and I could feel the explosions from the enemy panzers firing into the ridge.

Did you consider surrendering?

Well, many of our men were shouting to each other to surrender. But this was a situation, which I'm sure many soldiers will know about, where trying to surrender was probably more dangerous than staying damned still. Those Shermans were determined to clear us off the ridges there, and they were firing and firing like devils, and they were blowing up the top of the ridge with high explosive.

I saw a man stand up and raise his hands, but he was hit by shrapnel and he was bowled back down the ridge, over and over. I did not want to suffer that fate, and I also did not want to be taken as a prisoner. I was due to be married at the end of the summer, and I didn't want to be carried off to some prison camp away from my beautiful wife-to-be. I had a cousin who was in a prison camp in the USA, which sounded as far off as the moon. I was desperate to avoid capture.

Do you think that your attitude to capture was common?

This varied greatly between individuals, I think, and also on the stage of the war. I know that some of our men had the view that being captured by the British or Americans would be a relief, or even an adventure, and they felt they would be well treated compared to what happened on the Eastern Front. But I think that attitude changed after France was lost, when we saw the Americans attacking Germany itself.

My own experience, when I was a prisoner of the Americans in 1945, was very frightening, but that was a discovery I only made later.

Remember also what I have just said: that the immediate circumstances of the situation are often what decide a soldier to surrender or not. Does it feel 'safe' to surrender, compared to the risks of not surrendering? Every moment is different in that respect.

But for me, on June 6th, we were saved from the necessity of making this choice, because at that moment our own artillery began to bombard the Allied panzers very effectively. We started hearing the sound of shells coming over the ridge; they were good, fat shells too – it sounded like a battery of 128mm. We had a battery of these a long way down beyond the river, so I imagine they were finally on the ball. Our German artillery of the war is sometimes underrated, Herr Eckhertz, but in fact the fire that they could concentrate was impressive.

I heard the shells coming over, because they had a distinctive low whine, and I heard them explode beyond the ridge, towards the Shermans. The noise made my ears ring. I risked taking a look over the top of the ridge, and saw that the shells were exploding all across the minefield. One Sherman, I think the one that had knocked out our Stug, was hit, and burning badly. I saw some of the crew trying to get clear, but they were hit by one of these blasts, and thrown through the air a long way. The other Shermans were reversing in disorder down the lane that the mine clearers had created.

Those of us behind the ridge took the chance to retreat then, and we ran like men possessed by the devil, towards our deeper line of defences. This was a distance of about a kilometre, and we were strafed by Allied fighters as we ran. I think these were Mustang type planes; they shot us up with machine gun fire very accurately. My commander, who was being helped across the open ground, was killed in this strafing, and so was the man with him. We could do nothing to help them, because they were so slow; it was every man for himself by then. We aimed for some woods that would give us cover.

I remember that one of those Mustangs was hit by small-calibre Flak just as he pulled up on top of us. There was a 20mm Flak near the woods, well concealed under netting. I didn't see the plane get hit, because I was running like a madman, but I heard the Flak firing. When I got to the woods a moment later, I looked up and saw this Mustang, which was a beautiful plane, cartwheeling across the open ground. It was literally turning over from one wingtip to another, and its fuel was all spraying out behind it and leaving a trail of flames. What a sight that was. We were all transfixed at this sight, despite the danger. That Mustang span over and over, wingtip to wingtip, many times, burning brighter and brighter. I could see the pilot still on the canopy, sitting inside there. I'm sure that crash is burned into the memory of everyone who witnessed it, because it was such a vision of destruction. In a few moments, the whole plane crashed flat onto the ground and burned up completely. A lot of ammunition came shooting out and flew towards us at the trees.

The other Mustangs came back within moments and went berserk on that Flak gun. My God, they were like a pair of dogs tearing a rabbit to pieces. They shot it up from two directions, so the gun didn't know which way to turn. They shot the whole Flak to pieces, and then they came after us in the woods. We ran quickly to a ravine area inside the woods where our defences were set up, and we survivors of my Stug crew were taken to the rear to be assigned a new vehicle which was under repair. We were back in combat later that night in a new Stug.

Did you counterattack that same night?

We attempted a localised counterattack, yes. The spirit of the Wehrmacht was always that counterattack is the purest form of defence. That is why the Stug was such a valued vehicle for us: it could be used in attack and defence with equal effectiveness. By that stage, in the night of the 6th June, we were all exhausted, and we had to take amphetamines to keep us awake and energetic.

This was the 'panzer chocolate' amphetamine?

That's right. It was fantastic stuff at first, because it made you feel like new for three or four hours. But after that, my God! You had to take more of it, and then more, and it affected your judgement, by making you reckless or uncaring.

Were many panzer crews using these amphetamines?

The majority, I'd say. You had no choice, really. I mean, nobody forced you to eat it, but if you were fighting for twenty-four, thirty-six hours non-stop, you needed something, and if the officers offered it to you...why not? I have a very confused memory of the 7th of June, and after that we in the Stugs were pulled out of the line to refit the vehicles in the inland zone, although the Division stayed there fighting for many weeks.

I remember, on the way out of the line, we passed a lot of Hitler Youth boys in Panther panzers – these young lads were sixteen years old at the most. That shocked us a bit, seeing these boys coming in with these massive panzers. What kind of army was it that put Sunday

School boys in Panthers? God alone knows what the Allies thought of those Hitler Youth kids. They must have thought we'd gone insane.

Were you eventually captured?

Yes, but I was taken prisoner in the Reich itself. This was in spring 1945.

How were you treated as a prisoner? Just now you mentioned that your experience was frightening.

It was a terrible time. I was taken prisoner with many thousands of other Wehrmacht troops, and we were marched out of Germany along the roads. We ended up in Holland, I'm not sure where exactly, somewhere near a large river. We were put into a camp – well, I say *camp* but this was more like a stockade with a wire fence all around it, and no huts or buildings inside it. The land inside the fence was bare, with no shelter, just grass and weeds. We thought this was a temporary holding pen for a few hours, but night came on, and we slept inside the stockade with no food or water given to us. We were probably three or four thousand men, all lower ranks, with no officers among us.

The next day came, and the guards, the American sentries outside the wire, they threw in some packages of food and canteens of water, but this was grabbed by the first men who caught it, and most of us had nothing. This went on for several days. Germans in that stockade were collapsing from thirst and hunger, and fights were breaking out all the time over the little food that was thrown in. And all that the American sentries did was to stand outside the wire and watch us. What do you think of that?

I have heard rumours that this happened in the last weeks of the war, but I have never had a testimony to it. How long did this go on?

I got out of there after three days. By that time, the prisoners were rioting and trying to break down the wire, and the sentries were firing low over their heads. Some of the unconscious prisoners were trampled in all of that and killed. So the Americans took out about half the prisoners, of which I was one, by chance, and marched us away to other camps.

Conditions in the other camps were far better, more in line with the Geneva Convention. But that experience shook me and made me very suspicious of the Allies, as you can imagine. I'm sure that stockade isn't mentioned in any official records, though.

I don't wish to be insensitive, Herr Breslau, but I suppose after what our forces did during the war... and in general the Western Allies were very humane in their treatment of prisoners.

Oh, so you think I should keep quiet about this and not mention it again? Well, one day, the facts of this will come out and people will know what happened.

Thank you for giving me this very detailed account of the Stugs on June 6ᵗʰ.

—

THE WONDER WEAPON

K.L. Bergmann was a specialist weapons officer who served with the Wehrmacht from 1941-45. He passed away in the early 1980's.

Editor's note: the German word 'Taifun' ('Typhoon'), when applied to German weapons of World War 2, causes some confusion. The name was used for an experimental ground to air missile, and also for a method of combat employed by the Wehrmacht Sturmpioner (*Assault Engineer*) units, reflecting their use of shock tactics and assault weapons.

Confusingly, the word was also used for a powerful weapon using airborne explosive particles, which the Germans are known to have deployed several times on the Eastern front and again during the 1944 Warsaw Uprising in Poland. It is an experimental variant of *this* form of weapon which the next interview appears to be describing.

By coincidence, the British RAF used a fighter-bomber aircraft which was also named 'Typhoon.'

—

Herr Bergmann, I appreciate you making time
in your schedule to speak with me.

You are in fact the first person who has contacted me to discuss the situation in Normandy in June 1944. I find this rather surprising, considering my knowledge of the situation. To be honest, I have been waiting for someone to track me down and listen to my version of events in Normandy. I am glad that it is you who have located me, because you seem to understand the background quite well. How did you find me?

In a recent conversation I had with a certain German veteran of Normandy, I heard your name mentioned in connection with a rumour of an unusual type of weapon system. I have been unable to find out anything about this weapon, and probably all this was just a wartime rumour, but it did not take me too long to locate you by researching your name. And so I wanted to come here and ask you what this was all about.

Well, I have never made any attempt to conceal my name, my role in the Wehrmacht or my activities during the war. The fact is that the world has heard a very one-sided version of the Normandy situation, in my view.

What I mean by this is that the German forces, contrary to what most Allied historians might tell you, were really quite close to defeating the Anglo-American armies in Normandy during the period from the landings up until late July, when the American 'Operation Cobra' armoured breakout happened. It is correct that the German military was substantially outnumbered in July, and also that the Allies had almost total air superiority. However, we possessed a number of radical weapons which could certainly have pushed the Allies back into the sea, in my view, if they had been used promptly and effectively.

You say 'radical weapons.' Do you mean by this the use of the regime's 'wonder weapons' such as the V1, the V2 and that class of systems?

Not really.

On the subject of V1 and V2, those missiles certainly could have been used in a more effective, tactical way in the summer of 1944. The command, of course, opted to use them strategically against

London in the summer and autumn, thinking that this would desta-
bilise the English government itself. This proved to be a false hope
and a waste of priceless weapons. If only those systems had been
used against the invasion beaches themselves! The V1 was ready
at the time – it was used against London only a week after the
Normandy landings. Using that weapon, we could probably have
destroyed or damaged the Mulberry harbours and the fuel pipe-
line system which the Allies ran under the sea from England. This
would have had a profound effect on the ability to land and refuel
their vehicles. The same goes for the V2 rocket – if that had only
been available a couple of months sooner, we could have destroyed
the Mulberry harbours in June for sure. How the war would have
looked different then...

But, look, what I am talking about, more than this, was the class
of weapon which was already available to us, and which was in its
explosive effect actually just as powerful as the V rockets. I refer to
the 'Taifun' (*Typhoon*) class of bomb.

I have not heard of the Typhoon bomb. Can you explain?

Let me give you an idea of how it operated.

Before my posting to France, I was attached as a technical
officer to the German forces in the Crimea, where we used the
initial version of Typhoon for the first time. I saw it used against
the Soviet defences at Sevastopol, where the Russians were positioned in a series of very well-constructed concrete fortifications.
These forts were huge structures, similar in concept to the French
Maginot line bunkers, but in this case there was no possibility to
go around them as there was in France. It would have taken the
Luftwaffe many weeks of intensive raids to wear down these forts,
but the thickness of their concrete meant that they could resist
even heavy bombing.

When we used a Typhoon system on the site, however, these
huge buildings were ripped open from top to bottom, literally torn
apart by the blast wave. Even in the bunkers which were not blown

open, the Russian occupants suffered massive trauma from the effects of blast. This was the largest explosion that any of us present had ever witnessed; I believe its explosive force was much larger than the British 'Grand Slam' bomb which is often claimed as the most powerful conventional bomb of the war.

How did this bomb function? How was it deployed?

This was not a bomb that you could drop from an aircraft, you see. This early version of Typhoon was actually a very crude system. Essentially, it pumped a mixture of oxygen and coal dust into the interior spaces of buildings such as bunkers or tunnels. Our assault troops would force a gap into the structure, and then they released an oxygen-rich mixture into the inside. This mixture was released from steel canisters containing the oxygen and a pump which blew simple coal dust into the building.

How could ordinary coal dust form part of a weapon system?

Well, the intention was to replicate the conditions which existed in a coal mine leading to an underground explosion. In coal mines, the air is full of coal dust, which is highly flammable, and if the circumstances are right a spark can set off a catastrophic explosion in which all of the available air, being full of this flammable dust and oxygen, simply explodes. There were several such terrible explosions in German coal mines in the nineteenth century and again in the 1920's, and it was realised that in effect the air itself in the coal mine was being turned into an explosive element. It was as if the entire mine was pumped full of explosive gas – that is how devastating simple coal dust and air can be if they are mixed and ignited.

That is what inspired the *first* version of Typhoon.

When we used it on the Eastern front, in the Crimea, we filled the target buildings with this type of mixture as I have described, and then we ignited it with a flamethrower. The explosive effects were as I described to you.

The Russians themselves regarded the Typhoon as a chemical gas weapon, and we began to realise that in response they were assembling mustard gas and other poison gases in the Crimean sector. I believe this was another reason why Typhoon was not used more fully in the East, because of the risk of provoking a poison gas attack by the Soviets, which would have led to a stalemate on the Eastern Front. None of us wanted that, and so its use was dropped. It was employed again against the Warsaw rebellion, which the Russians didn't care about, and again its effects were devastating against tunnels and closed buildings.

But the Typhoon weapon was the reason that I was in Normandy in July 1944.

This is all new to me. Do you mean that the German forces were planning to use a primitive coal dust weapon against the Allies in Normandy? But against what targets? Surely it was the German troops who were inside the huge bunkers, not the Allies.

You do not know the full facts. You must understand that during 1943, we had developed a *second* variant of Typhoon, a much more powerful version, which we named Typhoon B. As a weapons specialist, I was personally involved in the design and development of this weapon. Typhoon B was a quantum leap forward in terms of the efficacy of this type of system...it was a very radical weapon indeed.

What was Typhoon B?

We had already learned to exploit the enormous explosive potential of mixing explosive dust or gas with air *inside* the target buildings, inside a closed space. Typhoon B was designed to use a similar airborne explosive system, but in a form which could be used out in the open, on the battlefield, against targets on the ground.

*It was a battlefield bomb? How did this function,
with the coal dust and so on?*

The system was essentially an explosive vapour which was released into the open air. The vapour consisted of a kerosene base, similar to aviation fuel, blended with particles of charcoal dust and aluminium powder. The charcoal and aluminium particles, which are in themselves explosive, served to accelerate the force of the explosion, and also to make the vapour heavier and less likely to be dispersed by the wind.

The vapour was launched by low-velocity rocket, using a rocket-firing vehicle of the 'Stuka Zu Fuss' *('Stuka on Foot' half-track)* type, which was widely available. The rockets fired canisters which were designed to release their vapour as they descended onto the target. This was extremely difficult to achieve, because of the probability of the liquid base detonating inside the canister. A vacuum system was used to prevent this. When a number of these canisters had been launched, they filled a large volume of air with their explosive gas; this volume could be up to one hundred cubic metres. Essentially, the target had this complete volume of explosive vapour suspended over it.

The volume then had to be ignited, and this was done by immediately firing a secondary bombardment of incendiary rockets. These incendiaries would simply detonate the complete mass of explosive vapour hanging in the air. The nature of the explosion was astonishing, because it created a blast wave which expanded across the ground for an enormous distance.

We tested a small prototype version of this weapon on the Eastern front, in controlled conditions. I observed the detonation and the effects on the landscape, which were enormous. As you can imagine, the shock wave was able to pulverise any structure immediately below it, and any Russians who were either in the target area or in a radius of many hundred metres were killed outright. The effect of blast wave is to remove the air from a man's lungs and arrest his heart muscles, and death is almost immediate, although there are often no outward signs of injury.

I am amazed that I did not know about this system.
How often was this used on the Eastern Front?

It was never actually used against Russian forces in the field, in combat.

Then how were Russians killed by it?

This was a controlled test.

Do you mean that prisoners were there, under the blast?

Let's move on. I was talking about the Typhoon B technical side... the problem with it was that it was such a difficult and unpredictable system to use, because local weather conditions had to be completely mild and calm, with no breeze to disperse the vapour, and if the concentration of explosive gas in the air became slightly too diluted, then absolutely nothing would happen. But when it could be made to work, the effect was almost Biblical in its devastation, I can tell you. And the conditions in Northern France in summer are far better for deploying a weapon like this than the wind-blown steppes of Russia, that's for sure.

Are you telling me that the German forces were
planning to use this weapon in Normandy?

Well, it would be incredible, surely, if an army had access to such a weapon and did *not* plan to use it on a major battlefield which was pivotal to the outcome of the entire war. That would be like saying that we had the Tiger panzers, but decided not to use them. And you must bear in mind that the Typhoon B system itself was evolving all the time and was greatly improved by mid-1944. We had developed a denser vapour, which was less likely to be thinned out by breeze, and a self-detonating canister which released its cloud of gas and then ignited the cloud itself as it hit the ground when it was empty.

This was an extremely complex munition with which I was involved closely, from late-1943 for about nine months. I was not a scientist, you understand, but I was a technical officer responsible for the launching system and the fuse arrangements on the new canister design.

How did these weapons come to be sited in Normandy?

We were moved from the test phase in the East, over to France in March 1944. When I say 'we,' I refer to my artillery unit of which I was the technical officer. We were two platoons of fifteen men each, equipped with the Famo-Hanomag type fully armoured half-tracks. The half-tracks were fitted with rocket launching racks in the 'Stuka Zu Fuss' pattern. We also had several Nebelwerfer class rocket mortars.

Our Typhoon B canisters could be adapted to fire from either system, although our preference was for the half-track launcher. The aiming system was crude, but with such a powerful weapon at close range it did not need to be extremely accurate. We were based at Saint Omer in the Pas de Calais region, which was generally considered the most probable site for an invasion if the Allies attacked France. We were briefed to be ready to deploy our system at six hours' notice anywhere in a one hundred kilometre radius inland of Calais. So it was clear to us that we were to be used in the opening stages of a landing, as a response weapon.

Could the Typhoon system, as you have described
it, be used on a coastal target?

The weapon could not be used on a beach target, because of the effect of the offshore winds. But we must remember that in 1944, we expected the Allies to invade France by capturing a large port for unloading vehicles and supplies, because an army needs harbour facilities for this. We certainly did not think it was possible at the time to land large numbers of tanks, trucks and so on directly from the sea onto a beach. At the most, we thought that the Allies would assault the seafront sector of a port city, as they had tried to do at Dieppe in 1942.

This is an important point; the regime expected the invasion to be achieved through an existing port, not directly onto beaches.

Absolutely. Because if you start to calculate the volume of armour, vehicles, supplies that would have to be landed in the days after a full-scale invasion of France – how could such volumes be landed directly onto the sand? We believed that it had to be done through a port, and Calais was the closest distance to England, only thirty kilometres. Of course, we made the mistake of thinking that if *we* could not do something, then it could not be done. We had no idea that the Allies would bring over their concrete Mulberry harbours and create an artificial port there on the invasion beaches.

So, with this expectation of a seizure of Calais, your Typhoon unit was intended to be used against Calais?

We would deploy it wherever we were ordered to deploy it.

We reconnoitred thoroughly in Calais and its surroundings, in addition to the port itself. We assembled enough of the canisters to be able to launch three separate Typhoon B explosions of the maximum power, which would be greater than the controlled test explosions we had caused on the Eastern front.

We planned to launch the canisters from a range of about five kilometres, which would mean that we would have to be in shelters to avoid being injured by the blast wave ourselves. The half-tracks would fire six of the vapour-delivery rockets, which had the canisters fitted as a warhead. The last rocket to fire was fitted with the self-detonating canister, which would ignite the vapour produced by the complete salvo. As a failsafe, in case the detonator failed, we would launch a salvo of incendiaries from a Nebelwerfer mortar into the vapour zone directly after the final canister was launched. In this way, we could be sure of igniting the volume of gas and producing the explosive effect.

I really must ask the question, Herr Bergmann. What would the effect of this explosion have been on Calais?

Well, it would certainly have destroyed the port facilities, if we had targeted that. It would have knocked over the concrete quays and destroyed any vessels moored there. The blast wave would have largely destroyed the warehousing zone, and also the residential zone across about half of the city. Remember: although the weapon was based on kerosene, the addition of the charcoal dust and aluminium meant that it was not an incendiary bomb, but a blast bomb. The shock wave would travel out at a rate which I think was roughly supersonic speed, and it would radiate outward in a circle.

The way that you describe this bomb, it seems to resemble an atomic bomb in its effects.

That is exaggerating, and of course we knew nothing of atomic bombs then, but this would still be one of the largest explosions yet produced by mankind. It would immediately deny the use of the port to anyone. Any Allied troops who survived the blast could then be swept up by our forces moving onto the zone from inland. Also, the psychological effect of the weapon would be massive, as a warning to the Allies not to attempt another invasion.

And was it anticipated that the civilian population of the city would be evacuated before the explosion?

That would have been impractical, you must understand. Even the German garrison soldiers themselves were unaware of the presence of the Typhoon system in France. There was no point in briefing them on our presence. If the port was captured, we then had to destroy the port; that meant that the garrison had failed in their task anyway, to be quite frank.

That was the official view that we were given, but I have another perspective to add. We have to remember that the German garrison at Calais contained many troops who had been posted there for two years or even three years. Some of these men, including some of the senior officers, had started relationships with local women, and in some cases it must be said that there were children born as a result.

This is not a criticism of the garrison, because of course such things happen in any army when troops are posted to a city for any length of time. This is the way of the world, after all. But the result of this was that I would not have trusted the garrison to conceal the fact of the Typhoon weapon. Word would have spread, that is the way of these things.

Does this mean that you intended to use this weapon against Calais, knowing that the remnants of the garrison would be present, and that the city would be populated with civilians?

Really, Herr Eckhertz, the way you say this makes it sound shocking. But the Allies themselves were bombing French civilians on a daily and nightly basis. In the build-up to June 6th there was a very intensive bombardment by heavy bombers against railway junctions, roadways and storage yards. It was far more intensive than anything I saw the Luftwaffe do in Poland or France in 1940, and it went on from around February right up to June.

I'm not sure how many French civilians were killed by this Allied bombing, but our estimates at the time were around 40,000 French people – that is more than the British said were killed in the 1940 blitz against London.

Do you see what I am driving at, Herr Eckhertz? Surely my point is logical. Destroying Calais with the Typhoon B system was no more destructive than what the Allies were already doing to France in the guise of 'liberating' the country. Using Typhoon B would have been a necessary action in the defence of Europe; that is how we saw it. And it would have deterred further attacks on us, saving many lives of both troops and civilians.

Wasn't that the American justification behind using the atomic bombs on Hiroshima and Nagasaki? To save lives in the long term?

Herr Bergmann, you are combining many separate issues here. My intention in interviewing you was purely to make a factual record of what took place in France on June 6th.

Would you prefer me to confine my comments to a description of the events?

The events, and also your personal reactions and thoughts; that was my intention. Forgive me, but your reference to the Typhoon B weapon and the plan for Calais has really taken me aback.

Then I shall tell you about my unit's activities in Normandy. I must ask that this conversation is not made available to the press in any form for the foreseeable future, unless I authorise it.

I give you that assurance.

Well, then.

To start with the day of the invasion, my team of course was still based near Calais. I recall that the night of the 5th to the 6th was noisy, with substantial bombing around Calais and to either side. This was not unusual in itself, as I have said, and I personally saw no reason to consider this anything other than a heavy night's bombing. I was billeted in a house in the Saint Omer district near to Calais; the building contained our two rocket platoons, and adjacent there was a sunken area where we stored our half-tracks and we dug a pit to store the Typhoon rockets and canisters themselves.

I can bring the scene to my mind now. That night of the 5th, I sat at the mess table with our commanding officer of artillery and the junior officer in charge of the men. The ceiling lamp swayed and the power cut out, and we sat there in the darkness. I was desperate for a cigarette, but we couldn't smoke on the site, and we all suffered in silence, drinking French red wine.

At around two am, a courier arrived by motorcycle, with an instruction to make ready our systems and to be ready for a possible landing or raid by the Allies. There was also a letter for us to present to all Field Police and security units, ordering them to give us the utmost cooperation. We immediately went to our magazine pit and moved the rocket and canister crates inside the half-tracks. This was an exciting phase, because the weapon was to some extent my child, and I wanted to see it at work.

Your emotion was excitement?

Yes, it was. I was excited to be in charge of the technical side, after such lengthy preparations. I had the utmost confidence in our system, while of course I regretted the necessity of using it.

Following our predetermined plan, we activated our radio sets and left our base for the higher ground to the West, from where we would be able to survey the Calais area. We had the three half-tracks, each with rocket cradles, the rockets and canisters, and two wheeled trucks following us with spares, extra fuel for the vehicles and supplies for the men. We were now a self-sufficient unit, and we could exist for at least ten days independent of the rest of the army. The men themselves were heavily armed, with the newest MP44 machine guns and MG42 mounted on the half-tracks, and a supply of Panzerfausts. With this formidable little battle group, we reached the high ground and began to observe what was unfolding.

303

What kind of overview did you have from your position?

We could see to the shore, including Calais itself, and to the South West we could see down towards Boulogne. Of course, we were a long way East of the invasion in Normandy, but there were Allied aircraft moving overhead in large formations, which were arranged like grids. This was a worrying sight as they moved through the rain-clouds. Flak was not heavy, and the explosions of bombs from the South were very clear to see. From our vantage point, we could see the blast waves of the bombs radiating out across the landscape in concentric rings, because the wave threw up the rain droplets which were reflected in the moon and other flashes.

I knew that our weapon system would make a shock wave far stronger than any of those bombs, stronger probably than a thousand of them detonating at once. We made radio contact with our command, and awaited their orders. We waited throughout the night. When the light came up, there were still large aerial formations overhead, including Lancaster type bombers which were very distinctive in their black colouring. We noticed that all the aircraft had black and white stripes marked on them. No Luftwaffe planes were visible. In this way, we waited into the morning.

What information did you receive about the Normandy
landings which were happening to the West?

It was a confused picture up until about midday on the 6th. We were told to keep radio silence, and then we were told to report every thirty minutes, and finally we were ordered to arm the Typhoon rockets in readiness. At that stage (although I did not know this at the time) the command firmly thought the Normandy beach landings were a diversion or feint, intended to distract us from the Pas du Calais. We had expected such a diversion to be staged in Normandy or in Belgium, so this only confirmed our view that Calais itself was the real target.

Arming the rockets was a simple process, and we equipped each of the half-tracks with the full complement of six rockets plus canisters. In the meantime, in the afternoon of that day, the 6th, we began to see groups of our vehicles moving West. These vehicles were often shot up badly by the Allied Jabo fighters. The worst Jabos were the American Thunderbolt type, which was noticeable for its wide engine radiator, and the British plane, called the Typhoon, which were both absolutely lethal to our ground forces.

I observed through binoculars in the late afternoon of the 6th, on a road to the West, when three of our Panzer IV vehicles were moving towards the West. These panzers were strung out with about one hundred metres between each one, and behind them was a support group of trucks and a mobile Flak on a half-track. Well, a line of these Thunderbolts came down from the West, out of the sun on that side, and just made one pass over this column. They were using rockets under their wings, and these rockets were tipped with explosive that caused an absolute storm of fragments to fly around where they detonated.

I was about two kilometres distant, but I saw clearly the explosions shoot up the roadway, looking horribly like red flowers...as if these huge red flowers were suddenly sprouting along the road, one after the other. These bursts ran right through our three Panzer IVs, and tore them up. Their armoured screens came off, and also the tracks, and the rockets went right into the engine of one of the panzers and simply blew it to pieces. Then the trucks and the Flak vehicle were hit, without the Flak even firing a shot. Those vehicles were completely torn up, with the wheels all flying off and the cabs exploding – all with the crews inside. This only took perhaps five seconds from start to finish, but my God, after those few seconds the three panzers and all the support wagons were knocked to pieces and burning.

I began to be concerned for what would happen to our system if we were hit by such strafing, and we made huge efforts to conceal our vehicles in culverts under foliage and nets. When we finally received the order to move to the West, towards the beaches, we moved at night to avoid the Jabo planes.

But this was the following week, on the eleventh or twelfth of June.

*By that stage, was the Normandy landing still regarded as a
diversionary attack, or acknowledged as the main attack?*

That is difficult to say. I was often in discussion with armour officers or the intelligence command. It became clear that the Allies
were building up in great strength behind their beach heads in
Normandy, which suggested they wanted to break out of where we
were containing them, indicating that this was more than a diversion. At the same time, we found it difficult to accept that they
would not want to capture a port. They were moving North towards
Cherbourg, apparently, and there were also rumours that they were
going to capture the Channel Islands, you know - Jersey and those
strange places, and use them as a jumping off point, like a group of
aircraft carriers.

Another view was that *everything* in France was still a feint, and
the main attack would be through Holland to separate France from
the Reich.

All of this uncertainty was very frustrating for us, and I heard
some of the infantry officers say that it was hard to order their men
to fight and die against a fake, diversionary landing. But I think in
those days, around the twelfth of June, there started to be a general acceptance that the beach landings really were in fact the main
strike, and it was in Normandy, around the beach heads, that we
would have to push them back to the water.

As we moved West at night, in fact, this became clear to me
as I began to see the amount of armour that we were assembling
around the beach head pockets. This was in the phase when the
21st Panzer and the Waffen SS panzers were encircling the Allied
pockets, which were still very small areas of land.

As we moved into Normandy, although it was dark, there were a
lot of flares burning in the sky and I could see long lines of Panther
type panzers along the roads. They travelled with their turrets
rotated to the rear, which I asked about and they told me that this
was to disguise the typical outline of the panzer if seen from above.
Most of these Panthers had foliage tied to their upper surfaces, and

some of them had planks of wood and even roof tiles arranged over them, to resemble buildings from the air. This made an impression on me, and I halted our small column and had the men wrap foliage completely around our half-tracks.

What do you remember most strongly today about entering the Normandy battle zone in mid-June 1944?

The level of destruction was the most immediate thing. The destruction achieved by the Allied bombing was staggering, even for me. I can tell you this, Herr Eckhertz: if our Luftwaffe had been able to deliver such destruction on a battlefield in Russia in 1941 or 42, then we would have been more successful in our endeavours there.

As we came through inland of the Deauville area, towards the front line, there was a series of parachute flares from the North which forced us to take cover between two houses. I jumped down from the half-track and went up to the top of one of these houses to see the battlefield area with my binoculars. Everything was destroyed – everything.

A train line had a civilian train demolished on the tracks, with the locomotive and the carriages bunched up like some monstrous caterpillar frozen in its movement. To either side, cattle which had been in the fields were dead with their legs in the air – scores of these cattle. Cultivated fields were full of craters. A village of fifty or sixty houses was smashed apart. What impressed me most was a creek running close to the front line, which was literally on fire; I mean that the water was running with flames which must have come from spilled gasoline or some form of incendiary attack. This creek ran down over a weir and the fall of the weir was burning with fire.

In the middle of all that was the tail of a Lancaster bomber, just lying there and burning. The glass turret of this tail plane was pointing up, and the flames were burning inside the glass. I thought that I could see a human form in there, perhaps the body of the tail gunner – but as I looked, the whole structure dissolved away into the flames.

Beyond that, one of our tank destroyer vehicles had been caught in the open, and it was nose down in a crater. I saw its crew simply sitting on the ground, apparently stunned, with their bodies trailing smoke. Nobody came to help them. Everywhere around were wrecked cars and trucks with their tyres burning.

I remember that my father had told me about things he had seen in the 1914 war, where the mud, he told me, stretched out in front of him like a sea, full of burning craters. My father always impressed that on me: the burning craters of France. Looking at Normandy, I concluded that mankind had made some progress from 1914: not only the craters were burning, but every possible thing was smashed and wrecked.

What were your orders on entering the combat zone?

We were to be ready to use our weapon system not against a port, but against enemy panzer groups preparing to attack our lines. At this point, we were taken to the South and held in hiding with the reserves, first for a week, and then we were told that our system would have to wait for a critical moment to be used. This waiting and waiting was infuriating for us. We could hear the battles happening to the North, and we followed the news hour by hour on our maps. But we waited, into July, and right up to the third week of July. Finally, around the third week of July, we were told that the critical moment was now in sight, and we moved up to the front with our half-tracks and all our gear.

Our intelligence was that the Americans were assembling a huge force, apparently of many hundreds of panzers of the Sherman type, apparently intending to break out of the Saint Lo zone and enter South across the plain. This is what is now known to be the 'Operation Cobra' breakout action. This was a grave danger, because if their panzers could break out they would advance rapidly to the South and East. There was also a concern that the English and Canadians were massing to break through past Caen. Taken together, these potential attacks had the capacity to drive the

German forces out of Northern France, which indeed was what very soon happened.

But it was thought that our Typhoon weapon, if used accurately in the right conditions at this very moment, was capable of destroying a large concentration of armoured vehicles at one blow – potentially an entire armoured Division. We could halt the American 'Operation Cobra' before it started.

How could one blast destroy so many tanks?

We knew from discussions with our own panzer troops that a tank does not have to be destroyed for it to be rendered out of action. The shock wave of the Typhoon B weapon would crush any tanks in a radius of about one kilometre, but tanks present to a radius of three or four kilometres would be prevented from moving. The shock travels through a tank, you see, and causes damage to the engine, such as breaking the fuel lines and starting fires. It also unbalances the gun mountings, and blows off the tracks – and of course, there is the damage to the crew inside, and the potential for detonating the ammunition.

We knew that the Allies had a tendency to amass their tanks in very tight groups before an attacking operation. Don't take my word for this, just look in 'Time' magazine and those other magazines for pictures of the Shermans in Normandy. Some of them are packed so closely together that it looks like a parking lot. Of course, they did this because they had no fear of air attacks, but it certainly created a very dense and vulnerable target for a powerful blast weapon.

The technical aspect was complex. This was a different mission to what we previously envisaged, which was the destruction of a port city, and the new task was in some ways much more demanding for us technically. We would receive little notice of the exact location of the enemy tanks, and we would have to take up firing positions rapidly, coinciding with the right wind conditions.

On the other hand, because the tank concentrations were now many kilometres inland, the atmospheric conditions might be *more* favourable; on the coast in France, there is always a slight breeze, whereas a few kilometres inland in the middle of summer, the air can be very hot and still, at times completely windless, which would be ideal for the release of our explosive vapour. Of course, the French weather is changeable, and if a strong breeze blew in at the time of launching, then the vapour would be dispersed, the weapon would not ignite and so the whole launch would be wasted.

Given all these factors together, we moved to a point near Saint Lo, and we housed our weapons at dawn in a small stone quarry which was covered over with netting and foliage, an ideal conceal-ment point. We constantly checked and maintained the vehicles, the canisters and rocket systems so that all was prepared. At sunset, a cou-rier from the command came to us, with an escort of field police vehi-cles and a detachment of Panzergrenadiers. The courier was under orders to guide us to a firing point, which was within range of a huge assembly area for Allied tanks north of Saint Lo. When we arrived there, we were met by intelligence teams who briefed us in detail.

Intelligence from French and aerial reconnaissance had shown that there was a large assembly of tanks in fields near a place which was named Ariel. I took that as a good omen, as it's such a classical name. This was an area in a slight depression, which presumably the Allies intended for concealment, but in fact this would assist the concentration of the explosive gas, as it would hold the vapour in place. The weather conditions were ideal, being an estimated fifteen degrees Celsius overnight, and with no wind movement dis-cernible at all. It was believed that the Allied tanks would break out at first light, and so we had to launch our weapon during the night. We decided on launching at one am, by which time we believed that the tank numbers would be at their greatest.

How many Allied panzers were involved?

I don't know exactly; possibly around four hundred armoured vehi-cles of different types, of which I believed we could destroy at least half by using the three groups of canisters together simultaneously across a zone. The blast wave would be destructive to a radius of about ten kilometres. The psychological effect on the Allied troops would be very shocking, of course, and their commanders would have no way of knowing whether or not we had further such weapons in reserve.

In reality, we did not yet have more supplies, but these were expected from Germany around the end of July. So, if the system worked, the opportunity was for us to stun the Allied advance, as a slaughterhouse man stuns a bull before slaughtering it. Once the stun blow was delivered at Ariel, our panzers would advance through the wreckage of the American zone, drive to the sea and split the Americans off. We would then have more Typhoon weapons available to use against the British tanks in turn. As the intelligence officer said to me, and he expressed it well, 'The Allies thought they could kick in our door, but we will bring the house down around their heads.' This was the plan on the evening of 24th July.

We moved to a point just inside our lines, protected by our Panzergrenadiers. All our other armour was pulled back out of the blast zone. We had some infantry units in our front line, of course, and they would suffer in the blast, but this was an unavoidable factor.

You would sacrifice the German infantry in the blast?

It was not practical to remove them. The Allies would notice any withdrawal, and might surge forward, threatening our launching site. As it was, we expected that we ourselves would become casualties of the blast; perhaps not fatal casualties, but probably with permanent injuries, loss of hearing or lung damage. But we were facing the loss of France itself if the Allies broke out fully, because there was then nothing to stop the Shermans racing on to Paris and then beyond.

We knew that the loss of France would lead to a siege of Germany, potentially the loss of the Reich itself...the stakes were as high as for any action in the war, you must understand. We were saving the Reich itself with our Typhoon B explosion; that was the calculation, you see.

I need hardly enquire as to whether your Typhoon was used successfully.
If so, this would have been one of the decisive moments of the war.
Perhaps it would have changed the course of the war itself.

Of course it *might* have. If we could halt the 'Cobra' breakout, and drive the Allies from France, and then use our Typhoon system on the Eastern front, imagine the consequences. Let the Reds attack us with their armies of one thousand T34s or two thousand T34s. Our system was improving all the time, its technical aspects were becoming more manageable, and before long we would have it in a form that could be used in windy or cold conditions. The East might be ours to conquer again. All this was in my mind as we were readying the three half-tracks at Saint Lo. I felt the weight of history itself on me, I can say that without exaggeration.

What ultimately happened? Did you launch the weapon,
and it failed to ignite, or what was the outcome?

It got to 12.45 am, and the whole device was primed. We had the vehicles pointing north towards Ariel, and we had deployed our infra-red rangefinder to adjust the rocket trajectory as precisely as possible. The escorting soldiers had been ordered to dig a protection trench, and they had created one about three metres deep and long enough for all of us in the Typhoon crew. We had the electrical firing cables running to the trench and connected to the firing battery.

My God, the night was so hot, it was so airless and still – it was perfect for our purposes. I warned the troops to take cover and to expect the biggest explosion imaginable, although in reality I knew that nobody could imagine the scale of the blast we were about to create. It came to 12.50 and 12.55, and I decided to fire the weapon earlier than planned, because the air conditions were so well suited at that moment. I felt the hand of destiny on my shoulder at that moment, believe me. I knew we were on the brink of a historic action.

Such thoughts are often punished by reality, of course. In reality, the launch was not destined to take place.

What happened to prevent it?

A soldier's bad luck, nothing more. The enemy began a bombardment on us – not, I am sure, because they knew what my unit was doing, but as part of some attempt to realign their front before their breakout. At first I was not alarmed, but this barrage came towards us across the meadows, and before we could move the half-tracks the shells burst on our position.

I had a periscope with me in the trench, because I wanted to film the launch process, and through this I saw one of the shells land close to the half-tracks. One of the vehicles was knocked onto its side, and with that blast, the canisters exploded. Because they were not dispersed into the air, their explosive power was not equivalent to the full-scale Typhoon system. The kerosene simply ignited in its liquid form, not the vastly more potent aerosol form accelerated by the charcoal dust. There was just a huge fireball of the fuel, which completely destroyed the three half-tracks, and rose up over us to a height of maybe a hundred metres.

Everything stopped for a few seconds; I suppose that everyone on the battlefield must have watched this fireball. The Allies probably assumed that they had hit a fuel supply dump, because the explosion was about the same. Our infantry probably decided something similar. In the heat of this fireball, the metal end of the periscope, which was exposed, partly melted, and we down in the trench suffered burns to our skin. But that fireball was slow and burned in a messy way, not at all like the sudden, rapid explosion that was planned from the aerosol bomb.

Well, that was it. That was the end of our attempt, and we were not authorised after that to rebuild the system. And so the Allies escaped this demonstration of our power.

What impact would this have had on the Allies, do you think?

It would have been a body blow to them, both materially and mentally. We knew that they were afraid of our most modern weapons, especially the Panther panzers and the Messerschmitt 262 plane, and a demonstration of our rocket technology in this manner would have been devastating. I believe it could have prevented the loss of France in 1944. That was its power.

Why was the system not progressed after that?

After that experience, the launch at close range from vehicles was considered too unreliable and too prone to being disrupted by the enemy. Research took place into other ways of delivering the blast. We must also remember that the Reich had in preparation a number of weapon systems which could possibly have been adapted to delivering the Typhoon very effectively. Not the V2 rocket, because that was supersonic and simply too fast in its impact. But the V1 rocket would have been an excellent delivery weapon, if used in salvos fitted with the canisters. If you have seen newsreel films of a V1 falling to earth over London, the way it falls is ideal for releasing the gas mixture.

We were also working on a Typhoon bomb that could be launched from an aircraft such as the Messerschmitt 262, which was far faster than anything the Allies had dreamed of. There were also glider bombs steered by remote control radio commands, which the Luftwaffe used very effectively against Italian warships in 1943, I believe. These glider bombs were in effect missiles steered by remote control, and if we imagine using them with our Infrared mechanisms, well, that would be a devastating missile indeed.

But our research in these delivery systems was slow under the chaotic conditions that existed in 1944-45, and no breakthrough was achieved. The other problem was the availability of the high grade aluminium powder for the explosive mixture, which was becoming almost impossible to obtain at the end of the war.

You see, Herr Eckhertz, there were many ways that Typhoon B could have been used, if we had pressed ahead with its development and matched it with the best delivery method. Truly, the Typhoon could have changed the outcome of the war, I believe, just as the atomic bomb finally did. But of course, *that* is one field, and one field alone, in which the Americans were vastly beyond us in technology: the atomic field.

You think that the German scientists were not
close to creating an atomic bomb?

I think it is unlikely, because the fact is that none of us understood what an 'atomic bomb' was. I speak as someone who attended University and studied physics, and I often had discussions on this subject with other technical officers who also had an interest in atomic science.

I remember that, since the 1930s, there were theories that a powerful bomb could be created using radioactive materials such as radium. What I thought this meant, and my technical colleagues also thought this meant, was that a bomb could be made which would disperse radioactive material such as radium, and in this way it could poison a wide area by dispersing the dangerous substance. I did not understand that the radium itself would be the explosive matter.

In fact, in August 1945, when I read about the American atomic bombs dropped on Hiroshima and Nagasaki, my first thought was 'Well, they have built a Typhoon weapon like ours! They have built a giant Typhoon bomb which works in the air and spreads poisonous radium. This is how they have blown up a city and poisoned the people with radiation.' I thought that was what it meant when the newspapers said the Americans had 'used the power of the atom.' I had no real understanding of materials such as Uranium and the way it could be made to explode by itself. It was only by reading the press that I understood that this process was entirely new to science.

Where were you in August 1945, when you read about Hiroshima?

I can tell you exactly: I was in a factory converting German military vehicles into agricultural tractors.

I had surrendered to the Americans in April 1945, on the river Elbe, when they were overrunning the whole of Western Germany.

By that stage I was in the role of a normal artillery officer, and I was considered to be nothing special at all. I was in an American prisoner camp until July 1945, at first in Germany, and then in in a British camp in Northern Ireland. The Northern Irish were the most cheerful people I have ever encountered, before or since. Everything was a joke to them: the war, the world, life, everything was the subject of humour.

In August 1945, I was offered the chance to return to Germany to work in the tractor plant, as the authorities knew I had engineering skills. The factory took light tanks, half-tracks and similar vehicles and turned them into farm tractors. This was an excellent idea, because agriculture was a priority for us, and these thousands of tracked vehicles were available in running order.

But Herr Bergmann, what did the Americans and British say about your knowledge of the Typhoon weapon? You shared the design with them?

No, I did not discuss the Typhoon system during my interrogation. The questioning was very quick, and the interrogators were more interested in the location of supply dumps, concealed bombs and other immediate concerns. They had no reason to think that I was anything other than a basic artillery officer.

I *thought* of telling them, but then I thought that it would complicate matters for me, and the longer I kept quiet about it, the more problems I saw if I did tell them. And as the Typhoon programme had all come to nothing anyway, the concept was not a threat to them, surely. So my war experiences came to an end, and I came back into the civilian sphere, where you find me today. If anyone was to ask me now, 'What do you know about Typhoon?' then I would tell them, as I feel that I have done nothing wrong, and I have nothing to hide. But, as I said to you when we began speaking, you are the only person who has made the effort to contact me regarding Normandy.

You have given me a remarkable account of an important aspect of the war. I need some time to reflect on what you have told me, to put it into perspective.

I ask only, Herr Eckhertz, that you do not publish this interview in the general press, I mean the newspapers and the like, without my express permission. I am glad that I have had this opportunity to discuss the events, but I do not wish to be under public scrutiny. I am sure that you can sympathise with my wishes in this respect.

I appreciate your sentiments fully, and I think you are right to ask for discretion in this matter. This is not something which I would want to publish for the foreseeable future.

—

Postscript To Book Two

By Holger Eckhertz
July 2015

I sincerely hope that the reader has found new insights, understanding or interest in this second book of interviews with German veterans of D Day. Looking back over the transcripts, I am struck by a number of common elements which I would like to highlight.

In the first volume of these interviews, I noted that there were three themes which seemed to come out strongly in those particular conversations: the Germans' *motivation* in defending a 'United Europe,' their apparent shock at the *aggression* of the Allied troops, and the overwhelming *firepower* and air superiority of the Allies. In this second book, I feel that these three elements are again strongly present – but there are also further issues which are very noticeable in these veterans' remarks.

One such issue is the highly diverse and ambiguous *relationships* which sprang up from 1940 to 1944 between the German troops and the local French population. The question of the German attitude to the French is a complex one: part 'protector' and part exploiter, the individual attitudes of the Germans themselves seem to vary enormously depending on circumstances and prejudices. The added complication of the attachments between German servicemen and French women is a human aspect to June 6th which has, I feel, been chiefly lost to the historical record.

Another theme which emerges (which has also received surprisingly little attention from historians) is the presence of large numbers of *Russian* troops in Normandy among the Static Infantry Divisions. General Rommel is known to have remarked that he felt it was asking too much to order 'Russians to fight Americans for Germany in France' – but the exact combat performance of these troops on June 6th and the ultimate fate of those who surrendered (which must surely have been many) appears to be unclear. If, as one veteran in this book asserts, the captured Russians were taken directly from the beaches and repatriated to their deaths in the USSR, this is an event which should be explored further.

One last point which is noticeable in both volumes of these transcripts is the matter of the *Dieppe Raid* some two years before D Day. At Dieppe, Allied troops (predominantly Canadian) attempted to take control of the port and town for a limited time on 19th August 1942, in a 'coup de main' attack which proved abortive and highly costly in casualties and prisoners. It seems that the memory of Dieppe remained long in the Germans' minds as an example of Allied failure in seaborne landings, to the extent that the reaction of many troops on June 6th was to immediately make comparisons with Dieppe. Whether this psychological impact was ultimately beneficial to the Allied mission is something to be considered.

I hope that this book serves in some way as a marker to the incalculably important events of June 6th and all its military, political and human repercussions, both for those involved and for those of us born long after the battle ended.

—

For further astonishing World War Two reading, try Wolfgang Faust's unforgettable account of his breakout from the Berlin-Halbe Pocket in April 1945, entitled 'The Last Panther.'

An intensely personal description of the German Ninth Army's attempts to escape Russian encirclement against all odds in the last weeks of the war, this is combat writing at its most unflinching. It's a phenomenal memoir of panzer battles, the collapse of the Third Reich and the suffering of civilians and troops on all sides, as the war comes to an apocalyptic conclusion in the idyllic meadows of Germany.